SECRET MARVELS of The WORLD

CONT

LONGTITUDE
−180°/−120°

ⒾN WHICH WE ENCOUNTER DISAPPEARING
ISLANDS, BOATS HEWN FROM PUMPKINS
AND A ONE−EYED TROLL LURKING
BENEATH A BRIDGE

LONGTITUDE
−120°/−60°

ⒾN WHICH WE ENCOUNTER MYSTERIOUS
MOVING ROCKS, A CAVE OF GIANT
CRYSTALS AND A MUSEUM AT THE
BOTTOM OF SEA

LONGTITUDE
−60°/0°

ⒾN WHICH WE ENCOUNTER AN ISLAND
TEEMING WITH SNAKES, A SHIMMERING
PINK LAKE AND THE WORLD'S BIGGEST
MUD−BRICK STRUCTURE

ENTS

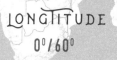
OCT 2 7 2017

SOUTH COUNTRY LIBRARY
22 STATION ROAD
BELLPORT, NY 11713

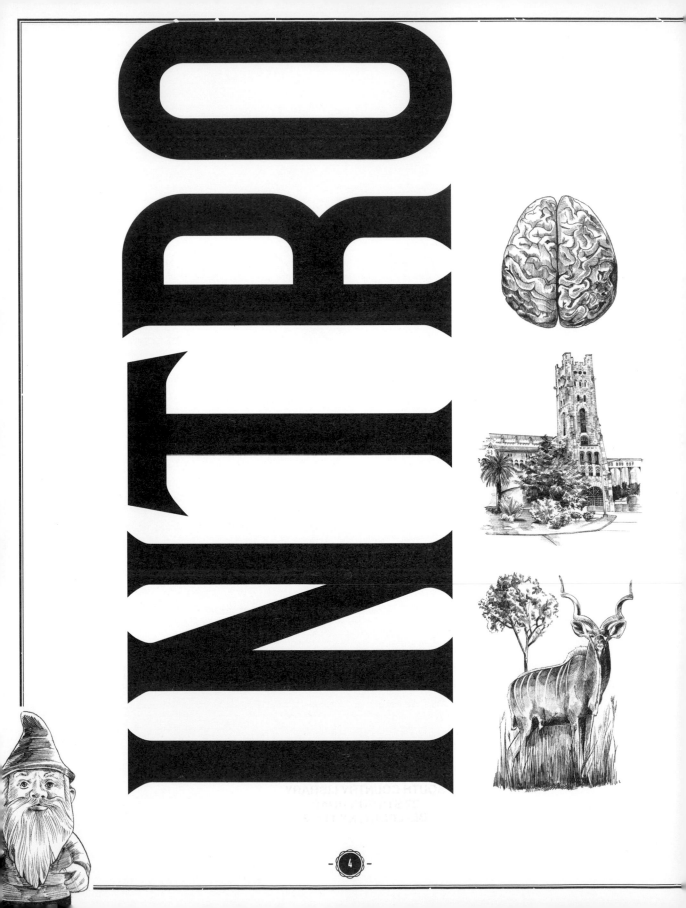

INTRO

Move over, Grand Canyon.
Au revoir, Eiffel Tower.
See you, Sydney Opera House.
Angkor what?

If you think you know about the world's most amazing sights, it's time to look again. This book celebrates under-the-radar places, from the mysterious and the mesmerising to the downright bizarre. In these pages are rainbow eucalyptus trees, a stomach-churning cocktail, ghost towns, a bridge made of trees, an underwater museum, a town called Hell and a band of Caribbean swimming pigs.

Some of these marvels are entirely man-made – Nebraska's eye-popping replica of Stonehenge made entirely from vintage cars (page 47), for example, or Indonesia's so-called 'Chicken Church' (page 249) – while others are a curious accident of human endeavour, such as Ohio's eerie abandoned ghost ship (page 55). Some needed no intervention from us whatsoever – take the Mexican cave filled with gargantuan, glistening crystals (page 49) or the disappearing island of Fonuafo'ou (page 9), which prove that this planet produces astounding phenomena without a hint of fanfare, while most of us are busy elsewhere, snapping selfies in front of their better-known cousins.

Because these marvels don't pay much attention to country borders, nor have we: the places in this book are arranged not by continent or country, but loosely by their line of longitude. It's a hat-tip to the way our planet resists attempts to impose order upon it, with the most surprising and wonderful of results.

In a time when technology has given us a better understanding than ever before of the hows and whys of life, these places show us we don't know the half of it. As the human race strives above all towards profitability and efficiency, there is a delight to be found in those marvels made by human hands not to chase success or increase the bottom line, but for the simple joy of it. It's a life lesson we could all learn from: taking time out from hectic schedules to appreciate the mysteries and wonders our planet has to offer.

But first, of course, we need to know where to look for them. Fortunately, wherever you are in the world, there will be a sight to enthrall you nearby. These pages are filled with a few hundred ideas of where to start. Happy marvelling!

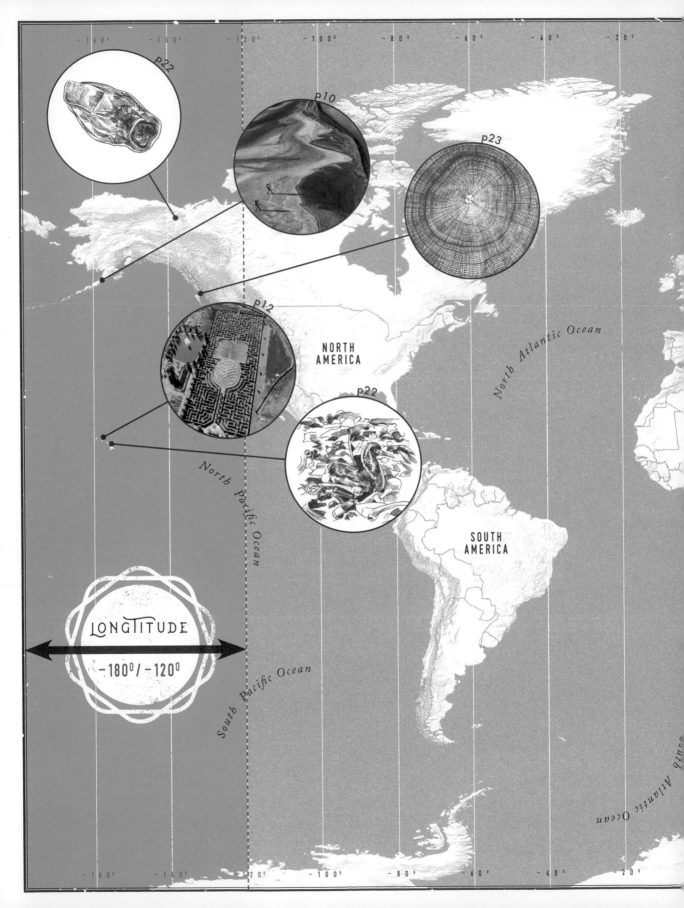

p22

p10

p23

p12

NORTH
AMERICA

p22

SOUTH
AMERICA

North Atlantic Ocean

North Pacific Ocean

South Pacific Ocean

South Atlantic Ocean

LONGTITUDE
-180° / -120°

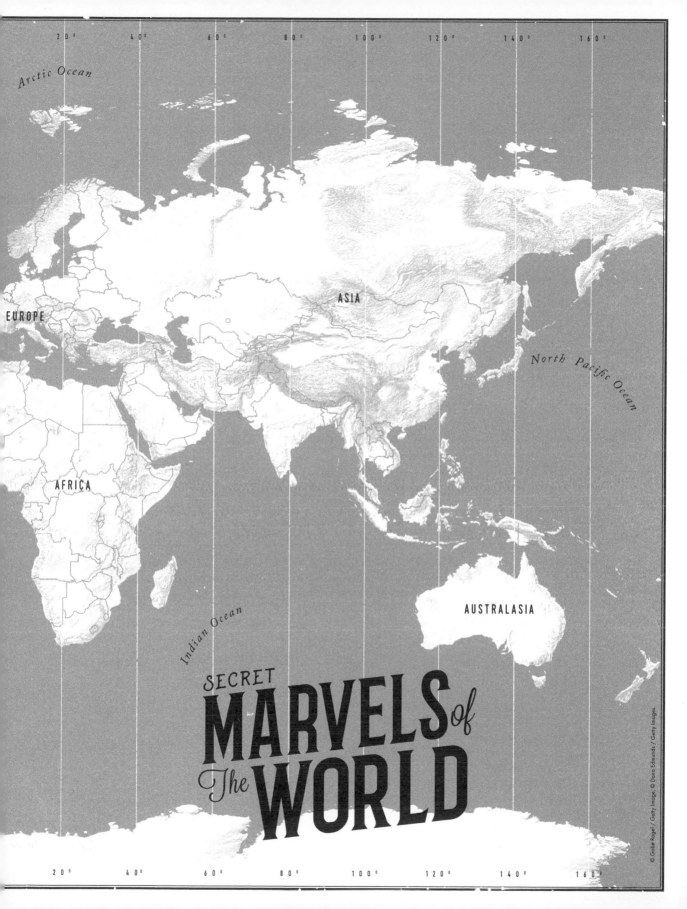

Waitavala Water Slide

Steamy, dreamy Taveuni seems purpose-built for doing sweet nothing. But too many days of languid lolling was making me feel as if I'd been bonked on the head by a coconut. It was time for action, and on Fiji's Garden Island, 'action' means only one thing: water slide! No chlorinated chute here; this is a slick, scenic series of smooth-rock cascades that slice through the rainforest with surprising speed.

Wobbling on slippery boulders, I gawked as the local kids surfed, goofed and grandstanded down the gushing slide. Me? I went down on my bum, hit every bump and plonked into the water below with all the grace of a drunk giraffe. But injuries, indignity and all: it was the ride of a lifetime. By Tamara Sheward

The slide, on the Waitavala Estate, is a 20 minute walk from Waiyevo on Taveuni's west coast.

© Jason Edwards / Getty Images

ⓉONGA, -20.3167 / -175.4167

FONUAFO'OU DISAPPEARING ISLAND

The British vessel *HMS Falcon* reported in 1865 that it had discovered a new landmass in the central part of the Tonga Islands that was 50m high and 2km long. Naturally, they named it Falcon Island. Unsurprisingly, that didn't last. Tonga immediately changed the name to Fonuafo'ou (or 'new land'), planted a flag and claimed it for the king. Not 30 years had passed before the island vanished in 1894, only to re-emerge from the Pacific two years later even taller at 320m. This ephemeral isle – the tip of an underwater volcano – has disappeared and reappeared at least five times over the years in a series of fiery eruptions. Current status: missing.

🕊 *Check up on Fonuafo'ou (presently a shoal) on the monthly ferry from Niuafo'ou to Vava'u.*

© ERIC CHENG

ⓉONGA, -20.5369 / -175.3801

HUNGA TONGA-HUNGA HA'APAI

It was January 2015 when tiny Hunga Tonga-Hunga Ha'apai first peeked its head out of Mother Earth's belly to greet the light of day. Formerly a quiet subterranean volcano, it burst through the surface of the Pacific with such bravado that its ash plumes diverted flights for days. When all the geothermal fireworks were done, the world's newest island was 500m long and 250m high, with a sulphurous milky-green lake in its central crater. The seahorse-shaped landmark may have made a stunning debut, but its role on earth could be just a cameo. Scientists believe the fragile island (it's best to not set foot on it) will likely erode back into the sea in a matter of years.

🕊 *You can charter a boat to take a look in Tonga's capital, Nuku'alofa. It's a 45km journey.*

© Ho / Reuters

ⓀAWAII, USA, 21.4023 / -157.8237

HA'IKU STAIRS

Otherwise known as the Stairway to Heaven, this flight of 3,922 steps steers itself up to the giddy apex of Oahu's breathtaking Ko'olau Mountain Range. In a plotline straight from *Lost*, the stairs were created in 1943 to provide access to a top-secret radio facility. That base was decommissioned in the 1950s, but the stairs remained, tempting photographers and risk takers alike with the most spectacular views over one of the most spectacular islands on the planet. The staircase is technically off limits, but few pay attention to that when it offers the chance to view paradise from the heavens (and Instagram it). A non-profit group, the Friends of Ha'iku Stairs, is dedicated to its upkeep and preservation.

🕊 *Access is via the John A Burns Freeway, 20 minutes north of Honolulu. www.haikustairs.org.*

© Matthew J. Bielecki / Getty Images

ALASKA. USA. 56.9036 / -158.0990

ANIAKCHAK NATIONAL MONUMENT

More people explore space each year than visit Aniakchak National Monument, a collapsed volcanic crater that contains some of the rawest wilderness in North America. Fresh off the angry Bering Sea, waterfalls of billowing clouds spill over Aniakchak's steep crater rim during wet weather, adding a ghostly sheen to the 'lost world' of giant bears and barren tundra below. If you're up for adventure, you can backpack into the crater using sinuous animal trails, before white-water rafting out along the foamy Aniakchak River to the sea. Hikers will need foldable kayaks, lightweight camping equipment and lots of courage.

Fly into the tiny settlement of Port Heiden and hike from there. See www.nps.gov/ania.

© Gabe Rogel / Getty Image

WORLD'S LARGEST MAZE

Covering over 12,000 square metres, the Pineapple Garden Maze is the world's largest. Officially recognised in 2001 by Guinness World Records, the signature attraction at the Dole Pineapple Plantation features hedges grown entirely out of Hawaiian plants. Wander through a garden of croton, hibiscus, panax and pineapple and see if you can beat the fastest times through the maze – winners receive prizes for finding eight 'secret stations' that are hidden within the structure's plant-formed walls.

The fastest times recorded were around seven minutes, but the average wanderer takes 45 minutes to complete the maze. It's at its best just after a heavy rain, when the plants are at their most colourful.

☛ *The Plantation is on Kamehameha Hwy, about 40 minutes from Waikiki.*

'If you never thought you'd visit London, Paris, Poland and the wonderfully named Banana on the same day, think again'

ⓀIRIBATI, 1.8721 / -157.4278

Kiritimati

If you like to be in the right place at the right time, why not spend Christmas on Christmas Island? There's historical precedent: Captain Cook stopped here and named it on 24 December 1777. Kiritimati is pronounced 'Krismas' – 'ti' is pronounced 's' in the language of Kiribati, which, yes, is pronounced 'Kiribas'. Lying just above the equator in the Pacific Ocean, and remote from pretty much everywhere else, Kiritimati is the world's biggest coral atoll. Theme a visit around brilliant place names, birds and bonefish and you can't go wrong.

If you never thought you'd visit London, Paris, Poland and the wonderfully named Banana on the same day, think again; these are the practical, political or eccentrically personal names of the island's four early settlements. Though on a very different scale to its namesake, London is (of course) the capital of this former British colony. Paris is (of course) across the channel! Its once-thriving coconut plantation, and that at nearby Poland, were named by a homesick Frenchman with aspirations to grandeur and his Polish mechanic. The journey by boat across the channel is an adventure in itself, starting with finding a local boat owner willing to make the trip; there is no public water transport. And Banana? The site of the first banana gardens is still a sizeable village, and minibuses heading to and from London offer a good opportunity to chat with locals heading to town.

After locating a mechanically sound car, and an owner willing to hire it out, take a road trip to visit the island's biggest population – seabirds. If you're used to looking up when birdwatching, here's a tip. On Kiritimati, look *down*. There are no Christmas trees (!), and the lack of tall vegetation means that birds such as boobies and terns breed on the ground. Towards the southeast end of the Bay of Wrecks – no prizes for guessing how that name came about – the road runs alongside a vast, noisy, smelly and completely fantastic breeding colony of sooty terns. In the salt-blasted shrubs, keep an eye open for *bokikokiko*, the small and lively Line Islands Warbler; it's a big tick on the must-see list for serious birders.

East of the island's main lagoon, salt flats interspersed with shallow lagoons are famous for fly-fishing for bonefish. If you like the idea of such a tongue-twisting activity, hire a local guide and head for the water. If it's too rough for a boat ride or you don't want to wade in the water, you can cast a line from the back of a pick-up truck. Don't even think about doing this alone, though – it's *extremely* easy to get lost and sun-crazed in the island's interior, and going Christmas crackers is a sure way to ruin a marvellous adventure.
By Virginia Jealous

🡒 *Fiji Airways flies weekly to Kiritimati from Nadi (Fiji) and Honolulu (USA).*

MAUKE, COOK ISLANDS. −20.1546 / −157.3445

THE DIVIDED CHURCH

The Bible reckons a house divided cannot stand, but the Ziona Church tells a different story; literally split in two, it's been a Mauke landmark since 1882.

The church was a joint project between two neighbouring villages of the same denomination; all was going a treat until the two fell out over the interior colour scheme. Arguments – pink versus red, teal against turquoise – enflamed the villages; unable to reach a compromise, a wall was built across the middle of the church, separate entrances were constructed, and each village set to painting their side with a polychromatic passion. Though each flock finally had the rainbow rooms of their dreams, the decor dispute had taken its toll; while one congregation worshipped, the other would be right outside, playing noisy, disruptive games.

After years of cold-shoulder Sundays, a pastor finally convinced the villages to hold communal services. The wall came down, the church was given a neutral-palette makeover and villagers took turns singing hymns, though the separate entrances remained, and the pulpit – in the centre of the nave – retained a dividing line which speakers were (and still are) expected to straddle. This harmony holds today, so much so that the interior has recently been repainted in all of its original bold, clashing colours. Visitors are welcome to attend Sunday services (and to use whichever entrance they wish).

🕊 *Air Rarotonga flies between Rarotonga and Mauke every day but Sunday.*

HAWAII, USA, 20.7575 / -155.9884

RAINBOW EUCALYPTUS TREES

The road to Hana is one of the most incredible drives anywhere on the planet, featuring an overwhelming abundance of sights, sounds and colours as the road winds its way down to the sleepy town nestled in the fragrant bosom of Maui's rainforest. Perhaps the most extraordinary thing you'll see on this journey is the 'painted forest' of rainbow eucalyptus trees: a quirk of nature producing trees that literally look like frozen rainbows. The reds, purples and greens are particularly vivid within these spectacular oddities of evolution, thanks to sections of bark shedding at different times during the year. The real beauty of this phenomenon, however, is that the process is ongoing, so the multicoloured streaks continuously evolve, forming a grove of living kaleidoscopes.

🦐 *The rainbow eucalyptus grove can be found at mile marker 7 on Maui's Hana Highway in Hawaii. You can also see some of the trees at the nearby Ke'anae Arboretum.*

'One side is a graveyard for the Japanese community. The other side is a Chinese cemetery. Beyond the wharf is an ancient Hawaiian burial site'

⌖HAWAII, USA, 20.8836 / -156.6870

Pu'upiha Cemetery

'Go to the ancestor tomb and ask for permission to tell the story. Maybe you don't believe. Maybe you do. But go.'

I'm talking with Dr Busaba Yip, curator of the Wo Hing Museum on the Hawaii island of Maui, to learn the story of a local burying ground. Outside downtown Lahaina on Maui's west coast, historic Pu'upiha Cemetery sits on prime oceanfront property, directly in the sand.

Pu'upiha Cemetery might look like any palm-lined Hawaiian beach – if it weren't for the gravestones. Inscribed with Asian characters, the majority of the headstones set into the sand date to the early 1900s.

Most visitors come to Maui to relax on the beach. Most don't plan to stay for all eternity.

Dr Yip tells me that one side of the cemetery, opposite the Lahaina Jodo Mission (a Buddhist temple), is a graveyard for the Japanese community. The other side, closer to Mala Wharf, is a Chinese cemetery. Beyond the wharf is an ancient Hawaiian burial site. Something about the location, she explains, has made it a spiritual place.

Many Chinese and Japanese people emigrated to Hawaii in the late 1800s to work in sugar plantations and mills. In the early days, these communities sent the bones of their deceased home to their own countries to be buried. But as years passed, they began to bury their dead in Hawaii.

On the Japanese side, large headstones are placed across the sand, while on the Chinese side, small stone posts in orderly rows mark the plots. Overlooking the site and the ocean below is a red concrete monument, which Dr Yip tells me is the Grand Ancestor Tomb.

Dr Yip, who holds a PhD in traditional cultural studies, will tell you that she's a Taoist who believes in honouring the spirits of the ancestors. Every year, she joins her Japanese neighbours at Pu'upiha Cemetery for the O-Bon festival, where they release lanterns, symbolic vessels for the spirits of their departed loved ones, into the sea.

I go to this cemetery in the sand, and I stand before the ancestor tomb.

I ask the ancestors for permission, for guidance, for support. The waves break steadily against the shore, and I listen.

I look out over the graves. The surf laps the beach. And still, I listen.

Maybe I don't believe.
But maybe I do.
By Carolyn B. Heller

☞ *From downtown Lahaina, follow Front St north and turn left onto Ala Moana St. The Cemetery is near the water.*

'It's a weird and wonderful place, populated by oddballs and eccentrics, ideal for kayaking isolated rivers with moose and bears for company'

ALASKA, USA, 64.0753 / −141.9361

Chicken, Alaska

I wanted wilderness. I wanted adventure. I wanted to drive the open road. Heading off to Alaska across the Top of the World Highway, a winding mountain road only open in summer, seemed like the ideal plan. Until I arrived in Chicken.

A handful of log cabins in the middle of nowhere, surrounded by wilderness, Chicken is a tiny speck in a landscape that is colossal, unforgiving and raw. And, oh, it has a saloon with a cannon that shoots panties into the air. In fact, it's hard to find the bar among the sheer number of knickers, baseball hats, license

plates and handwritten notes pinned to the walls.

Chicken is one of Alaska's last gold rush remnants – when the highway closes in October the population drops to single figures and the village succumbs to isolation and the Arctic winter. During the summer a trickle of prospectors, intrepid RV drivers and thrill seekers make their way here to try their luck in the creeks, to learn about frontier history or tick one more kooky adventure off their list.

Early prospectors arrived here in the late 1800s and only survived their first winter thanks to the abundance of ptarmigan (a type of wild grouse). By 1902,

the tent city needed a name. The miners wanted to call it after the local bird but no one could agree on the spelling, so they opted for Chicken instead. The gift shop is full of 'I got laid in Chicken' mugs and 'Cluck it' T-shirts, the creeks still spit out sizeable nuggets now and again and you can tour a working mine or even pan for gold. You can also cheat and hire a metal detector or just slip back to the gift shop and buy a bag of gold flakes instead.

It's a weird and wonderful place, populated by oddballs and eccentrics, and ideal for kayaking down isolated rivers where your only company are moose and bears. That is, if you

don't arrive during Chickenstock, the annual music festival, when almost 1,000 revellers descend on the village to listen to folk and bluegrass, and yes, do the chicken dance. With music blaring, merry punters stumbling to the public outhouse under the midnight sun and women blasting their knickers from a cannon, there's a strong whiff of the old Wild West. Anything goes when you're this far from civilisation.
By Etain O'Carroll

☛ There's no public transport and the highway closes from October to April. You could fly from Tok, but that's cheating. See www.townofchicken.com.

HAWAII, USA, 18.9705 / −155.5994

PLASTIC BEACH

A time-honoured Pacific melting pot, this stretch of coast on the southeastern tip of Hawaii's Big Island is officially called Kamilo Beach ('the swirling currents' in Hawaiian). Once, a combination of powerful tides and trade winds delivered all kinds of valuable flotsam to the ancient Hawaiians here, including logs from the Pacific Northwest to fashion into canoes. In recent years, however, the ocean has been delivering a different bounty: astounding amounts of plastic debris from the so-called 'Great Pacific Garbage Patch'. Today, on what is now known as 'Plastic Beach', you're likely to discover ephemera from every side of the ocean, not to mention a lesson on the wastefulness of mankind and the unrelenting power of nature.

☛ The beach is near Naalehu, via a maze of sharp volcanic rock. Tread carefully or come by 4WD.

DAWSON CITY, CANADA, 64.0623 / −139.4334

THE SOURTOE COCKTAIL

The legend of the Sourtoe Cocktail begins in the 1920s, when rum runners Louie and Otto Linken were caught in a blizzard and Louie's toe became frostbitten. Fearing gangrene, the brothers amputated Louie's toe with an axe and some rum (for anaesthesia and courage). To mark the event, they preserved the toe in a jar of booze.

Decades later, Captain Dick Stevenson found the jar and brought it to the Sourdough Saloon. There he used the toe to garnish the drinks of those brave enough to join the 'Sourtoe Cocktail Club'. Today, visitors can become a club member by gulping down a digit-embellished shot (but lips must touch the toe).

☛ The Sourdough Saloon is on the corner of Queen St and Second Ave in tiny Dawson City.

VANCOUVER, CANADA, 49.2641 / −123.0965

DUDE CHILLING PARK

One day in 2015, a new sign appeared in a small Vancouver park. Looking just like the official signposts that display the name of every public park in this British Columbia city, this one suggested that the name of little Guelph Park had been changed – to 'Dude Chilling Park'.

Many local residents assumed that the city was simply acknowledging the growing hipster population in the surrounding neighbourhood. In fact, the sign was an installation created by local artist Viktor Briestensky. When the city removed the sign, however, community members protested, and Briestensky offered to donate his work. This 'artwork' now permanently overlooks the park where, on sunny days, many dudes are indeed chillin'.

☛ The park is on Brunswick St between East 7th and 8th Aves.

© Michael Wheatley / Alamy

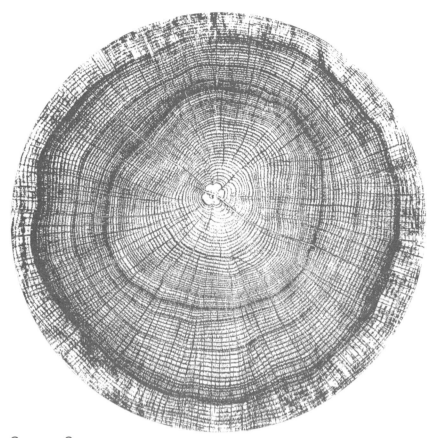

BRITISH COLUMBIA, CANADA, 53.6367 / −132.2096

THE FELLED GOLDEN SPRUCE

There once stood a tree unlike any other. Its boughs were bright yellow, and it stood out against the old-growth rainforest of Haida Gwaii in British Columbia as though sunlight poured from its very branches. The strange colour was the result of a rare genetic mutation that caused the tree to lack the chlorophyll normally found in spruces. Against a backdrop of green, the 50m golden spruce was an unusual sight.

The tree was a popular stop on visitors' itineraries, and central to legends of the indigenous people, the Haida, who named it K'iid K'iyass (Old Tree). That is until 1997, when, after standing for over 300 years, the 2m-thick tree was cut down by an environmental activist called Grant Hadwin in protest against the destruction of nearby forests.

But the golden spruce lives on. Cuttings taken from the original tree were distributed across BC. At Port Clements, some 10km north of where the golden spruce fell, an offspring grows behind a barbed-wire fence – at around a metre tall, it's a mere echo of the original. Just outside town, the Golden Spruce Trail takes hikers to the edge of the Yakoun River, where the tree could once be seen. Now the decaying trunk of the golden spruce rests on the riverbank.

☞ *Hwy 16 connects Port Clements to the main Haida Gwaii transport hub of Skidegate Landing. Take Bayview St out of town, heading southbound for 6km; the Golden Spruce Trailhead will be on your right.*

'I hiked the windswept beaches, overnighting in abandoned settlers' cabins while wandering the 40km of driftwood-strewn sands'

CALIFORNIA, USA, 39.9428 / -123.9640

California's Lost Coast

As long as I can remember, I've been fascinated by grey-roading – the art of exploring the faintest and most obscure back roads on the map. In my early twenties, I became obsessed with California's Lost Coast, a 100km stretch of tantalisingly undeveloped shoreline in northern California, where the legendary Route 1 abruptly parts company with the Pacific Ocean, heading inland to avoid a series of rugged coastal cliffs and giving way to a sketchy tangle of unpaved logging roads.

I had to see it for myself. On a bleak January weekend, my friend Keasley joined me on a reconnaissance mission. Armed with his ancient Plymouth Valiant, we ventured into the unknown. Big disappointment. Between the driving rain, deep ruts, steep, muddy inclines and failing brakes, our death-defying journey of discovery was prematurely thwarted by a collapsed bridge in a godforsaken river valley a few kilometres shy of the coast.

Failure only egged me on. A few months later I tried again. Following an unmarked dirt road Keasley and I had bypassed, I reached a steep slope swooping down to the sea. Eureka!

I had discovered, by accident, Sinkyone Wilderness State Park – a sleepy piece of paradise straddling spectacular bluffs above the storm-tossed Pacific. As ruggedly dramatic as California beach classics like Malibu, Monterey, Mendocino and Big Sur, this place only gets a fraction of the visitors. Exhilarated, I pitched my tent under a massive old eucalyptus, falling asleep to crashing waves and waking to the sound of grazing elks' hooves inches from my head.

Over the ensuing years I set off to discover the rest of the Lost Coast on foot. I hiked the windswept beaches of King Range National Conservation Area, overnighting in abandoned settlers' cabins and wandered the 40km of driftwood-strewn sands between the Mattole River mouth and Shelter Cove. Further south, the Lost Coast Trail revealed equally mesmerising landscapes: the Sally Bell Grove of old-growth redwoods, the dizzying coastal views from Anderson Cliffs, and the skeletal lightning-struck ghost tree at Needle Rock.

Decades later, this coastal wilderness lives on, saved from mass tourism by its remoteness. Elk still graze unfazed atop lonely bluffs, and the access roads remain untamed. Meanwhile, 30km east, a stream of redwood-seekers cruises along California's Avenue of the Giants, oblivious to the coastal marvels they're missing. *By Gregor Clark*

☛ *To reach the Lost Coast, leave US 101 at Garberville and head west toward Shelter Cove. Then branch north or south.*

'Suddenly, in the middle of the forest, we're in a street–art gallery. Seven mangled rail cars sit at weird angles, each tagged in vivid colours'

BRITISH COLUMBIA, CANADA, 50.0815 / -123.0555

Whistler Train Wreck Site

My husband Alan and I are hiking near Whistler in British Columbia, hunting for a new trail to an unusual attraction: a wrecked train that's become an outdoor art installation.

In 1956, a freight train travelling too fast through a rock canyon derailed near this Canadian mountain community, 120 kilometres north of Vancouver. To clear the rail line, a logging company towed the damaged train cars into the woods, where they were abandoned.

Eventually, local graffiti artists found the wreckage in the old-growth forest and started using the derelict rail cars as a canvas.

For years, the only way to reach the site was to hike along an active rail line – not the safest choice. But Alan and I are attempting to find our way to a recently constructed suspension bridge over the Cheakamus River, which has made this unexpected artistic hub easier to reach.

As long as you don't miss the turnoff for the path.

Retracing our steps, we find an entry to the Sea to Sky Trail, a long-distance hiking route that extends through Whistler into the BC wilderness. We follow the trail into the woods and soon spot a sign, 'Train Wreck Site and Suspension Bridge'. The path takes us down to the churning river and over the wooden bridge that sways gently as we cross.

And suddenly, in the middle of the forest, we're in a street-art gallery. Seven mangled rail cars sit at weird angles in a sun-dappled grove, each tagged and retagged with vividly coloured paint. We spot a *Simpsons*-style cartoon on one and a mishmash of designs sprayed on another, all but obscuring its 'Canadian Pacific' logo. Peeking inside, we find the head of a bodhisattva and a Zeus-like figure with a flowing white beard.

It's not just graffiti artists who have customised the train wreck site. Mountain bikers have built jumps and rails surrounding several of the train cars, creating a renegade bike playground.

We snap plenty of photos before making our way back over the bridge and through the woods. Just a short distance from North America's largest winter sports resort, it feels as if we've discovered a secret art gallery. It's not secret, of course – but you do have to know where to look.
By Carolyn B. Heller

☛ *South of Whistler, the train wreck is a 30-minute walk along the Sea to Sky Trail, which you can pick up behind the Hi Whistler Hostel.*

CALIFORNIA, USA, 37.8085 / -122.4402

THE WAVE ORGAN

Everyone sees the bay when visiting San Francisco, but how many people get to hear the bay? The unique Wave Organ is both a visual and auditory work of art where visitors can fill their senses with their surroundings. Located on a small jetty in the Marina District, the site takes in fine views of the Golden Gate Bridge, Alcatraz, Fort Mason and further out across the bay.

The concept for the Wave Organ came to artist Peter Richards when he heard a recording of sounds coming from a vent pipe on a dock in Sydney, Australia. In collaboration with San Francisco's well-loved, hands-on science museum, the Exploratorium, Richards worked with master sculptor George Gonzales to build the piece.

The sounds are the most distinct at high tide as water rushes in and out of 25 organ pipes fixed in concrete at various levels and locations around the jetty. The site itself is a thing of beauty, constructed out of a multi-level hodgepodge of granite and marble reclaimed from a demolished cemetery. The low groans from the pipes can be subtle, so take time to take deep breaths, calm the mind and listen closely to music made by the sea.

The Wave Organ is a public site near St Francis Yacht Club (www.exploratorium.edu/visit/wave-organ).

NEVADA, USA. 39.2872 / -118.0270

THE SHOE TREE

Draped with sneakers tied together by their laces, the Shoe Tree is a welcome sign of civilisation for road-trippers. The homely tree borders Highway 50 in central Nevada. Dubbed the Loneliest Road, Highway 50 crosses miles of high-desert emptiness, linking Fallon in the west with Great Basin National Park in the east. According to lore, the Shoe Tree was born when a newlywed couple quarrelled while camping beneath its branches. The angry bride said she was going to walk home. The groom tossed her shoes in the tree, telling her to try. They reconciled, but a shoe-throwing tradition was born. Vandals cut down the original tree in 2010, but a new cottonwood – called Shoe Tree, Jr – has taken the job.

☞ From Fallon follow Highway 50 east for 80km.

OREGON, USA. 45.3825 / -122.7612

THE GIANT PUMPKIN REGATTA

Humankind has accomplished many feats throughout the course of history: mastering fire, developing agriculture and landing on the moon. But few compare to carving out a giant pumpkin and using it as a boat.

The West Coast Giant Pumpkin Regatta in Tualatin, Oregon, is the culmination of aeons of human engineering, and it's hilarious. After carving out the centres of giant pumpkins, paddlers don fancy-dress costumes and race across a lake towards glory. Not particularly known for their seaworthiness, the pumpkins bounce and bob across the water – and sometimes the paddler manages to stay inside. An associated festival also features a giant pumpkin weigh-off, best-costume prizes, a pie-eating contest and tons more.

☞ The festival is held every October in Tualatin, Oregon, just south of Portland.

FREMONT PUBLIC SCULPTURES

◉WASHINGTON, USA, 47.6494 / -122.3495

A 16ft-tall bronze Bolshevik, a giant troll hidden beneath a bridge, a Cold War rocket that didn't make lift-off, and a row of cement commuters waiting for a train that never comes. Welcome to the weird and wonderful neighbourhood of Fremont in Seattle where the community motto is *de libertas quirkas* (freedom to be peculiar) and the streets are decorated with outlandish public art.

Located three miles north of downtown Seattle, Fremont is an irreverent quarter in a city well known for its free spirits. Abutting Lake Union, the tree-lined streets regularly fall victim to 'art attacks': spontaneous sculptures and exhibits that spring up anonymously overnight before disappearing again just as quickly. More permanent are the half-dozen pieces of public sculpture.

Close to Fremont Bridge and testimony to Fremont's love of wit and humour is *Waiting for the Interurban*, a study in cement of five commuters and a dog standing forlornly at an imaginary tram stop. It is Fremont tradition to dress the quintet up in clothes or other paraphernalia to celebrate a sporting victory, satirise a political event, or simply make an artistic statement. Needless to say, the statue is rarely naked.

A few blocks away is another notorious creation – the *Fremont Troll* (right) a one-eyed monster crushing a Volkswagen Beetle in its fist. Winner of first prize in a local arts council competition in 1990, the statue (created by artists Steve Badanes, Will Martin, Donna Walter and Ross Whitehead) was an early example of Fremont's wry contrarianism and has been prowling under the George Washington Memorial Bridge ever since.

To regain your sense of direction, gravitate towards the *Guidepost*, Fremont's community totem that points in multiple directions and announces itself as the 'center of the known universe' (an unsubstantiated Fremont claim). The guidepost will direct you towards the next head-scratching oddity, the *Lenin* statue, a fierce-looking study of the Soviet strongman that was rescued by a Seattle teacher from a junkyard in the former Czechoslovakia soon after the Velvet Revolution. It's technically for sale, should you fall in love with it.

Lenin seems to striding hurriedly towards the *Fremont Rocket*, an unused piece of Cold War hardware now grafted on to the side of a shoe shop

© Wolfgang Kaehler / Getty Images

that once playfully emitted steam if you pushed a coin into a slot and waited. These days the most supersonic it gets is when it is lit up at night.

Slightly more down to earth are Fremont's *Apatosaurs* down by the ship canal, two life-sized topiaries made out of creeping ivy. Like most of Fremont's sculptures, the dinos were salvaged – a community group bought them for $1 from the Pacific Science Center in 1999. Sit for a moment and contemplate their pleasant greenness (and their weirdness) and then be on your merry way.

☛ *Fremont lies three miles north of central Seattle. Buses 5, 40 and 62 run to and from downtown.*

'So the ghosts wouldn't find her, Sarah Winchester's house and its constant construction were to form a labyrinth to keep her safe'

CALIFORNIA, USA, 37.3182 / −121.9511

Winchester Mystery House

The Winchester Mystery House is an unsolved mystery with as many twists as a Jason Bourne thriller – but here the plot moves on real-life hidden passageways and doors to nowhere. Built non-stop, 24 hours a day for 38 years, the house has over 160 rooms and more weird quirks than your Great Aunt Marge, including cabinets that lead into rooms, staircases that go up then down and chimneys that don't reach the roof. The house feels haunted, yes, but it's also an exceptional example of late 19th-century architecture, including Tiffany stained-glass windows and finely etched doorknobs.

Sarah Winchester was the solo mastermind behind the house.

Heir to the Winchester rifle fortune – 'the gun that won the West' – she allegedly became interested in the occult after the untimely deaths of her child and husband. A medium told her the bad fortune was caused by spirits of those who had been killed by Winchester guns and wanted revenge. She spent the rest of her life trying to outwit the ghosts.

Sarah left her home in Connecticut and bought an unfinished farmhouse in San Jose, California. She was extremely secretive so most of what we know about her life are rumours. It's said that she always wore a veil over her face and fired staff (that she paid generously) if they saw her without it; a bell tower chimed for lunch and dinner but also at midnight and 2am – the times of the departure and arrival of spirits. She spent every night in a different bedroom so the ghosts couldn't find her, and the house and its constant construction were to form a labyrinth to keep her safe. Some staff claimed that she held nightly séances.

It's impossible not to think of Sarah and her superstitions as you wander the home and property. Each turn to a wall, room after room or skylights installed in the floor, is a chilling reminder of a woman possessed, by what, no one will ever know. Employees have reported creaking floors, smells of chicken soup coming from the kitchens and there have been sightings of people resembling Mrs Winchester's old employees and even Sarah herself. It's impossible to visit without at least one chill running up your spine.

☛ *Visit by car or take the number 60 VTA bus from Santa Clara Station. There are guided tours daily. See www.winchester mysteryhouse.com for details.*

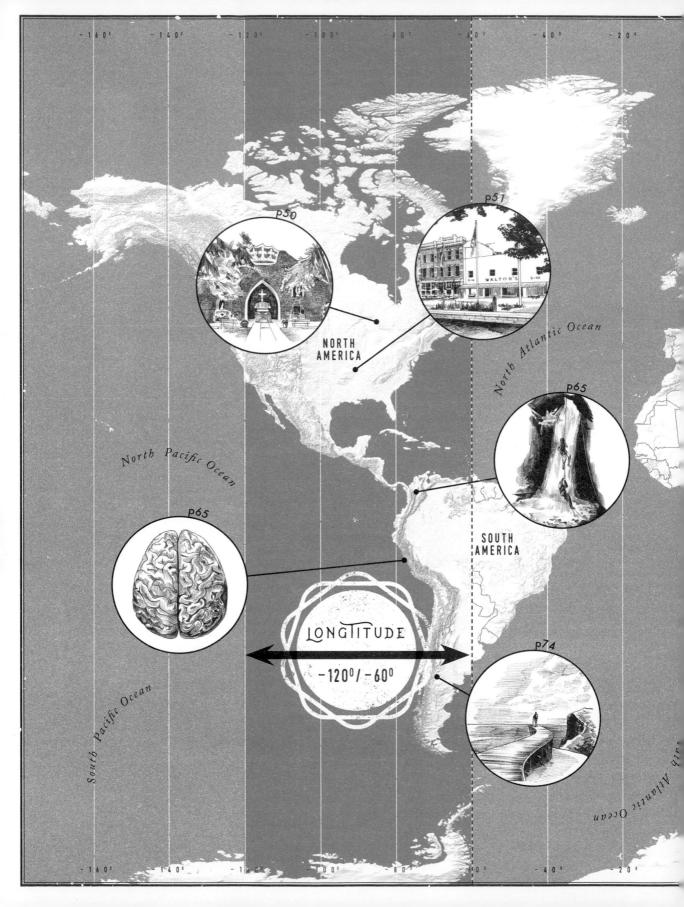

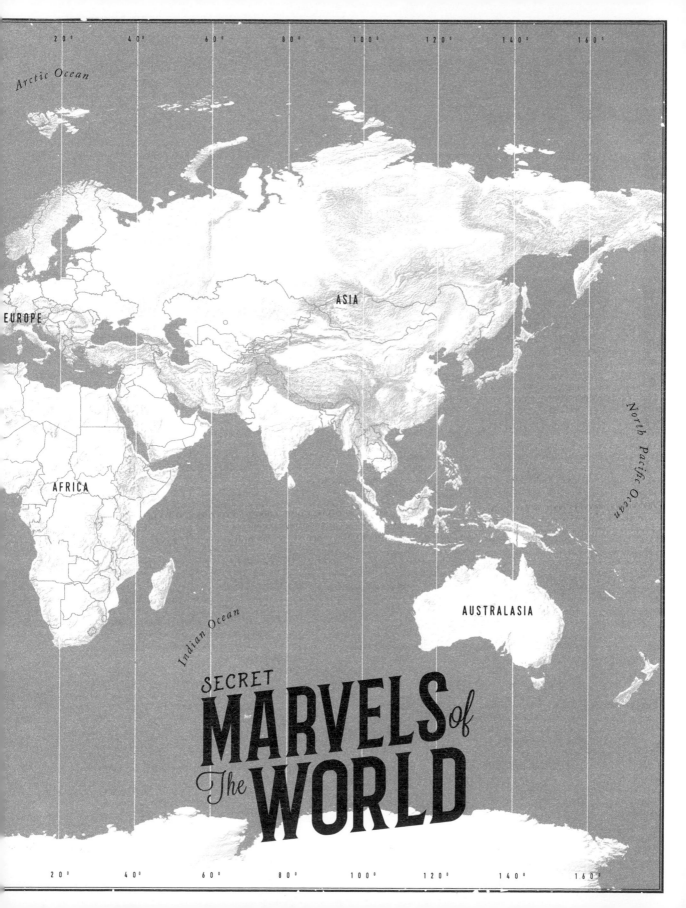

'Boulders dotted the parched earth before me. In their wake, trails were carved into the dirt. How did the rocks move? Some weighed 600 pounds'

ℂALIFORNIA, USA, 36.6813 / −117.5627

Racetrack Playa

As my Jeep Liberty slammed over the washboard ruts of Racetrack Road in Death Valley National Park, I tried to keep my bones from rattling right out of my body. With miles of washboard ahead and empty desert all around, I felt vulnerable and alone. But then again, that was the point.

My goal? Observing the mysterious moving rocks of the Racetrack Playa, a dry lake-bed in the northern wilds of the park. I was living in Los Angeles at the time, trying to break in as a screenwriter. But success was elusive. As a goal-oriented person, I decided to tackle a series of challenging outdoor adventures. Mini-successes would keep me fired up.

But then I met Racetrack Road. A 20-mile unpaved nightmare in a desert valley flanked by dark mountains. How nightmarish? The park recommends 4WD. A spare tyre is also smart. Cell phone coverage? Nope. And did

I mention that Charles Manson and his followers holed up in the southern reaches of Death Valley after the Helter Skelter murders? Misfits and malcontents were no strangers here.

Teakettle Junction finally appeared, a solitary mileage marker typically draped in teakettles. The playa was six miles ahead. Anticipation overtook fear as I drove. After reaching the south-playa parking area, I left the Jeep. Approached the lake-bed.

Boulders dotted the parched earth before me. In their wake, trails were carved into the dirt. How did the rocks move? Some weighed more than 600 pounds. That question had bedevilled observers for decades. Aliens? Supernatural forces? Freakish weather? Scientists solved the mystery in 2013. In winter, a thin sheet of ice occasionally covers the playa. As the ice warms, it cracks apart. Winds push

these ice patches into rocks that have tumbled from surrounding mountains. The wind-driven ice floes shove the rocks across the slick lake-bed. After temperatures rise, the ice vaporises, leaving the boulders.

I walked, took pictures. Mesmerising. But I had a long journey back, so I didn't linger. My return? Bumpy, but fun. I'd accomplished my goal. Even better? I'd seen something rare, which triggered a sense of lightness and wonder. Maybe there was magic left in the world. And though the mystery has since been solved, the stark beauty of the setting and the rarity of the phenomenon keep the place amazing. *By Amy Balfour*

The boulders dot the southern end of the playa. Don't walk across the playa when it is wet; don't drive or cycle across it at any time. The western border of the park is 370km from LA.

© John Delapp / Getty Images

'Retired undertaker David H Brown collected discarded glass embalming fluid containers from funeral homes to build his dream woodland cottage'

ⒷRITISH ⒸOLUMBIA, ⒸANADA, 49.4052 / -116.7415

The Glass House

If you were an undertaker, what would you do with the thousands of glass bottles of embalming fluid left over from preserving a career's worth of dead bodies? Well, if you are David H Brown, a Canadian funeral director, you build your house with them.

My windshield wipers are working overtime as I drive north on Highway 3A in eastern British Columbia, searching for this oddity known as The Glass House. The drenching rain nearly obscures the views of Kootenay Lake and the wooded hills. Patches of fog along the snaking tree-lined road give it a slightly sinister start-of-a-horror-movie air, though perhaps that's just my imagination.

Brown constructed his Glass House in the 1950s from more than 500,000 empty embalming fluid bottles. Deciding that this funeral industry byproduct could be put to good use, the retired undertaker collected discarded glass embalming fluid containers from funeral homes across western Canada to build his woodland cottage.

When I pull in at The Glass House, set in forested gardens overlooking Kootenay Lake, I'm surprised to find that it looks like a fairy-tale castle. It has turrets, rounded walls and rectangular merlons jutting up from the roof. The exterior appears to be made from thousands of square glass bricks and, even on this grey day, it sparkles. Bright red paint trims the windows, the glass cross-hatched with diamond-shaped glazing bars. Colourful flowers bloom along stone ledges, and vividly painted, oddly lifelike gnomes peek out from under the bushes.

The interior of the 111 square metre house is more pedestrian, preserved as it was 50 years ago. An old sewing machine sits atop a wooden table, a vintage baby carriage on a braided rug nearby. The pine-panelled kitchen has yellowing Formica counters and a white Frigidaire stove. The only hint that this house isn't a typical 1950s suburban bungalow is a display of photos detailing its construction, depicting walls of glass rising between the pines.

In the garden, it's a fairyland again, with bridges and paths through the woods, incorporating more embalming fluid bottles. A testament to one man's weirdly compelling vision, The Glass House was David Brown's dream home. To this funeral director, using the byproducts of his industry wasn't eerie, but sensible, practical, even a bit fanciful. Cute garden gnomes and all. *By Carolyn B. Heller*

🡒 *The Glass House, 11341 Highway 3A, is just south of Boswell and 40km north of Creston in BC. It's open daily for tours from May to October.*

'I climbed to the mountain's cross for a panoramic view of the 150ft length of the monument and the abandoned vehicles surrounding it'

CALIFORNIA, USA, 33.2541 / -115.4726

Salvation Mountain

Salvation Mountain is a living prayer in a desolate wilderness. It is at once so unique and so out of place that you must enter it. Some cry at first sight, while others fall to their knees in prayer, and even those who visit out of curiosity often leave as pilgrims.

It was the life's work of Leonard Knight. Born in Vermont in 1931, he was a drifter until a religious epiphany struck in 1967. Using his bare hands, he began building an adobe and straw mountain on a low mesa in the baking hot desert of Southern California near the Salton Sea in 1984. His simple mission was to share his religious fervour with the world, spelling it out in paint on his mountain, and it consumed him until his death in 2011. The result is a surreal merging of mountain and prayer book.

The mountain face declares 'God is Love' over a massive red heart, the work peaks at just over 50ft and is topped by a gleaming white cross. It is framed by painted waves that Leonard called his 'Sea of Galilee'. The mountain boasts trees, flowers, and waterfalls among countless prayers, coated with an estimated 100,000 gallons of paint in a rainbow spectrum.

I followed a yellow path past a towering wall that holds both the sinner's prayer and various biblical quotes, to the 'Hogan', a circular room decorated eclectically with the cast-off detritus of the desert, and an homage to the local indigenous people. Next I visited Leonard's 'museum' of towering walls, held in place by a forest of surreally twisted, multicoloured trees, all winding towards heaven like giant fingers, in bold Day-Glo colours. I wandered through a maze of dead ends, which Leonard said always brought the visitor back to God.

Finally I climbed to the base of the mountain's cross for a panoramic view of the entire 150ft length of the monument, and the graveyard of abandoned vehicles surrounding it, each of which is covered with prayers. At the centre is the rusting truck that Leonard Knight called his home for 31 years.

Salvation Mountain is listed in the Congressional Record as a national treasure, and has appeared in some half a dozen films. It's maintained by volunteers, some of whom live on site, all of them eager to greet visitors and answer questions while soliciting donations of paint for the non-stop maintenance the monument requires. *By James Dorsey*

 Salvation Mountain is just outside the town of Niland, which sits on Highway 111. See www.salvationmountain.us.

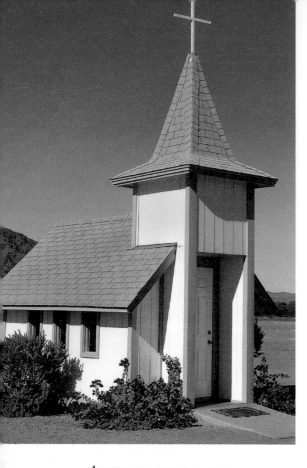

ARIZONA, USA, 31.5395 / -110.7562

Telles Family Shrine

The first time I stared into the Telles Family Shrine, I couldn't make sense of it. A collection of bright candles, many of them burning, filled a small cave at the top of a roadside staircase 4km south of Patagonia, Arizona. The walls of this lonely grotto were black from candle smoke. What was this place? I learned that Juanita and Juan Telles created it in 1941. They promised to keep the candles burning if their sons returned safely from World War II. They came home alive, and the promise was kept. Today, the Telles family is gone, but locals keep the candles burning. By Amy Balfour

ARIZONA, USA, 32.7655 / -114.4141

PAUSE-REST-WORSHIP CHAPEL

It's easy to feel despair driving north from Yuma into the scorching desert of western Arizona. Behind you? The lonely Bridge to Nowhere as well as Yuma Territorial Prison, once dubbed the Hellhole of the West. Ahead? The ghost town of Castle Dome and the mysterious Yuma Proving Ground, a military research facility. But wait... is that an itty-bitty church? Yep, it's the Pause-Rest-Worship Chapel. A farmer built the 8ft-by-12ft structure in 1995, to commemorate his late wife. A storm destroyed it in 2011, but the community rebuilt it. The blue-and-white chapel seats 12 and even has stained-glass windows.

🐌 *The chapel is 24km northeast of Yuma on Highway 95.*

🐌 *Patagonia is 96km south of Tucson, Arizona.*

UTAH, USA, 39.8107 / -110.3386

NINE MILE CANYON

Tucked away in the fiery sandstone mountains of rugged Utah is one of the world's largest – and oldest – outdoor art galleries. Nine Mile Canyon (which is actually 46 miles long, but was originally formed by Nine Mile Creek), contains thousands of ancient petroglyphs, carved by the native Fremont and Ute tribes between AD 600 and 1300. The scenes – scattered throughout the canyon and easily accessible from the road running through it – depict everything from war and sacrifice to animal husbandry and family dynamics.

This spectacular visual storytelling is best explored with a local guide, who will help you peel away the respective layers (historically, not literally – there are signs everywhere reminding people not to touch the fragile rock art). A guide will also be able to point out petroglyphs, which you might otherwise have missed, as well as a number of (remarkably intact) ancient dwellings called pit houses. One way or another you'll need transport, but the canyon is a great day trip option with plenty of picturesque picnicking spots along the 160km round trip from the town of Price. Visitors are advised to pack plenty of provisions for the journey though (there are no shops or restaurants en route), as well as the free brochure detailing the canyon's main sites, which can be grabbed from the Carbon County Visitors Centre in Price.

Nine Mile Canyon is accessible from Price, southeast on US Route 6 then north on to Soldier Creek Rd.

EASTER ISLAND, CHILE, −27.0800 / −109.3105

THE NAVEL OF THE WORLD

Easter Island – or Rapa Nui, as it's called locally – will take your heart and your soul in a few days. One of the most isolated places on Earth, this tiny speck of land is blessed with an extraordinary array of archaeological sites. Apart from the iconic *moai* (giant statues) that are scattered amid an eerie landscape, you'll also be mesmerised by the so-called Navel of the World, a perfectly round-shaped stone that lies on the island's north coast. The legend claims that king Hotu Matua himself brought this stone here, symbolising the navel of the world. It's magnetic – when a compass is placed on the rock it loses its direction.

☛ *Get here by bike, car or scooter from the island's main town, Hanga Roa. Access to the site is free.*

ⓝEW ⓜEXICO, USA, 36.3021 / -106.0453

RA PAULETTE'S SANDSTONE CAVES

It's been a quarter of a century in the making. American artist Ra Paulette has spent most of his adult life digging, carving and chiselling out a series of underground caves in the soft sandstone rocks of the New Mexico desert. Using just hand tools, and with only his pet dog for company, he has created more than a dozen caves in all, dotted at various locations near Santa Fe.

The scale and detail of Paulette's work is staggering. He's dug chambers, tunnels, doorways, staircases, recessed seats, ledges and niches. On the walls he has sculpted bas-reliefs and cornices, some loosely based on plant life, others psychedelic. All the caves are illuminated by grandiose skylights reaching up towards the desert floor above them.

Some were commissioned from Paulette by local residents, and have been fitted with mod cons. They now sell for hundreds of thousands of dollars. Not that financial gain was a motivation – on many of the commissions he was paid just US$12 an hour. Instead, it was the artistic impulse that drove him.

'The fact that the cave is underground and you feel the earth around you, yet the sun is pouring in – those are the juxtapositions of the two metaphors of our life,' he explains in *Cave Digger*, a documentary about his life's work. 'The within and the without. It's a perceptual trick that brings out deep, expansive emotionality.'

 The caves' exact location is not advertised but Origin (originnewmexico.com) offers tours for US$25.

①MARIETAS, ②MEXICO, 20.7006 / -105.5687

Hidden beach

The secret beaches of the Marietas are a sought-after sight in their own right, and the so-called Hidden Beach is the cherry on top. Sliding off the side of a catamaran, I swim with the tide until I reach a thin slit – like the lip of a closed clamshell – between the surface of the sea and the arid island above. I duck under the waves, quickly resurfacing in a rocky chasm that leads towards the doughnut hole, ringed by a spit of peachy sand, at the island's core. Archaeologists and volcanologists have posited theories of the island's strange shape based on evidence of ancient deity worship and modern-day bomb testing – today it's an anomaly dutifully captured on Instagram by its visitors. By Brandon Presser

🦷 *A short boat ride connects the Marietas to Riviera Nayarit, serviced by the international airport in Puerto Vallarta.*

①NEBRASKA, USA, 42.1423 / -102.8580

CARHENGE

No one knows who built Stonehenge, or why. But we do know who built Carhenge (American artist Jim Reinders) and why (as a tribute to his father, and because it's cool). Dedicated on the summer solstice of 1987, these automotive Nebraska monoliths are fast becoming a cult destination. The sculpture consists of 39 classic American automobiles, painted grey and assembled in exactly the same formation as Stonehenge (the honour of depicting the heel stone goes to a 1962 caddy). Reinders, who erected the installation on the farm he owned in Nebraska, admitted its construction took 'a lot of work, sweat and beers'.

🦷 *Carhenge is 5km north of Alliance, NE. Opwn daily; entry is free (carhenge.com).*

© Education Images / Getty Images

◎SOUTH ◎DAKOTA, USA, 45.7406 / -102.2322

MONUMENT OF HUGH GLASS

The story of frontiersman Hugh Glass is so incredible that it's difficult to sort fact from fiction. He set out on a fur-trading expedition in 1823, but was attacked by a grizzly bear near the border of present-day North and South Dakota. Bleeding and unconscious, Glass was not expected to survive. His companions, unable to carry him to safety, buried him in a shallow grave and left him behind.

Glass survived. Driven by revenge but unable to walk, Glass crawled 200 miles to Fort Kiowa. The true story lacks a climactic ending, however. accounts differ on whether Glass had a change of heart or simply never had a chance to enact his vengeful plan. He was killed by Native Americans in 1833.

🦷 *A marker stands in Sandhill, South Dakota. Nearby Lemmon has a statue.*

CAVE OF THE CRYSTALS

Journey 300 metres towards the centre of the Earth to this science-fiction-worthy cave of translucent, gargantuan crystals. Humans are dwarfed by glistening pillars – some up to four metres thick – that crisscross the cavern like Escher staircases. Other blocks of shorter obelisk-shaped shafts line the walls. Some say the cavern looks like a cathedral, others are reminded of Superman's icy lair, but everyone agrees that it is one of the most astounding sights on the planet.

Surviving here requires a helmet, a respirator and an ice-packed suit to protect against the 50-degree Celsius temperatures and high humidity, but even with the proper attire, visits can safely last only about 20 minutes. The cave was closed to the public shortly after its discovery in 2000 when a mineworker snuck in and was roasted alive.

Some of the crystals are estimated to be around 500,000 years old and are likely the largest specimens ever discovered by humans. The mineral is selenite, a soft substance that's easily damaged – it can be scratched by a fingernail. The caves were naturally filled with water but have been pumped dry by the mining company. When, or if, the mine floods the chambers again, the crystals will begin to grow anew, but they will also be lost to human sight and research, possibly forever.

☛ *The cave is closed to the public but open by arrangement to scientists. See www.naica.com.mx for up-to-date information.*

INDIANA, USA, 41.5577 / -87.4895

GROTTO OF THE BLESSED VIRGIN MARY

Motoring past the tidy green lawns in Munster, Indiana – a working-class community near Chicago – you barely notice the low-slung buildings of Our Lady of Mount Carmel Monastery behind a thicket of trees. But the Discalced Carmelite Fathers have been here tending their trippy, fluorescent rock grotto for more than 60 years.

The barefoot monks, as they're known, arrived from Poland after World War II. One of the friars was also a geologist, so when they decided to build a one-of-a-kind shrine to the Virgin Mary in 1954, this guy knew just what to do. First came 250 tons of sponge rock for the grotto's dark, twisting, three-storey caverns. Then came the bright-hued bits of

rose quartz, blue fluorite and other minerals that glimmer in starry designs from the walls. The real eye popper, though, is the Fluorescent Altar. Flip the light switch and the stones around Mary's statue jolt to life. You don't see the message at first, but then the rocks start to glow yellow and green and 'Hail Holy Queen' appears in all its psychedelic glory.

More ultraviolet goodness radiates in the nearby Memorial Chapel, where there's a shrine to Jesus raising the dead. The monks show the sun dropping, hands clawing from the earth, yellow crosses marching across the ceiling – conveyed entirely with glow-in-the-dark rocks. Even Michelangelo would rub his eyes in wonder.

☞ *The monastery is open on Sundays, from April through to October, or by appointment. You'll need a car as it's a 50km drive from downtown Chicago. See carmelitefathers.com/shrine-visits/.*

ARKANSAS, USA, 36.3728 / −94.2094

WALMART MUSEUM

How did Walton's, a typical 1950s
five and dime store from the tiny town
of Bentonville in Arkansas, become the
ubiquitous retail behemoth known as
Walmart? Visit the place where the empire
began at the Walmart Museum, housed
in the original building on Main St in
Bentonville. Details such as the preserved
ceiling and floor tiles give visitors a
glimpse into Sam Walton's world as he
pioneered the deep-discount no-frills
business model. The meticulously curated
museum provides a comprehensive look at
how Walton turned the idea of the variety
store into the worldwide phenomenon of
Walmart and forever changed the retail
landscape in America.

☛ *The museum is free and open daily.*
See www.walmartmuseum.com.

ALABAMA, USA, 34.6733 / −86.0445

UNCLAIMED BAGGAGE CENTER

Scottsboro's Unclaimed Baggage Center delivers the goods
in more ways than one. Part jumbo-sized second-hand
store, part museum of an extraordinary range of lost items,
this labyrinth of lost goods is awe-inspiring in scale and an
excellent place to pick up some cheap cowboy boots.

There's a simple idea at the heart of this place: once
airlines have paid passengers compensation for losing their
bags they still need to dispose of them. What waits within
the store are racks of (laundered) clothing, piles of electronic
devices and enough quirky items besides to happily pass
half a day. Staff also run insightful demonstrations of the art
of unpacking someone else's lost bag and deciding what
gets to go on sale here.

☛ *The Unclaimed Baggage Center, two hours drive from*
Nashville, opens Mon-Sat. See www.unclaimedbaggage.com.

CAYO, BELIZE, 17.1175 / -88.8905

Actun Tunichil Muknal

The cave was black. The weak beam of my headlamp lit only as far as my next step. But when our guide, Juan Carlos, shined his powerful light on our surroundings, the space suddenly opened up. It was a vast cavern, hanging with magnificent stalactite and stalagmite formations. So this is what the underworld looks like, I thought. We had journeyed almost a mile into Actun Tunichil Muknal, in the Cayo district of Belize, following in the footsteps of the ancient Maya. A millennium ago they frequented this cave network, seeking a route to the underworld and a way to communicate with its gods. Our small group of travellers had come to see what they had left behind.

After an hour of wading and climbing, we gathered on a dry ledge. 'You will walk where I walk and stand where I tell you to stand,' Juan Carlos instructed. 'There are artefacts all over this

place and you don't want to be stepping on them.' He shone his light on the ground, where a broken pot lay at our feet. Several other examples were strewn around the chamber. Juan Carlos explained that the pots were used for food offerings and blood-letting rituals. Scholars believe that a Maya ruler would slit his tongue or the tip of his penis, then mix the blood with incense and burn it as an offering to the gods.

After spelunking through the cave and discovering thousand-year-old artefacts, it was hard to imagine what might come next. But Juan Carlos had saved the best for last: his light illuminated a 1500-year-old skull. Other bones were scattered nearby, all belonging to a 40-year-old male. They don't know how he was killed, but he almost certainly was a victim of human sacrifice.

That was the first of many skeletons we discovered in Actun

'Our guide's light illuminated a 1500-year-old skull. Other bones were scattered nearby, almost certainly from a victim of human sacrifice'

Tunichil Muknal, which contains the remains of 14 individuals – all of whom were sacrificial offerings – including a complete skeleton of a young woman. Encrusted in calcium carbonate, the so-called Crystal Maiden sparkles in the beam of a light.

Before we left, Juan Carlos set a scene for us. 'Imagine this room lit with torches,' he said, shining his light on the stalactites and stalagmites, which cast shadows on the walls. 'Imagine the air is filled with chanting.' Then, referring to the hallucinogenic morning glories we'd seen outside, 'Now imagine that you are high. No wonder the Mayans believed that they were communicating with gods in this mystical place.' No wonder indeed. *By Mara Vorhees*

☞ *The caves are accessible only by licensed guided tour. Try www.pacztours.net or www.cavesbranch.com.*

ROATÁN, HONDURAS, 16.3107 / −86.5453

BAY ISLANDS UNDERWATER MUSEUM

Tired of the same old humdrum museum routine? Are you over the informational headsets, long queues and mobs of people? Then trade those cargo shorts and trainers for a swimsuit and some flippers and head over to the Bay Islands Underwater Museum. This unique exhibition is located off the coast of Roatán, one of Honduras' picturesque Bay Islands. Shunning traditional exhibits for one filled with adventure, the museum leads snorkelling visitors into the glittering Caribbean waters, where they will discover a number of rather unique sunken treasures: Maya statues, Paya artefacts, Garifuna canoes, old anchors and even a Spanish galleon. Guides will fill you in on the background of these items before you hit the surf for your underwater scavenger hunt, giving you some background about colonisation in this part of the Americas and the subsequent fight for independence.

The experience isn't purely an historical one, however. The Bay Islands are known as one of the world's pre-eminent locations to observe coral reefs, and abundant wildlife thrives among the museum's installations. Brightly hued fish swim around the sunken artefacts, while golden starfish and striped shrimp move across the sandy ocean floor. Corals punctuate the seascape, and crabs duck in and out of their hiding spots.

☛ *The museum is in west Roatán, accessible from the main road. Several tour operators coordinate visits.*

⊕ KENTUCKY, USA, 39.0810 / -84.8486

ABANDONED GHOST SHIP

South of the Ohio River in Petersburg, Kentucky, lies the 186ft *Sachem*, its rusting prow sticking sharply out from the surrounding vegetation, the hull tilted slightly askew in the muddy banks of the river tributary. The ship's sombre present betrays its colourful past, however. First setting sail in 1902, the boat served as a luxury yacht, carried Thomas Edison, trained naval soldiers, fought in two world wars, and appeared in a pop music video before being banished to its current isolated locale.

Originally dubbed the *Celt*, the ship was commissioned by wealthy Delaware railroad executive J Rogers Maxwell; it was sold in 1917 and leased to the US Navy, who outfitted it with depth charges designed to sink World War I U-boats. Renamed the *Sachem*, it took on a new

military life – in an effort to improve their anti-submarine technology, the navy gave it to Thomas Edison, who used it to conduct experiments in New York Harbor and sail to Florida and the Caribbean. After the war, the ship was sold, serving as a fishing vessel before returning to the line of duty a second time during World War II. Renamed yet again, the *USS Phenakite* was primarily a training and patrol boat, guarding both the Key West Harbor and the Long Island Sound. After World War II ended, the ship sailed as a tour boat in New York City for over 40 years. It made an appearance in Madonna's 'Papa Don't Preach' music video before it was bought one last time, this time by a Cincinnati native who sailed the ship inland to its final resting place, where it has languished for more than 30 years.

☛ *The ship is located on private property, so accessing the site by foot is trespassing. Sachem is accessible by kayak via the Ohio River and the Taylor Creek tributary.*

GRANADA, NICARAGUA, 11.9313 / −85.9628
SAN JUAN DE DIOS

In 1886, construction began on the Hospital San Juan de Dios, a shining example of neoclassical architecture in Granada. Today, however, the hospital more closely resembles a horror movie set, its chequered hallways hauntingly empty of patients and doctors, its courtyards overgrown and its ornamental façade crumbling, trees sprouting through its neglected walls. The building officially opened in 1905 and closed in 1998, and while there are plans to renovate it, no progress has come to fruition. Recent visitors have reported that the area is now protected by security guards, but some are happy to show urban explorers around.

☛ *The hospital is a 15-minute walk west from Parque Central on Calle La Libertad. Taxi drivers know it as el antiguo hospital.*

GEORGIA, USA, 34.2696 / −84.7518
OLD CAR CITY

Cadillac Ranch in Texas isn't the only rural automobile installation worth visiting in the car-crazy USA. Old Car City in White, Georgia, is a fascinating mash-up of open-air classic car museum and nature preserve. Spend an afternoon walking the six miles of nature trails as they wind through one of the most beautiful junkyards in the world, filled with more than 4,000 complete cars from no later than 1972. The forest has reclaimed many of the cars, creating an ethereal, post-apocalyptic atmosphere.

Run by Dean Lewis as a labour of love, the 34-acre lot was originally purchased by his parents in 1931 as a site for a general store. They started a car dealership here as well, and Lewis has kept up this tradition for decades.

☛ *Old Car City, an hour's drive from Atlanta, opens Wednesday to Saturday, 9am-4pm (www.oldcarcityusa.com).*

Diquís Delta, Costa Rica. 8.8689 / -83.4710

DIQUÍS SPHERES

Scattered around the Diquís Delta on the west coast of Costa Rica are giant stone spheres – the only remnants of the mysterious Diquís civilisation that existed between 300 BC and 1500 AD. Their purpose remains unknown, though theories suggest that those spheres found aligned in a certain way may have functioned as solar calendars, while others were symbols of an individual's power (the bigger the sphere, the more powerful the chief).

You can see them in public parks in Palmar Sur and Sierpe, though the best place to view them is the Sitio Arqueológico Finca 6 museum between the two, where the spheres have been left in their original alignments.

 The museum opens 8am to 4pm Tuesday to Sunday. Buses run between Sierpe and Palmar Sur.

GEORGIA, USA.
32.4525 / −84.9791

LUNCHBOX MUSEUM

Readers of a certain age will remember the days of toting your lunch to school in a metal box, usually with a matching thermos tucked inside. If you want to see your old lunchtime pal again, chances are you'll find it at the world's largest lunchbox collection in Columbus, Georgia.

Located in the backroom of an antiques shop, this isn't a museum in any usual sense of the word, but rather a haphazard, extensive collection of varied lunchboxes featuring pop culture icons ranging from Star Trek to Peanuts to Strawberry Shortcake to Pac Man.

☞ *The collection is open daily; entry to the museum is $5. See www.lunchboxmuseum.com.*

CORDILLERA, COSTA RICA.
10.1845 / −84.3918

PARQUE FRANCISCO ALVARADO

If you're travelling through central Costa Rica, take a detour to Zarcero, a small town located in the western part of the Cordillera. There, you'll find Parque Francisco Alvarado, perhaps the country's most unusual public green space. Situated in front of the stately 17th-century Iglesia de San Rafael, the park started off as your average topiary garden before its gardener, Evangelisto Blanco, decided to let his creativity flow in the 1960s, shaping the trees into dreamy, Dalí-esque forms. Today, the spot continues to function as an interactive botanical art exhibit thanks to Blanco's continued efforts. Wind your way through a tunnel of 'melting' arches, or snap a photo with whimsical dancers, animals and dinosaurs.

☞ *Buses make the drive to Zarcero from San José, Grecia, Alajuela, and San Ramón.*

GEORGIA, USA.
33.7984 / −84.3272

CENTER FOR DISEASE CONTROL MUSEUM

Fans of disaster movies and *The Walking Dead* will be familiar with the Center for Disease Control, in Atlanta, Georgia. Whenever any pandemics, fictional and real, sweep across the planet, all eyes turn to the CDC for guidance and reassurance about the security of global health. The CDC museum focuses on the agency's achievements in studying, treating and preventing disease, as well as highlighting important artefacts in its history. In addition to the permanent collection, there are rotating exhibits on topics such as diabetes prevention, interactive exhibits that let you do things like try on a hazmat suit, plus art and photography on health-related themes by artists such as Norman Rockwell.

☞ *This Smithsonian affiliate is open Monday to Friday; entry is free. See www.cdc.gov/museum.*

GEORGIA, USA.
34.8890 / -84.2207

TANK TOWN USA

If you're in Morgantown, Georgia, with an insatiable urge to destroy things with heavy machinery, head on over to Tank Town USA. Its motto is simple and accurately describes the fun to be had here: 'Drive Tanks, Crush Cars'. The main attraction is the tank-driving course, which you can work your way around – the end of the course is where the car-crushing action happens.

If you've always wanted to work on a building site, you can fulfil those dreams here as well – take a 20-ton construction excavator for a spin and dig holes to your heart's content.

☛ Open most weekends, 11am to 6pm, from April to November. See www.tanktownusa.com

© Epa European Pressphoto Agency B.V. / Alamy

GRAND CAYMAN, CAYMAN ISLANDS. 19.3792 / -81.4064

HELL

The phrase 'to hell and back' takes on a very literal meaning when you visit the island of Grand Cayman. Tucked away in the middle of a tropical paradise, you'll find the quirkily named Hell, a group of ancient limestone rock formations in West Bay. Spiky, black and barren, the rocks evoke the infernal underworld, but the site itself delivers a healthy side of camp to go along with its spooky atmosphere. The local post office and gift shop has been painted bright red and emblazoned with the greeting 'Welcome to Hell'; stop in, meet the resident 'Satan' – who actually goes by the name of Ivan Farrington and enjoys making hell-themed puns – and send postcards to all your friends with the official Hell postmark.

☛ Hell is a 15-minute drive from Seven Mile Beach, on the Hell Road. Free admission.

© Hank Shiffman / Shutterstock

TUNGURAHUA, ECUADOR.
-1.4158 / -78.4262

SWING AT THE END OF THE WORLD

High up in the Ecuadorian jungle, a treehouse perches precariously on the edge of a canyon. The Casa de Arbol is actually a seismic observation station built to keep an eye on Tungurahua, the active volcano next to it. Yet it's the crude swing, a plank suspended by two ropes hanging from a tree branch, that attracts daredevil visitors. There are no safety features – no harness, no net – so those who choose to push off over the canyon take their lives into their own hands. The reward? A head-spinning view of the canyon floor, and perhaps a glimpse of an erupting volcano as you swing over its lip.

☛ The swing is 10.5km up a steep, winding mountain road from the nearby town of Baños.

© Kalypso World Photography / Alamy

'The pièce de résistance is the artist's own house, a maelstrom of murals, arches, lurid faces and swirling ceramic trees and flowers'

HAVANA, CUBA, 23.0898 / −82.4831

Fusterlandia

Cuba's most remarkable work of art isn't a sculpture or a painting, but a whole city neighbourhood. Fusterlandia is the unofficial name for Jaimanitas, a quiet Havana suburb with a history rooted in fishing that, these days, is better known for its giddy array of mosaics, murals and whimsical Gaudí-esque street art by talented Cuban artist José Fuster.

Fuster's project began as a spot of home decoration in the mid-1990s, but quickly morphed into something more ambitious. By the 2010s, his decorative ceramics and imaginative paintings had covered several city blocks, encompassing street signs, public spaces and more than 80 local houses. Doused in bright Caribbean sunshine, the intricate tilework, curvaceous parapets and kaleidoscope of colours create a spectacle that makes Barcelona's Park Güell look positively sedate.

Welcoming you to the 'show' is the Jaimanitas neighbourhood sign etched with words *'Homenaje a Gaudí'* (Homage to Gaudí) arranged in a vivid mosaic. The father of Spanish *modernisme* isn't Fuster's only influence. Nearby, a public bench set in front of a wave-shaped wall is covered in tiles painted with Picasso-like visages.

Yet, despite the modernist bent, Fusterlandia is inherently Cuban. At a street junction a block away, a huge mural depicts the landing of the *Granma* yacht in Cuba in 1956. Aboard the ship, you can pick out the figures of Fidel Castro, Che Guevara and Camilo Cienfuegos. Equally head-swivelling are reproductions of the Cuban flag, surreal studies of Cuba's patron saint, the Virgin of Charity, and a line of joined-up houses (Fuster's neighbours) emblazoned with the words 'Viva Cuba' with a different letter marked on each chimney.

Fusterlandia is renowned for its community engagement. Benches, bus stops, street posts and even a doctor's surgery all get the Fuster treatment. Tucked under a wall next to the artist's home is a chess park containing a life-sized chessboard with several Alice in Wonderland-like kings, queens and knights.

Fusterlandia's pièce de résistance, however, is the artist's own house, a maelstrom of murals, arches, lurid faces and swirling ceramic trees and flowers. The multi-levelled complex is centred on a small pool replete with mythical maritime themes (recalling Jaimanitas' fishing background) and enlivened with mermaids, fishermen and a giant octopus.

For a bird's-eye view, climb up to a small observation deck where you can look down on everything and absorb the fantasy, exuberance and, above all, overriding sunniness. Fuster's house is also home to his *taller* (workshop) where it is possible to acquire a piece of the master's art or, if you're lucky, watch him at work. *By Brendan Sainsbury*

☛ Jaimanitas lies 20km west of central Havana. Bus P4 stops nearby, or you can take a taxi. Entrance to Fuster's house is free.

⌖FLORIDA, USA, 25.5005 / −80.4443

CORAL CASTLE

This massive sculpture park was a nearly 30-year labour of love – or more accurately, heartbreak. Built entirely by hand using primitive tools, the fantastical sculptures are the creation of Latvian immigrant Edward Leedskalnin who spent 28 years sculpting them out of coral stone found near his home in Florida. Leedskalnin's sculptures comprise over 1100 tons of coral, all carved as a monument to the woman who left him a day before their planned wedding. Leedskalnin never married, and his love never came to see the monument he built for her.

Much mystery surrounds Leedskalnin's building methods. He was a small man, barely 150cm tall and under 50kg, yet he laboured alone for nearly three decades building sculptures reaching up to 7.5m in height, most of them carved out of a single piece of stone. He also constructed a wall around the sculpture garden, measuring 2.5m tall, 1.2m wide, and 1m thick.

Leedskalnin never revealed his engineering secrets, and he worked at night by lantern light so no one could watch him or observe his methods. He came from a family of stonemasons in Latvia, but modern scholars are still uncertain about how he was able to complete such extensive building work on his own. The sculpture garden, about 45 minutes south of Miami, was added to the National Register of Historic Places in 1984.

🕭 *Coral Castle is open daily. Admission includes a tour of the sculpture garden (www.coralcastle.com).*

①LIMA, ℗ERU, -12.0453 / -77.0271

CATACOMBS OF THE MONASTERIO DE SAN FRANCISCO

The catacombs beneath the Franciscan monastery in Lima hide a gruesome secret – the human remains of some 25,000 people. The skulls, tibiae and femurs are artistically arranged in geometric shapes – particularly concentric circles – in circular pits about 10m deep. Lit up for dramatic effect, these displays, presumably created by the monks, suggest a ritualistic purpose. They are spine-chilling and beautiful at the same time, and can be observed through the floor grates of the Monasterio de San Francisco.

The Franciscan crypts – a series of labyrinthine tunnels with vaulted ceilings – date back to the 16th century. From then, until the early 19th century, they served as a burial place for members of guilds and brotherhoods, with bodies stacked on top of one another along the passage walls and covered in lime to accelerate the decomposition process. After decomposition of the flesh, the bones were then moved to the ossuaries and arranged in an artistic fashion. The custom of burying the dead underneath the church persisted until 1808, when the use of the catacomb burials was banned by decree, and they were subsequently closed off from the outside world.

Forgotten over the decades, the catacombs were uncovered again in 1943 and opened to the public in 1950. It is believed that subterranean passages link them to the cathedral and other churches in the near vicinity.

👉 *The monastery is located in the historic heart of Lima and is open between 9.30am and 5.30pm. The catacombs may only be visited as part of a guided tour. See www.museocatacumbas.com.*

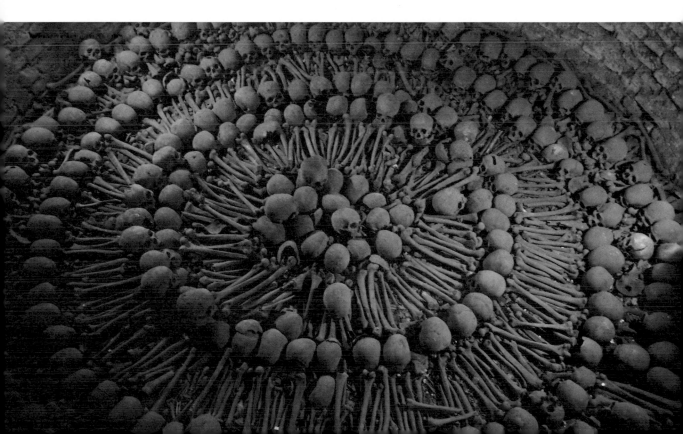

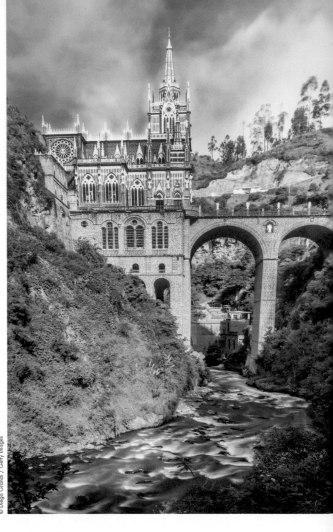

© Diego Grandi / Getty Images

CORDILLERA, PERU, -6.8640 / -78.1426
SOMBRERO OF CELENDÍN

In the highlands of the verdant Cordillera Central in northern Peru, the town of Celendín is known for its handcrafted straw hats. So much so, in fact, that the gazebo in one of the town's squares has been transformed to look like a giant version of just such a hat, with people congregating in the ample shade offered by its wide brim. The iconic high-topped straw hats themselves are a work of true craftsmanship: they are made using *toquilla* straw (also used in the making of Ecuador's world-famous Panama hats), with individual strands woven and tightened by local craftsmen. A bespoke hat takes anything from a few weeks to months to be crafted.

🐾 *Celendín is about 100km northeast of Cajamarca; buses connect the two.*

NARIÑO, COLOMBIA, 0.8056 / -77.5859
SANTUARIO DE LAS LAJAS

Practically hanging over the abyss, the Las Lajas cathedral perches 100m above the Guáitara River canyon, connected by a bridge to the side of the ravine. The construction of this Roman Catholic edifice that resembles a castle is rooted in miracles. According to legend, a local Amerindian woman and her deaf-mute daughter were caught in a storm here in 1754. When they took shelter in the gorge, they saw the image of the Virgin Mary in the stone, and the girl became able to hear and speak. When a blind man later regained his sight here too, pilgrims in search of miraculous healing followed and, in 1949, the humble chapel built around the image finally became a church.

🐾 *The church is 2km outside Ipiales; take a taxi. From the drop-off it's a steep 10-minute walk downhill to the church.*

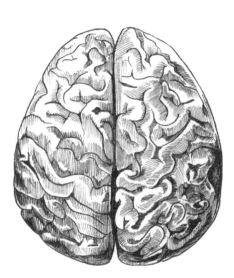

Ⓛima, Ⓟeru, −12.046026 / −77.015925

MUSEO DEL CEREBRO

An unprepossessing building down a decrepit street behind Lima's Institute of Neurological Science hides a remarkable collection. More than 3000 neatly labelled, formaldehyde-filled jars line the walls, the brains inside them displaying damage caused by diseases from neurological disorders and substance abuse to tumours, strokes, Alzheimer's and even mad cow disease. Neuropathologist Diana Rivas oversees the collection and performs autopsies in the same building, acquiring more specimens. While most visitors tend to be neurology students and academics, Rivas also educates the general public about preventable diseases by letting them see the effects up close.

🖝 *The museum is in a fairly rough part of town. It's best to take a taxi.*

Ⓐntioquia, Ⓒolombia, 5.6396 / −75.8096

LA CUEVA DEL ESPLENDOR

In the green mountains high above the little town of Jardín, a river runs through 'the Cave of Splendour'. The roof of the cave has been worn down by the gushing stream over the centuries, and a luminescent waterfall cascades through the hole in the rock. The cave has become a popular destination in recent years for hikers and equestrians, with sweaty travellers making a beeline for the deep, refreshing pool at the base of the waterfall as the reward for their exertion. Getting there is half the fun, with beautiful views of the surrounding mountains en route, followed by a steep scramble down a riverbed trail to the cave itself.

🖝 *The cave is 12.5km from Jardín. Take a Jeep to the trailhead, then go on horseback or on foot with local guides.*

'One curandero slowly passes a guinea pig over the prone body of a woman, then brings it to her ear, as if listening to what it has to say'

ⒸLIMA. ⓅERU. -12.0464 / -77.0428

Lima Witches' Market

The women arrive with the dawn, many on overnight buses from the mountains. Their traditional layered petticoats and bowler hats identify them as *curanderos* (mystical healers) and they gather each week at the witches' market in Lima, where hundreds of the faithful wait to be cured.

They are from and of the mountains, living a life unchanged in centuries; a merging of Catholicism, Santeria and folk superstition, but also of the modern world. They gather in a huge tent under banners that list their websites and mobile phone numbers, and photos that display their medical specialities. Business cards list their healing tools of eggs, coca leaves and even live guinea pigs, all of which they claim can cure anything from broken bones to cancer. Each stall offers displays

of fetishes and totems that will cast spells or repel the evil eye, a belief taken seriously here.

One *curandero*, a plug of cocoa leaves tucked in her cheek, slowly passes a guinea pig over the prone body of a woman on a table then brings it to her ear, as if listening to what it has to say. The woman has complained of stomach pains and the *curandero* assures her the guinea pig has identified her problem. It is cancer. Not to worry, though, as the *curandero* now passes an egg over the afflicted spot while chanting an incantation. The woman is then told to rise and go her way. She leaves, believing she is cured. Another man stands on his broken leg after healing hands are laid on it and walks out the door without a limp. A lady claims an evil spell has been cast on her unborn child so a

hand-held magnet is used to suck out the offending entity. A line of patients, all waiting in absolute faith, applaud as each patient leaves cured.

This is traditional folk medicine in its purest form and the *curanderos* have practiced it for generations. Lima is a world capital with modern medical facilities and Western ideals; its people are not uneducated but sophisticated city folk who hold beliefs in both the old and new. A stylishly dressed woman in heels, holding her baby, grasps my hand as she leaves, tears streaking her face. '*Gracias a Dios,*' she says. 'Thank God.'
By James Dorsey

☛ *The Witches Market takes place in the La Victoria neighbourhood of Lima, part of the 20-block mercado.*

BIG MAJOR CAY, THE BAHAMAS. 24.1836 / -76.4564

PIG BEACH

The Bahamas, an alluring chain of islands surrounded by luminous turquoise waters, is an ideal place to bask in the bright Caribbean sun or snorkel with rainbows of fish. Turns out it's also the best place in the world to hit the sands with some rather unusual local beach bums: swimming pigs. The southernmost beach on the uninhabited Big Major Cay, part of the Exuma Cays, is a porcine paradise, home to a gaggle of wild pigs that love nothing more than to take a daily ocean dip.

You can ask Bahamians about how these porky paddlers arrived in such a place, but you'll receive a wide range of answers. Some locals believe that ships carrying livestock to Nassau wrecked off the coast of the islet, leaving the animals to swim ashore to the cay; others think that they were intentionally brought by explorers (perhaps even Columbus himself) and pirates. Whatever their origin, the pigs are a hit with visitors looking for an unconventional day at the beach. While the animals are indeed feral, they are known for their friendly nature and have a habit of swimming out to greet passing boats, their snuffling snouts poking out of the gentle waves.

 The Exumas, 60km south of Nassau, can be accessed via flight or ferry (www.bahamasferries.com).

SANTA CATALINA, COLOMBIA,
8.8608 / -76.4181

VOLCÁN DE LODO EL TOTUMO

If you have ever fancied the idea of writing around in a massive vat of mud with a boatload of half-naked strangers – and who hasn't, right? – then Colombia's mud volcano just leapfrogged to the top of your bucket list. Volcán de Lodo El Totumo, 50km northeast of Cartagena on Colombia's gorgeous Caribbean Coast, is a 15m-high volcano-shaped tower filled not with molten lava but creamy, lukewarm, mineral-rich mud that makes for an immensely satisfying bath of supposed therapeutic pleasure. According to local lore, a priest, believing the 'volcano' to be the devil incarnate, turned the once fire and ash-spewing composite into a healing mud bath. If that is to be believed, then the fun-filled mound of dense and sexy sludge is surely the work of the Lord himself!

~~~~~~~~~~~~~~~~~~~~~~~~~~~~~~

🕨 *Organised tours run from Cartagena. The volcano is open dawn to dusk.*

© Matthew Micah Wright / Getty Images

VIRGINIA, USA, 38.2476 / -75.1545

ASSATEAGUE ISLAND'S FERAL HORSES

Assateague, a barrier island off the coast of Virginia, is most famous for its herd of wild horses. There are numerous theories about how these feral horses arrived on the island, ranging from them surviving a shipwreck off the Virginia coast to the more likely explanation that the herds were originally kept on the island by their mainland owners in order to avoid livestock taxes. These horses are beautiful and fascinating to observe, forming bands of up to 12 that roam the island together. The horses can be viewed by visiting the Assateague Island National Seashore, which stretches across 37 miles of pristine coastline and is split by the borders of Maryland and Virginia.

~~~~~~~~~~~~~~~~~~~~~~~~~~~~~~

🕨 *The park is open year-round. For more information, see www.nps.gov/asis/learn/nature/horses.htm.*

© FOTOS593 / Shutterstock

ANTIOQUIA, COLOMBIA, 6.2236 / -75.1783

EL PEÑÓN DE GUATAPÉ

Partially covered in sparse greenery, a giant stone rises steeply from the verdant, hilly grounds around the small town of Guatapé to a height of over 650 feet. Worshipped by the indigenous Tahamies people centuries ago, the monolith was first officially scaled in 1954 by a group of friends; the five-day climb was made using a series of boards wedged into the single crack in the otherwise smooth rock. Today, visitors can ascend the rock and the lookout tower at the summit using the 649-step masonry staircase wedged into the crack. The show-stopping vista from the summit – a series of lakes and islands – was created when the area was dammed in the 1970s.

 Take a bus from Medellín to Guatapé (two hours). From the turnoff to the rock it's a 20-minute walk.

WELLINGTON ISLAND, CHILE. -49.1390 / -74.4530

VILLA PUERTO EDÉN

Is this the rainiest place on the entire planet? Quite possibly. Villa Puerto Edén, a tiny fishing village among the fjords of southern Chile, is drenched with a precipitation of nearly 6000mm a year. Because of all that water, roads would get washed away, so instead the locals – all 176 of them, according to the latest census – get around town using pedestrian boardwalks or in their boats.

Not far from the southern tip of South America, the village is also one of the most isolated places on the planet, accessible only by sea. Public transport is not always straightforward: one local ferry company, Navimag, services Villa Puerto Edén

as part of its four-day journey through the fjords.

When you arrive here, on the east coast of the enormous Isla Wellington, that long journey will seem worth it. (Provided, of course, you can see through the veils of rain.) What first hits you are the ramshackle but brightly painted houses and huts overlooking the seafront. Looming behind them are mountains of the Bernardo O'Higgins National Park that remain snow-capped even in summer.

Villa Puerto Edén's claim to fame is that it is home to the world's last surviving members of the Kawesqar people. A handful remain, the last repositories of their language and culture.

Navimag offers a four-day ferry service to Villa Puerto Edén from Puerto Montt (on Fridays) and from Puerto Natales (on Tuesdays). Tickets start at US$550 per person; see www.navimag.com.

© Age Fotostock / Alamy

'We contemplated what we'd seen. Who drew these enormous animals? Who etched these straight lines into the desert surface? How? Why?'

Ⓝᴀᴢᴄᴀ Ⓓᴇꜱᴇʀᴛ, Ⓟᴇʀᴜ. −14.6939 / −75.1139

Nazca Lines

The little plane judders along the short runway of tiny Nazca Airport and takes off. There are eight of us inside – two pilots and six passengers. Soon we're high above the ring of greenery that surrounds the dusty cluster of streets of Nazca, flying over bare hills and vast desert. The desert is not featureless, however. Looking down, we can see ruler-straight lines etched into the stony ground, some converging and crossing over before disappearing into the distance. Seen from above, these roads to nowhere are longer than any airplane runway.

Then the animals come into view: a monkey with an intricately curved tail, a hummingbird with a long beak, a monstrous spider the size of the Empire State Building, a bird, a tree, a lizard. Their limbs are perfectly proportioned, the lines perfectly straight. We are glued to the windows in awe as the plane twists this way and that,

circling above each giant figure to ensure everyone gets a good look. Once back on the ground, we disperse to contemplate what we'd witnessed. Who drew these enormous animals? Who etched those straight lines into the surface of the desert? How? Why?

First brought to public attention in the 1930s, when commercial pilots began flying over Peru, the Nazca Lines – a series of miles-long straight lines, geometric shapes and giant animal figures scattered over some 500km of the parched Nazca Plain – have posed a puzzle to archaeologists and conspiracy theorists alike. It is believed that the geoglyphs were constructed by the ancient Nazca people who flourished here from around 200 BC to AD 600. The lines were made by removing earth and rust-coloured rocks from the surface of the desert, exposing 30cm of light-coloured sand beneath. The designs have remained largely

intact for up to 2000 years due to lack of rain, wind and erosion.

How the ancient designers managed to create such straight lines and perfectly proportioned animals remains a mystery, however, as does their purpose. Theories abound, some more outrageous than others: that the straight lines are ancient runways for alien spaceships, or that the animals are part of a giant astronomical calendar. Most recent theories suggest that the stylised animal and bird images either represented astrological phases or the totem (spirit) animals of different Nazca clans. As for the lines and trapezoids, it is possible that they were used in rituals to beg the gods for water in one of the driest parts of Peru.
By Anna Kaminski

🕨 *Best viewed from the air, the Nazca Lines can also be seen from the mirador (viewing tower) 20km outside Nazca.*

CHILOÉ, CHILE. −42.7137 / −74.1563
DOCK OF SOULS

The legend of Charon, the ancient Greek ferryman who transported dead souls across the river Hades to the underworld is well known. Less famous is the story of Chile's ferryman, Tempilcahue, who, according to ancient Mapuche legend, also transported dead souls to the afterlife.

Chilean artist Marcelo Orellana Rivera paid homage by building a huge wooden sculpture called *Muelle de las Almas* (Dock of Souls), on a promontory of the island of Chiloé, in southern Chile. It's a curved pier that stretches off the edge of a cliff, looking out across the Pacific Ocean. Sit here at sunset and you'll be tempted to catch the ferry to the afterlife yourself.

🐎 Drive south from the village of Cucao and park as close as possible. Make the final 45-minute hike on foot.

© Fotos593 / Shutterstock

ZIPAQUIRÁ, COLOMBIA. 5.0194 / −74.0095
Catedral de Sal

Colombia's salt cathedral, one of only three in the world, reeked of tourist trap to me. But as I descended 180m below ground into the otherworldly house of worship carved from 250,000 tonnes of salt, I quickly stood corrected. Located in the town of Zipaquirá, the stunning, dramatically lit sanctuary is a moving marvel bathed in cinematic crystalline. Ambling along the 14 small and maudlin chapels – each representing a Station of the Cross from Jesus' final journey – is an amazing passage through exquisite religious symbolism and mining triumph. If there is a God, he surely had a hand in the creation of the central nave (the world's largest underground church), where a mammoth cross, lit from head to toe, casts an unforgettable, ethereal glow. By Kevin Raub

🐎 Buses depart for Zipaquirá from Bogotá. The cathedral is open 9am to 5.30pm. See www.catedraldesal.gov.co.

San Antonio del Tequendama, Colombia, 4.5761 / 74.2967

TEQUENDAMA FALLS MUSEUM

Overlooking the eponymous 157m falls, this haunted-hotel-cum-museum has worn many hats over the years. It began its existence in 1923 as a luxurious fin de siècle French-style mansion, designed by architect Carlos Arturo Tapias. For years it attracted the upper strata of Bogotá society with its superb location and lush surroundings. It was due to be transformed during the 1950s into an 18-storey resort hotel, but expansion plans were shelved. As the Bogotá River feeding the falls gradually became more and more polluted with raw sewage from the capital, the stream of tourists slowed down to a trickle and, in the early 1990s, the hotel was abandoned and left to fall

into genteel decay and disrepair. It acquired a reputation as a haunted house after its picturesque yet precarious setting drew a number of unhappy souls here to shuffle off this mortal coil by throwing themselves off the cliff.

In more recent years, the mansion has been restored thanks to a collaborative venture led by the Institute of Natural Sciences of the National University of Colombia and the Ecological Farm Foundation of Porvenir. In 2013, it was transformed into a museum of biodiversity and culture, coinciding with clean-up efforts aimed at rejuvenating the Bogotá River and protecting the fragile ecosystems surrounding the building.

 The falls and the museum are 32km southwest of Bogotá. The easiest way to visit is by day tour.

'Along gravelled walkways, irregular steps and cinder-strewn paths, this stumble in the dark enlightens you to famous and infamous interments'

⒩EW ⒸYORK, USA, 41.0970 / −73.8616

Sleepy Hollow Cemetery

The rolling hills between the Hudson and Pocantico Rivers hum with history and hobgoblins. Lantern in hand, heart in mouth, you may confront these spirits of New York and New Amsterdam past on a walking tour of Sleepy Hollow Cemetery, terminating on the site where fictional Ichabod Crane met his demise at the hands of the legendary Headless Horseman.

Along gravelled walkways, irregular stone steps and cinder-strewn paths, this stumble in the dark (the 10pm to midnight Lantern Walk) enlightens you to some famous and infamous interments: the Rockefeller family's two-storey, Vermont-granite, Greek-themed mausoleum stands in stark contrast to Scottish steel magnate Andrew Carnegie's austere Celtic cross. Carnegie's philanthropic legacy is repaid with flowers, coins and notes left on his headstone; the Rockefellers' site remains bare.

Rockefeller's Standard Oil rival-cum-partner John Dustin Archbold's resting place is neo-modern – he covered all bets with a dash of Celtic, Russian, Greek and even Persian (peacock) iconography which vie for the attention of varied gods, ensuring a measure of sanctity, somewhere. Just up the road, the 'queen of mean', hotelier Leona Helmsley, interred with husband Harry, snarls behind stained glass – but without the dog to whom she bequeathed $12 million.

Pop icons of the past perambulate – the Ramones were briefly buried on a rolling hilltop here while recording a video for the film adaptation of Stephen King's *Pet Sematary* (the band are truly dead today); vampire Barnabas Collins of television's *Dark Shadows* conspired in a crypt which in real life served as a holding vault for stiffs when New York winters froze the ground solid (Mrs William Rockefeller waited two years here while the family's condo-crypt was being built.)

Wild creatures stalk the 90 acres of nooks and crannies: coyotes and foxes scamper in the shadows of this hardly disturbed wilderness, and screech owls linger in overhanging Linden branches. Twisted elms and tulip trees reach out for the unsuspecting hiker.

The tour concludes where the new Sleepy Hollow Cemetery – founded by Washington Irving himself – is separated from the old Dutch Burying Ground by a ribbon of horse-carriage path. Irving, a veteran of the War of 1812, gets a place of honour adorned with an American flag. Don't tarry in Tarrytown, however, because just beyond a copse of pines, in the graveyard of the Dutch Reformed Church, lies a certain decapitated Hessian mercenary, still prepared to ride out into the moonlit night.
By Brian Kluepfel

🐌 *The Cemetery is 2.5km north of Metro North's Tarrytown Station on the Hudson Line. The walk from there takes 30 minutes. Tours take place in November (www.sleepyhollowcemetery.org).*

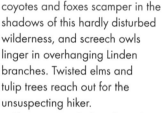

Ⓟatagonia, Ⓒhile. -51.5696 / -72.6050

CUEVA DEL MILODÓN NATURAL MONUMENT

There are many reasons for making the extraordinary effort required to get to this part of Chilean Patagonia. Heading to a cave where the skin and fur of a giant sloth was found may not, on first inspection, be one of them. But, given that a piece of this very skin was the thing that inspired Bruce Chatwin's own famous Patagonian journey, surely what's good enough for one of the world's greatest travellers is a secret worth exploring?

Your voyage here will be satisfyingly difficult: either a bumpy flight, a long bus ride or a stomach-churning ferry via dramatic fjordland to the north, bringing you to Puerto Natales, the nearest town.

Though the replica mylodon at the entrance adds a decidedly modern intervention, the secret here is the window into the every day lives of early humans who hunted and lived in and near these caves as early as 6000BC. There are several caves here as well as unusual rock formations and a lookout over the end-of-the-world scenery of Patagonia where you can contemplate their precarious existence. Your mind may also wander from the fate of the mylodon whose remains were found here to other exotic wildlife found at the cave – including, in a marvellous quirk of nomenclature, the Smilodon sabre-toothed cat.

☛ The cave is close to the main road to Torres del Paine National Park and is usually visited as part of the journey there. See www.cuevadelmilodon.cl.

ℂusco, ℙeru, -13.3289 / -72.1967

MORAY

In a remote part of the hilly Sacred Valley sits a perfect amphitheatre of grass-covered terraced rings. Left behind by the Incas, its exact purpose had long baffled archaeologists. Compared to the sophisticated masonry and elaborate stone cities the Incas left elsewhere, these concentric terraces seem simple but are in fact ingenious. Their design, their depth, variation in size and positioning in relation to the sun and wind all seem to suggest that they may have been an agricultural research station. The subtly varying climatic conditions on every terrace have resulted in the creation of different microclimates that correspond to the varied growing conditions across the Incan Empire. At its

height, the empire encompassed a huge swathe of South America, from the coast and jungle of Ecuador and the Peruvian highlands to the lakes, desert and mountains of Chile, with thousands upon thousands of subjects who required sustenance.

With a 15°C variation between the top and bottom terraces and soil samples proven to have been brought from different parts of Peru, it is likely that the Incas, remarkable agriculturalists that they were, used the terraces to test the growing prowess of different crops under varying climatic conditions, using modification and hybridisation to adapt potato, maize, quinoa, sweet potato and amaranth to make them suitable for human consumption.

🡆 Come to Moray either by taxi from Maras village, 5km away, or by guided day tour from Cusco.

PROVIDENCIALES,
TURKS & CAICOS, 21.8126 / -72.1378
CAICOS CONCH FARM

While visitor-friendly farms mainly feature animals of the fuzzy or feathered varieties, Turks and Caicos has taken things a step further with its most unconventional attraction: the world's first farm dedicated to growing sea snails, the famous queen conch to be precise. Conch is an integral part of the Caribbean menu, and is served in a number of ways – fried in golden fritters, chopped into fresh ceviche or salad, even cracked or grilled – and the facility tour will give you insight into how these tasty gastropods go from farm to table. Visitors also have the opportunity to see resident mascots Sally and Jerry, two full-grown conches, up close.

🔖 *Located on the eastern end of Providenciales, the farm is accessible by car. See www.caicosconchfarm.net.*

© Wanderluster / Alamy

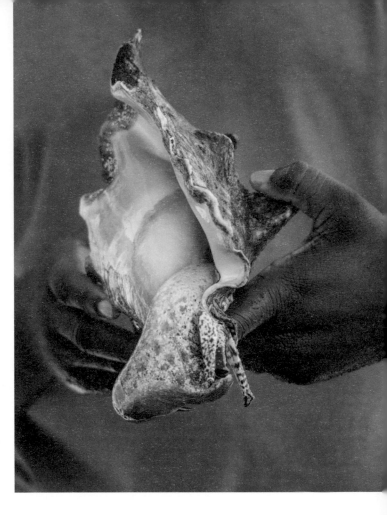

CUSCO, PERU, -13.5163 / -71.9778
GUINEA PIG LAST SUPPER

In the historic Catedral del Cusco, completed in 1654, on Cusco's main colonial square, a painting depicts a classic biblical scene but with a uniquely Peruvian twist. In the original image, Jesus and his disciples were scheduled to feast on bread and wine, whereas in *The Last Supper*, painted by Quechua painter Marcos Zapata in 1753, the plate in the centre of the table features a cooked guinea pig. Native to Peru, guinea pigs were consumed by the Incas and are still served in Cusco restaurants today. It seems somewhat remarkable that the Catholic Church tolerated this painting; perhaps the depiction of a local delicacy was seen as an effective way of converting the indigenous population.

🔖 *The cathedral is the main feature on Cusco's Plaza de Armas and is open between 10am and 6pm daily.*

© Y.Levy / Alamy

'VALPARAÍSO, CHILE, -32.5094 / -71.4721

PUNTA PITE

A coastal walkway unlike any other, a private park cared for by those living in its midst, or an art project that got entirely out of control? Call it whatever you want; Punta Pite is a mesmerising patch of Chile's Central Coast that shows how art can surrender to nature. This 11-hectare project was the brainchild of landscape architect Teresa Moller, who took a headland jutting out into the Pacific Ocean between the beach towns of Zapallar and Papudo and transformed it into a stroller's dreamland with narrow passageways and carefully crafted vistas.

A 1.5km route winds along the coast from a pebble beach to natural swimming holes where one can safely enter the sea. The path then climbs upwards along stone staircases (with no railings) to a clifftop lookout where sculptures by artist Gerardo Aristía are tucked within a patch of cypress trees. Moller employed 40 stonemasons to build the paths at Punta Pite out of hand-cut granite, the same material as the cliffs themselves. The goal was to create an organic mixture of walkways along the coast that didn't disturb the landscape, but rather challenged perceptions of it while heightening one's awareness of the natural surroundings. The end result is a humble, yet powerful, spatial experience for visitors to this stretch of the Chilean coast.

☛ *Free and open to the public, Punta Pite is an easy 3km walk (or drive) from the beach town of Papudo.*

CANAS, PERU. -14.3813 / -71.4841

Q'ESWACHAKA ROPE BRIDGE

Commonly used by the Incas 600 or so years ago, this is the last remaining example of a handwoven bridge made of *q'oya* (braided ropes), woven out of *ichu* (a local grass). Spanning almost 36m, the Q'eswachaka hangs high above the roaring Apurímac River. Each June it is renewed as a symbolic link to the past by four local Quechua communities that convene in nearby Quehue. The thin *q'oya* ropes made by local women are collected and braided into thicker, stronger ropes by the *chakarauwaq* (engineers). They then let the old bridge fall. The new bridge is celebrated by giving thanks to the *apus* (mountain spirits), with music and traditional food.

☛ *If you want to cross the bridge, visit in July or August, when it's new and strong.*

MÉRIDA. VENEZUELA. 8.5944 / -71.1488

HELADERÍA COROMOTO

Mmm, tasty garlic ice cream. There are bound to be some cuckoo flavours available at Heladería Coromoto, which offers over 1000 different types of ice-cream – the most of any ice-cream store in the world, according to the Guinness World Records. Sure, they're padded out by tongue-in-cheek options like Miss Venezuela, Tears of Love, Jurassic Park and Viagra Hope (blue colouring and honey), but many taste deliciously real, using authentic ingredients – try Prawns in Wine, Sesame Raisins, Cold Duck or Mojito. The original gourmet creation, Avocado, still gets a good licking; while Venezuelan dish Pabellón Criollo (beef stew with beans, cheese, plantains and rice) scoops up praise. Sit among the photo-plastered walls with a *barquilla* (cone) or 10.

☛ *From Plaza Bolivar in Mérida, walk west along Av 3 Independencia to the corner with Calle 29. Closed Mondays.*

ARUBA. 12.5470 / −70.0557

MORGAN ISLAND ARUBA WATERPARK

There's something unsettling about abandoned amusement parks, their cheerful colours dulled by the elements, ghostly remnants of thrill rides and playgrounds left behind by visitors long absent. Morgan Island Aruba Waterpark is no exception – lonely waterslides stand forlornly in the tropical breeze, the twisting tubes leading only to empty pools, expanses of cracked concrete and stagnant water puddles. Formerly pristine walls are scrawled over with graffiti of varying quality, and burned out roofs drape over the remaining structures. The park was only open for two years, closing its gates in 2010, but urban adventurers today will delight in its spooky solitude.

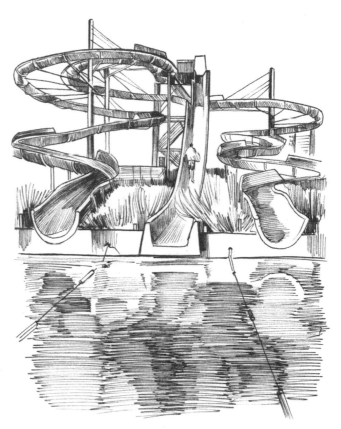

Morgan Island Aruba is next to Eagle Beach, and is currently unregulated.

© Vladimir Melnik / shutterstock

UYUNI, BOLIVIA. −20.4786 / −66.8335

CEMENTERIO DE TRENES

Corroded by time and the unrelenting salt winds that blow from the Salar de Uyuni – the world's largest salt flat – desolate train hulks sit eerily against the backdrop of a desert landscape. The Great Train Graveyard sits on the outskirts of Uyuni, a small town high up on the Andean plateau, a transport hub connecting several major cities and a distribution hub for mining companies. In the 19th century, British engineers built railway lines to connect Uyuni to Pacific ports, but the collapse of the mining industry in the 1940s and tensions with Chile meant that the trains were abandoned and left to rust. The 'cemetery' is particularly atmospheric in early morning or around sunset.

The Train Graveyard is located on the southwestern outskirts of Uyuni, a couple of kilometres from the centre. A taxi can get you out there; it's best not to go alone.

10 TOP BIZARRE DISASTER SITES

© Chronicle / Alamy

ⓑBOSTON, USA, 42.3684 / -71.0554

① Molasses Flood

The grim reaper has a nasty sense of humour. Destruction and death can arrive in bizarre ways, from armies of emus to breaches of royal etiquette, and the locations of these unexpected disasters make for grim viewing. One of America's oddest tragedies occurred in 1919, when 2.3 million gallons of molasses exploded from a storage tanker and gushed across Boston, killing 21 people and injuring many more.

☛ *There is a memorial plaque at Langone Park, in Boston's North End.*

ⓓDERBYSHIRE, ⒠NGLAND, 53.2871 / -1.6776

③ Eyam's Black Plague

In 1665, a tailor unwittingly brought Black Death into the heart of Eyam village by ordering a delivery of cloth. Fleas carrying bubonic plague were inside the parcel, and the resulting pandemic killed hundreds.

☛ *Eyam Museum (www.eyam-museum.org.uk) details the village's unlucky outbreak.*

ⓡRAKHINE STATE, ⓜMYANMAR, 19.0598 / 93.7715

② Crocodile Massacre of Ramree

One of World War II's most unexpected horrors occurred when Japanese soldiers were driven into mangrove swamps and promptly eaten by crocodiles.

☛ *Ramree is on Myanmar's western coast. The Guinness Book of World Records lists the event.*

Ⓐyutthaya, Ⓣhailand, 14.2326 / 100.57890

④ Death of Sunandha Kumariratana

Queen consort of Siam, Sunandha Kumariratana, drowned in 1880. Horrified onlookers didn't rescue her because of strict taboos about touching royalty.

☛ *Bang Pa-In Palace, Sunandha Kumariratana's destination that day, is 60km north of Bangkok.*

Ⓢumbawa, Indonesia, -8.2454 / 117.9953

⑤ The Year Without a Summer

The 1815 volcanic eruption of Mt Tambora, one of the worst in recorded history, unleashed snowfall and ruined crops across Asia and even further afield.

☛ *Mt Tambora is on the island of Sumbawa, which has ferry connections to Lombok.*

Ⓛondon, Ⓔngland, 51.5167 / -0.1302

⑥ London Beer Flood

A tsunami of beer swept through central London after a brewery vat burst in 1814. Eight people drowned. Reports that locals scooped up beer in celebration have been widely discredited.

☛ *The brewery has closed and London's Dominion Theatre stands in its place.*

Ⓩanzibar, -6.1607 / 39.1894

⑦ The 40-Minute War

The shortest war in history took place in 1896 between the United Kingdom and Zanzibar Sultanate. After less than 40 minutes of shelling, the Sultan lowered his flag and fled the palace.

☛ *Learn about this fleeting conflict at Stone Town's House of Wonders, in Zanzibar City.*

Ⓝew Ⓨork, USA, 40.7413, -74.0096

⑧ Titanic Landing Site

The *Titanic* was slated to reach New York's docks; instead, the RMS *Carpathia* arrived at Pier 54 to drop off survivors of the 1912 disaster. Only a faint sign, reading 'Cunard-White Star', marks the spot.

☛ *The pier forms a section of the Hudson River Park in Manhattan, New York.*

Ⓐustralia, -31.6475 / 116.4821

⑨ Great Emu War

In 1932, Australia's military tried to bring the emu stronghold of Campion under human control. But the quick-witted flightless birds ran rings about their would-be conquerors, despite the firepower.

☛ *Find friendlier Aussie emus at the world's oldest emu farm (www.emufarm.iinet.net.au).*

Ⓚrasnoyarsk Ⓚrai, Ⓡussia, 60.9645 / 101.8598

⑩ Tunguska Asteroid Strike

In 1908, 2000 sq km of Siberian forest was scorched by the air-burst of an asteroid that was completely vaporised before impact.

☛ *Lake Cheko, 750km northeast of Krasnoyarsk, is thought to have been formed by the strike.*

⑩

ARUBA, 12.4858 / −69.9722

FRENCHMAN'S PASS

The Caribbean's past is full of ghosts: the arrival of European explorers led to the decimation of native populations, pirates raided coast after coast, and slave ships moved millions of people through the region in dire conditions, delivering them to tragic fates. The history of Aruba mirrors that of its neighbours – originally settled by the Caquetio Indians (part of the Arawak tribe), Aruba was claimed by Spain in 1499 and, in 1513, the native population was enslaved and taken to Hispaniola. Indigenous people from the Venezuelan mainland began to migrate to the island after the Spanish abandoned it (there was no gold), and the Dutch West India Company took control in 1636.

Frenchman's Pass is the name given to a narrow stretch of land above Spanish Lagoon, a place with a scenic ambience at odds with its deadly history. According to island lore, French pirates attempted to invade Aruba in 1620, but met fierce resistance from the native people. The pirates attempted to drive their opponents away by smoking them out of a nearby cave, but the smoke from the fire asphyxiated them instead. Locals say that the cries of the indigenous people can still be heard at night, and reports of paranormal activity range from glowing balls of light to malfunctioning cars. Take the canopy-covered road through Frenchman's Pass, and you might just encounter a ghost of your own.

☞ *Take Route 1 south out of Oranjestad. Turn left at Route 4; then right on the road just past Rooi Bosal.*

CULEBRA, PUERTO RICO, 18.3287 / -65.3175

TANKS OF FLAMENCO BEACH

Puerto Rico's Flamenco Beach, located on the island of Culebra, is often lauded as the country's premier spot to soak up some sun, but this pearly little stretch of paradise wasn't always a laid-back place to relax. In the 1930s, the US Navy claimed all of Culebra's public lands and began using them for bombing practice and military exercises, activity that only intensified during the Vietnam War in the 1960s. In 1971, Culebra locals began protesting the US naval presence on the island, and their efforts eventually led to the discontinuation of military exercises there. Today, remnants of this era are still present – two rusting US tanks sink into the soft Puerto Rican sands. Puerto Ricans have covered one of them with art and graffiti, turning a solemn reminder of occupation into a brightly coloured symbol of civil resistance.

 Get to Culebra from the Puerto Rican mainland on the ferry from Fajardo. It's a 30-minute walk to the beach from Dewey.

USHUAIA, ARGENTINA, -54.8077 / -68.3052

Ushuaia Time Capsule

You'd think the end of the world would be lonely. But it's always busy near the harbour in Ushuaia, Argentina, the southernmost city in the world. Located on the archipelago of Tierra del Fuego, between the Beagle Channel and the Martial mountain range, Ushuaia is not just a hub for adventure travellers – it's the gateway to Antarctica. Travellers descend from cruise ships to wander the town, hungry for local specialities like freshly caught trout and king crab; tourists in North Face jackets come and go from boating and hiking excursions.

That's what I was doing, too, when I first laid eyes on Ushuaia's unusual time capsule. I had been out on a boat all morning, exploring the archipelago's cormorant colonies and snapping photos of the solitary lighthouse pictured on the cover of Jules Verne's novel *The Lighthouse at the End of the World* (1905). Back on dry land, it was starting to snow. I was hurrying along the sidewalk

when a strange sculpture caught my eye. Retro and geometric, painted a deep shade of green, the monument rose up from the plaza like a miniature pyramid. But it was the inscription that stopped me in my tracks: 'Do not open until October 2nd 2492.'

'2492?' It seemed like a mistake. I stepped closer to the time capsule so I could read the plaque. The capsule had been sealed in 1992, and was intended to be opened in 2492, the 1,000-year anniversary of Christopher Columbus' arrival in the Americas.

Inside the hermetically sealed container, the text explained, were six laser video discs of Argentinian TV shows, and hundreds of written messages addressed to the future citizens of Ushuaia. The technology would certainly be obsolete by the time the capsule was opened. What seemed more intriguing, I thought, were the thoughts expressed in the messages.

What did Argentinian people living in the early 1990s expect

for the future, I wondered? For Tierra del Fuego's indigenous groups, the past few hundred years had been tumultuous. The arrival of European settlers signalled the end of the Yaghan or Yámana, the nomadic people who originally inhabited the archipelago. Indeed, at that very moment, there was only one full-blooded Yámana still alive on the planet – Cristina Calderón, living across the Chilean border in Puerto Williams.

Calderón is the last speaker of the indigenous language of the Yámana. When she dies, she'll take untold stories with her; a certain chapter of the present will officially become the past. What would Ushuaia's contemporary residents have to say to those who will live here hundreds of years down the line? I'll never know – only time, a lot of time, will tell. *By Bridget Gleeson*

☞ *The capsule is on Plaza 25 de Mayo, by the boat harbour between the taxi stand and artisan market.*

'Inside the container were six laser video discs of Argentinian TV shows and hundreds of messages addressed to the future citizens of Ushuaia'

'El Tio is festooned in coloured streamers and surrounded by beer cans, cigarettes and the omnipresent cocoa leaves that keep the miners going'

POTOSÍ, BOLIVIA. -19.6183 / -65.7498

Cerro Rico

The mine entrance of Cerro Rico is daubed with llama blood; grim ritual comes as no shock. Humans by the thousands have perished here, crushed beneath the machinery of the Spanish empire. At 4000m, it's not only the altitude that takes our breath away, but the weight of history.

We strap into scuba-like rubber suits, heavy boots and helmets with headlamps. It would be hard to walk around in this stuff at sea level. The *mineros* (miners) rent this gear, along with iron bars and hammers, in their desperate daily search for a vein, any vein, in a despoiled paradise.

We sign our lives away in the tour office: 'dangerous place ... not responsible for accidents, injury, or death...' I scrawl my signature and make a sign of the cross, hoping any god, Christian or other, will bring me back.

Sputtering oxygen and squinting in the high-altitude sun, we trudge over to the sanguinary mine entrance. It's narrow, especially for non-Bolivians. We stoop and enter The Mountain That Eats Men.

It's damp, cold and littered with antiquated equipment – metal carts on rusting tracks, iron hammers and chisels to goad the earth into releasing just that little bit more. Men, old before their time, bend to their task, curved around a hopeful outcropping. Children, aged perhaps 10 or 12, labour alongside, faces as stony and cold as the rock itself.

We, too, are called to make a sacrifice, and it's a fun one. *El Tio* (the uncle) is a horned, devilish red figure who is, um, rather well-endowed. Guarding various portals, he is festooned in coloured streamers and

surrounded by offerings of beer cans, cigarettes and the omnipresent coca leaves that keep the miners going in this subterranean hell. I proffer a *boliviano* coin and bow to the spirit who rules this underworld.

We trek in and out, up and down, with a guide who still works a claim here. Exiting to harsh Andean daylight, we stretch our gringo limbs and thank our lucky stars we've reached terra firma again. The previous week seven unlucky Bolivians were felled by the killer gas which seeps silently through cracks in the stone. Cerro Rico is still the mountain that eats men.
By Brian Kluepfel

🐌 *Overnight buses from the main La Paz terminal take about nine hours; one daily flight departs La Paz's El Alto Airport.*

CÓRDOBA, ARGENTINA, -33.8679 / -63.9869

THE FOREST GUITAR

The young couple who dreamt up this project – a massive 'sculpture' of a guitar, 1km-long and crafted from thousands of cypress and eucalyptus trees - never saw the result. That's because Graciela Yraizoz, the woman who conceived the idea, died of a brain aneurysm in 1977, at the age of 25. In homage to his late wife, farmer Pedro Martin Ureta undertook the task himself. With the help of their children, he strategically planted 7,000 trees. Why the guitar? It was Graciela's favourite instrument. And why hasn't its creator ever seen the finished product? Ureta is afraid to fly – but he's happy with the aerial photos he's seen of his masterpiece.

🕊 *The Forest Guitar is in the province of Córdoba. It is sometimes visible on flights between Buenos Aires and Mendoza.*

SUCRE, BOLIVIA, -19.002138 / -65.236308

PARQUE CRETÁCICO

Sixty-eight million years ago, a vast ocean inlet reached as far inland as Sucre in Bolivia, with dinosaurs such as the Tyrannosaurus rex, hadrosaur and ceratops leaving their imprints in the soft clay shore. Today, 5055 footprints turned to stone can be seen on a near-vertical Cal Orck'o cliff, the most impressive belonging to a baby T-rex. Apart from the viewing trail that runs alongside the cliff – close enough to see the footprints but far enough away to protect visitors from collapsing parts of the cliff – the world's largest dinosaur track site includes the skeletons of a tyrannosaurus rex and a carnotaurus, as well sculptures of other dinosaurs in dramatic battle mode.

🕊 *Parque Cretácico is 5km outside Sucre, accessible by bus or taxi. See www.parquecretacicosucre.com.*

①MONTSERRAT, UK. 16.7103 / -62.1773

SOUFRIERE HILLS VOLCANO

In 1995, life changed forever for the residents of the small island of Montserrat, a British Overseas Territory in the southeastern Caribbean. On July 18, the Soufrière Hills Volcano erupted, sending massive pyroclastic flows across the south of the island and burying most of the capital, Plymouth, as well as the surrounding towns and forests. The eruptions left two-thirds of Montserrat covered in volcanic sludge and ash, permanently altering the landscape. The volcano awoke again in 1997, destroying the airport. The affected areas were among the island's most populated, and in the years after the eruptions the population shrank significantly, now standing at only 5000 people.

Today, the region resembles a modern Pompeii, the sloping grey face extending into the deep blue of the Caribbean Sea. Plymouth stands as a city immobilised, with rooftops and church steeples peeking out from the solidified ash, ghosts of a bustling urban life that once existed in the heart of tropical paradise. In these tangible reminders of the devastation, however, Montserrat is finding the silver lining – the volcano zone has become the island's biggest tourist attraction. Visitors can see the volcanic aftermath from a number of viewpoints, or visit the Montserrat Volcano Observatory to learn more about the 1995 eruption as well as the still-active volcano's most recent rumblings.

🐟 **Access Montserrat from Antigua via puddle-jumper flights with Fly Montserrat or ABM/SVG Airline.**

'The habitat these men and women lived in was nothing more than a pair of silos: two white metal cylinders, 4m in diameter, 6m high'

VIRGIN ISLANDS, USA, 18.3201 / −64.7272

Tektite Underwater Habitat

In the late 1960s, the US government sent groups of 'aquanauts' to live in an underwater habitat off the coast of Saint John in the Virgin Islands, to study the psychological effects of working in extreme environments. Little has been written about this bizarre, sci-fi-like experiment, which is why I set out to visit the only place in the world where you can learn what happened: the tiny Tektite Underwater Habitat Museum in Lameshur Bay.

It was here, in one of the least visited corners of Saint John, that aquanauts first gathered in February 1969 for a 58-day scientists-in-the-sea programme, the likes of which had never been attempted. The idea was to emulate the duration of future space missions and, in the process, set a new world record for saturated diving.

After breathing a mixture of 92 per cent nitrogen and 8 per cent oxygen for the two-month-long mission, the crew of four spent more than 19 hours in a decompression chamber before returning to the surface. An all-female team then took control of the facility in 1970 for a series of 10 shorter missions, sponsored in part by NASA. These women are credited with paving the way for the inclusion of female astronauts on future missions to outer space.

Wandering around the museum I learn that the habitat these men and women lived in was nothing more than a pair of silos: two white metal cylinders, 4m in diameter, 6m high, joined by a flexible tunnel and seated on a rectangular base at a depth of 15m. Scanning the 200-odd photos on display I see that this ethereal habitat had everything from a shower to a stove,

refrigerator and working TV set.

To get a better sense of the environment that these aquanauts studied for up to two months at a time, I strap on a snorkelling mask and swim into Great Lameshur Bay. I pass a school of barracudas, colourful angelfish and one lonely sea turtle en route to where the capsule once sat. Engineers dismantled Tektite several decades ago, but its foundation pads are still visible on the seabed. They're a testament to the fact that this lavish American experiment at the height of the Space Race was not just the stuff of science fiction. It actually existed, and in a setting that couldn't be more idyllic. *By Mark Johanson*

🖝 *The free museum, in the Virgin Islands National Park, opens daily from 9am to 5pm. See www.islands.org/tektite.*

'In 1985, weather conditions over the lake caused a standing wave that broke the dam. The saline waters slowly swallowed the town'

CARHUÉ, ARGENTINA. −37.1342 / −62.8111

Villa Epecuén

It's been compared to Atlantis or Pompeii. But let's go back to the beginning. Geographically speaking, Epecuén never seemed a likely pick for a luxurious getaway: the village was located in the outskirts of the province of Buenos Aires, hundreds of miles away from the capital on the road to nowhere in particular. But the resort was set on the shores of one of the saltiest lakes in the world. From the village's foundation in the 1920s through its 1970s heyday, the healing waters of Lago Epecuén drew a steady stream of vacationers; in summer, they'd arrive by train, checking into their hotels or enjoying a leisurely lunch before going for a dip in the lake.

That was before a rare and catastrophic natural event occurred, permanently altering the fate of the once-peaceful retreat. In 1985, weather conditions over the lake caused a seiche, or standing wave, that broke the dam. The saline waters slowly swallowed the town, submerging the streets, relegating hundreds of businesses and homes to the floor of a deep, salty lake.

Villa Epecuén was underwater: salvaging what little they could, everyone left. Fast-forward to 2009. The waters finally receded, exposing a damp ghost town of broken buildings and dead trees. The otherworldly remains of the underwater village fascinate archaeologists and photographers alike, but none of the original residents have returned – save for one, the octogenarian Pablo Novak. His favourite ice-cream parlour and nightclub are concrete shells now, but the lonely town's sole citizen holds fond memories of the way things were. *By Bridget Gleeson*

The ruins of Villa Epecuén are near the town of Carhué, which is an eight-hour bus ride from Buenos Aires.

BEQUIA, ST VINCENT & THE GRENADINES, 12.9921 / -61.2767

THE MOONHOLE

The Moonhole started out as the Caribbean dream of two American retirees, Tom and Gladdi Johnston, who moved to the island of Bequia in the 1950s to run a hotel. They became enamoured with a unique rock formation called the Moonhole, a magnificent arch that sometimes framed the moon. The two began camping there regularly, an endeavour that led them to build their new home in that very spot, despite not having any background as architects. Bringing in materials by boat and drawing blueprints in the sand, they built a labyrinthine structure that incorporated nature, shunning conventional rooms and floors for winding spaces and uneven levels; the walls, floors and structural elements were built of volcanic rock, hardwood, found ocean objects and even remnants of whalebone. Due to its isolated location, the home had no running water, instead relying on cisterns filled by the rain.

The eco-friendly house became a hit. Tom Johnston designed 16 other houses before he died in 2001, all evoking the same aesthetic as the original Moonhole property. Unfortunately, friction within the remaining Moonhole Company led to the neglect of the namesake house, and today it is off limits, as falling rocks from the arch are causing damage to the structures remaining roof. The Moonhole is only visible from passing boats, a ghostly skeleton of an idealistic venture.

Bequia is easily accessible from St Vincent via several daily ferries. One-way fares cost around EC$25.

CAPE BRETON, CANADA, 45.9620 / −60.7615

FÉIS AN EILEIN

Féis An Eilein translates as 'island festival' – and the use of Gaelic in its name is central to what this extraordinary community event is all about. Held in a glorious part of rural Cape Breton, Christmas Island prepares for its long winter quiet with an early autumn week of voice, music and dance that celebrates all things Celtic. There are story-telling sessions and song workshops, concerts and ceilidhs, walks, and plenty of chances to hear fiddlers work their musical magic. And if you've never been to a traditional Milling Frolic, now's your chance.

With a view to preserving the language and culture of the region's Scottish forebears – also recalled in the European naming of Nova Scotia, which means New Scotland – Gaelic is spoken and sung throughout the week. But don't let that discourage you! Daily language lessons are available, and newcomers are welcome.

Christmas Island is one of three in the world (the other two have their own marvels, and also get a mention in this book). This one is named, legend has it, after the burial place of a local Mi'kmaq tribal chief. He had strong connections with French settlers and had, as perhaps you guessed, taken the name Noel.

Féis An Eilein is held annually, in August. Fly to Sydney in Nova Scotia and hire a car for the 60km drive to Christmas Island. See feisaneilein.ca/feis/.

ANTARCTICA, −62.940930 / −60.555375

DECEPTION ISLAND

Deception Island sparkles in the remote South Shetland Islands archipelago skimming the northern edge of the Antarctic Peninsula. Deceptive in more ways than one, its secret harbour is ensconced in the caldera of a 'restless' volcano, always threatening to blow. Sail through the narrow opening to enter the horseshoe-shaped bay surrounded by black sand beaches and slopes of ash-covered snow and ice, which hide chinstrap penguin rookeries. After spying on the cacophonous breeding birds, sleuth through the island's industrial archaeology at its abandoned whaling station, partially destroyed by an eruption-induced mudflow and flood. And, naturally, don't forget to pack your swimsuit, since you can take a plunge into the island's heated geothermal currents for the ultimate polar adventure.

Reach Deception Island on an Antarctic cruise departing from Argentina. See www.deceptionisland.aq.

'The taxi driver looked at me in the rearview mirror. "Ferrowhite," he said. "You know it's haunted, right? People died there."'

BAHÍA BLANCA, ARGENTINA. -38.7903 / -62.2649

Ferrowhite

I tried to get on the bus. But all the kiosks around the main square – the little shops that sell the magnetic card you need to access the public transportation system – were closed. It was a Sunday, a quiet afternoon in late spring in Bahía Blanca, when most people are either finishing their family *asados* (barbecues) or indulging in the siesta that inevitably follows.

I hailed a taxi instead. There was no meter inside. 'How much to the port?' I asked. The driver hesitated, naming a price; I nodded, buckling my seatbelt.

'The port is big,' he said as we pulled away from the centre of town. 'Where do you want to go? The museum?'

'No,' I said. 'Take me to Ferrowhite.' He looked at me in the rear-view mirror.

'Ferrowhite,' he said. 'You know it's haunted, right?'

'I heard something about that,' I said. We were on a country road now, cows grazing in a field, the smells of manure and salty sea air wafting in through the open windows. Bahía Blanca is an important port, but the city itself isn't close to the water.

'Yes, there are ghosts there, and reports of extraterrestrial activity,' he said. 'People died there.'

Twenty minutes later, the fields turned into a dense grid of tin houses; beyond the streets, behind barbed wire fences and sea grass, huge barges floated in the bay. The driver took a sharp left at a traffic light, pulling on to a bridge. And then just past the grain elevators and a row of abandoned cargo trains, I saw it – Ferrowhite, suddenly looming grand and ghostly, a concrete castle on the water's edge.

The power plant was built by Italian immigrants in the 1930s. It's true that it was never a safe place to work: this was the site of a series of gruesome deaths, and the plant was abandoned for years before it was finally dismantled in 1997. Today, a small museum and cultural centre occupy the entryway, but most of the massive building sits empty – an elegant and eerie shell of a building, the glass windows shattered. There's no one to stop you from walking the whole way around it, even climbing inside the periphery of its ruins.

It's a fascinating and vaguely frightening sight, even if you don't believe in ghosts. There were still hours of daylight left, but no other people around. Before I got out of the taxi, I asked the driver, 'Can you come back for me in an hour?' *By Bridget Gleeson*

☛ *The museum is open daily; buses run from Bahía Blanca, or you can hire a taxi. See ferrowhite.bahiablanca.gov.ar.*

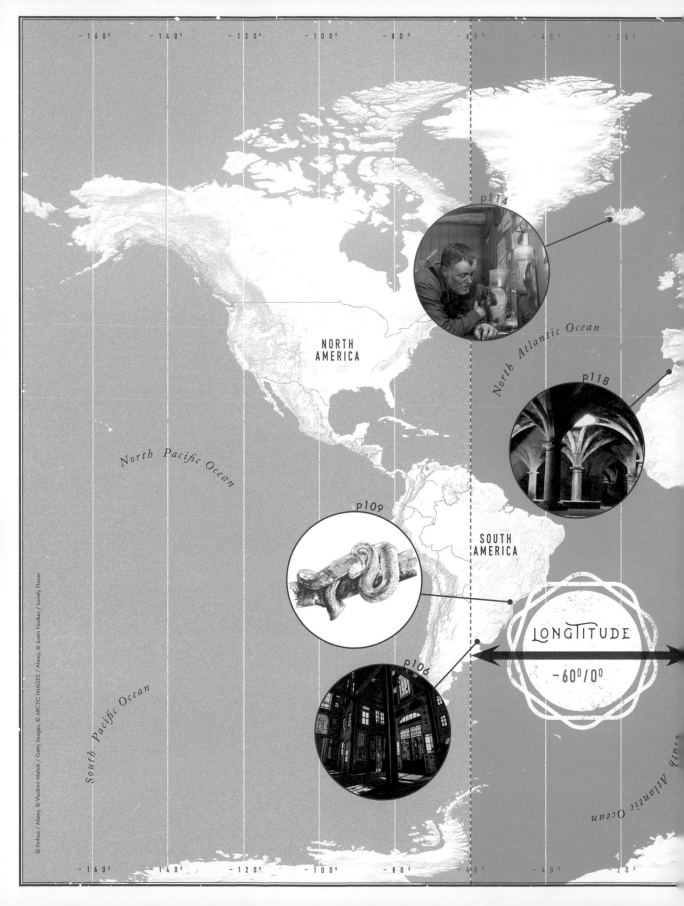

NORTH
AMERICA

SOUTH
AMERICA

North Pacific Ocean

South Pacific Ocean

North Atlantic Ocean

South Atlantic Ocean

p114

p118

p109

p106

LONGTITUDE
-60º/0º

-160º   -140º   -120º   -100º   -80º   -60º   -40º   -20º

-160º   -140º   -120º   -100º   -80º   -60º   -40º   -20º

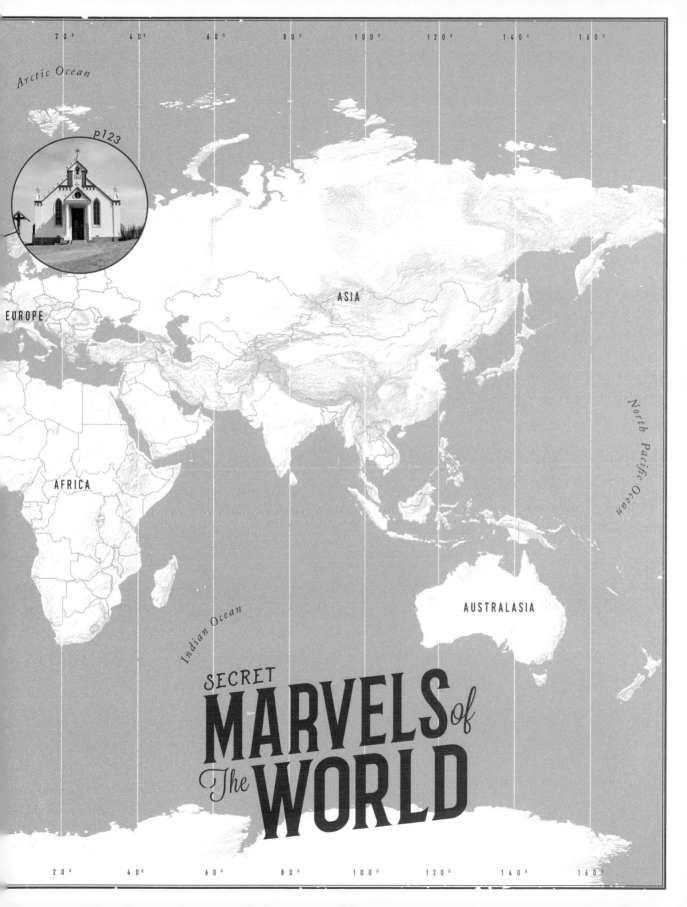

EUROPE

ASIA

AFRICA

AUSTRALASIA

Arctic Ocean

Indian Ocean

North Pacific Ocean

p123

SECRET
MARVELS of
The WORLD

BUENOS AIRES, ARGENTINA, -34.5612 / -58.5167

COLOSO

Electrical towers are often considered eyesores. In Buenos Aires, the artist collective Doma turned the concept on its head, transforming one tower into a robot-like sculpture. Coloso (meaning 'colossus'), the group's official entry at Tecnópolis 2012 – a popular art, technology, and science fair – is a massive 45m-tall creature. At night, he comes alive in neon colours, complete with an animated face and a beating heart.

Thanks to a sophisticated lighting system, Coloso exhibits a range of different moods: sometimes he winks his eyes and his heart seems to grow larger, sometimes he's expressionless, other times his smile is practically demonic. The 2012 version of Tecnópolis came and went, but Coloso remains a whimsical fixture on the scene, towering over the crowds during frequent art, music, and food festivals that take place on the grounds.

☛ *Tecnópolis is in the suburb of Vicente Lopez; frequent trains run from Buenos Aires' Retiro station.*

González Catán, Argentina. −34.7890 / −58.6066
CAMPANÓPOLIS

The year 1976 was a difficult one in Argentina. It marked the start of a brutal military dictatorship that would grip the nation for the better part of a decade. It was also the year that the Argentinian businessman Antonio Campana was diagnosed with terminal throat cancer. It's no wonder, given the grim circumstances, that the self-made millionaire decided to abandon reality – and build a fantasy world on an 80-hectare plot of land outside Buenos Aires. Campana made his fortune in the supermarket business: he had no training in architecture. But that didn't stop him from dreaming up the plans for a whimsical, fairytale-like village, nor did a legal battle over the land he'd purchased stop him from bringing his visions to life. Sourcing materials from salvage auctions – from doors, gates and fences to typewriters, an old elevator and metal scraps from discontinued railroad lines – he went to work at the construction of Campanópolis.

The doctors gave Campana five years to live, but he survived another 24. He devoted all of it to his enterprise: a medieval-style village with cobblestone streets, fountains, towers, a windmill, an artificial lake. Right up until his death, Campana continued developing his dream, planting more than 100,000 trees and bringing in myriad quirky antiques. Today, his sons maintain his unfinished masterpiece. You can peek inside on Saturdays, with a reservation.

☛ *Campanópolis is in González Catán. It's best to drive or take a taxi. See www.campanopolis.com.ar.*

BONITO, BRAZIL, -21.1442 / -56.5880

Gruta do Lago Azul

As we descend the crude stone staircase into the subterranean depths studded with stalactites and stalagmites, our guide explains that, most likely, no human had ever set foot inside this grotto until a member of the Terena tribe stumbled upon it by accident in 1924. As we descend further, my jaw drops as I stare down into a pool of startlingly blue water. The water is crystal-clear but the pool – one of the largest flooded cavities on earth – is so deep it seems bottomless. In 1992, a Franco-Brazilian diving team explored its 70m depths and discovered that the bottom of the pool was rich in prehistoric animal remains, from sabre-toothed tigers to giant sloths. By Anna Kaminski

☛ The cave is 19km from Bonito and access is by two-hour tour between 7am and 2pm; most lodgings in Bonito organise tours. Closed-toed walking shoes are mandatory.

Alto Paraíso de Goiás, Brazil. −14.1867 / −47.7897

VALE DA LUA

It has taken millions of years and trillions of litres of water to sculpt out the beautiful rock formations at Vale da Lua (Moon Valley), on Brazil's São Miguel River. Stretching along a 1km course of water, just beyond the southern edge of the Parque Nacional da Chapada dos Veadeiros, is a bizarre looking series of natural rock formations, caves, waterfalls, pools and crevices. It's a bit like a water park, but without the screaming tourists or garish swimming trunks. According to Brasilia University's Instituto de Geociencias, the endless curves are all caused by something known as fluvial abrasion, where the pressure of sand and continuously flowing water over several millennia has carved out the cups, bowls and smooth lines that you see today. And they are carving it out still – so it is, in effect, a constantly evolving sculpture.

There's a distinctly lunar feel to the entire landscape, hence the name Vale da Lua. Visitors can walk across the rocks, bathe in the rock pools and wade down many of the water courses. (Except during heavy rain when flash flooding makes proceedings very risky indeed.) But most amazing of all are the quartz crystals embedded within the rocks. Thanks to these, some visitors report feeling an added energy and healing power.

 Vale da Lua is on private property, 4km southeast of São Jorge village. The final approach is on foot.

BRAZIL. -24.485156 / -46.6756

SNAKE ISLAND

If you're afraid of snakes, you may want to look away now. Ilha da Queimada Grande, off the coast of Brazil, is home to the world's entire population of golden lancehead pit vipers – several thousand of them, in fact. Since the island is just 43 hectares in size, that averages out at about one snake every square metre, each armed with venom so deadly it can melt human flesh. No wonder the Brazilian government bans access to everyone except its navy and accredited researchers. Illegal wildlife smugglers sometimes sneak in, in search of snakes to sell on the black market. (Does this remind you of *Jurassic Park* yet?)

Thousands of years ago, Snake Island, as it has been nicknamed in English, was attached to the mainland, until rising sea levels eventually cut it off by a distance of 32km, allowing the golden lanceheads to multiply with abandon and evolve their particularly lethal venom. Since then they have survived by slithering up the trees to eat birds.

The island's Brazilian name translates roughly as 'Big Burning Island' since attempts were once made to clear land for a banana plantation. In the early 1900s a lighthouse was built. Several years later the island's last ever lighthouse keeper and his entire family were found dead after snakes crawled into their home and bit the lot of them. Since then the lighthouse has wisely been automated.

 You can only visit the island (150km from São Paulo) with a research permit from icmbio.gov.br.

CARAGUATATUBA, BRAZIL.
-23.7388 / -45.5494

VIADUCT PETROBRAS

Is this the ultimate white elephant? Back in the 1960s the plan was to build a high-speed motorway between Rio de Janeiro and Santos. One section, the 370m-long Viaduct Petrobas, was completed – but when government officials changed the route, the roads either end of it never were. Now, disconnected, abandoned and alone, this huge concrete elevated roadway looms 40m above the jungle floor, while plantlife gradually swallows it up. It may have been designed for motor vehicles, but nowadays the traffic is mostly climbers and bungee jumpers looking for somewhere unusual to practise their sports. Ladders link the jungle to the roadway.

☞ The viaduct is just southwest of Caraguatatuba. Small roads take you close, but the last stretch is by foot or 4x4.

VARGINHA, BRAZIL. -21.5594 / -45.4399

NAVE ESPACIAL DE VARGINHA

The Brazilian town of Varginha is South America's equivalent of Roswell, New Mexico. Ever since January 1996, when locals reported seeing UFOs and an alien creature ('5ft tall with a large head, thin body, V-shaped feet and red eyes'), the town has become a UFO pilgrimage site. Businesses cash in on the rumours of alien visitation, shops stock all sorts of ET souvenirs, and local media are ever keen to perpetuate the stories. In 2001, the town authorities devised a brilliant plan. They needed to construct a water tower, so they decided to disguise it in the shape of an enormous flying saucer. Christened the Nave Espacial de Varginha (the Spaceship of Varginha), it looms 20m above the town, and lights up at night, luring in ufologists from all around.

☞ Varginha is 400km northeast of Rio. The tower is on the junction of Praça Getúlio Vargas and Praça Mal Floriano.

Piauí, Brazil. −8.8366 / 42.5553

ROCK PAINTINGS OF PARQUE NACIONAL SERRA DA CAPIVARA

With its remarkable red stone arches and a riot of greenery erupting from between the cliffs, the 1300 sq km Parque Nacional Serra da Capivara is a Unesco World Heritage site famous for some 40,000 prehistoric rock paintings: the densest concentration of rock art on earth. Of the 300 or so archaeological sites, most consist of rock paintings dating back to 30,000-50,000 BC. This is the oldest and most compelling evidence of human presence in the Americas, which pre-dates other finds by about 30,000 years.

As visitors make their way around the 170 or so sites open to the public, using the four main driving circuits, walking trails and wooden walkways, the art on rock walls and inside stony shelters sheds light on the lives of some of South America's earliest inhabitants. Many images depict animals, hunting scenes, scenes of celebration and dancing, and sex scenes. The park's earliest inhabitants are believed to have been hunter-gatherers, followed by more sophisticated ceramic-crafting agricultural societies.

Some of the most important sites include the Boqueirão da Pedra Furada, with their 50,000-year-old remains of ancient hearths, illuminated at night. As visitors make their way between the rock art sites, the lucky ones may spot some of the park's abundant yet shy wildlife, including leopards, wildcats and armadillos.

A mandatory local guide can be arranged at most lodgings in São Raimundo Nonato, 35km away.

'From the air, the sweeping landscape gives the appearance of rolling bed sheets pitching across the world's most picturesque bed'

MARANHÃO, BRAZIL, -2.4859 / -43.1284

Parque Nacional dos Lençóis Maranhenses

At first glance, it seems a mirage. A translucent, postcard-perfect lagoon – blue as blueberries, clear as crystal – surrounded by towering sand dunes as far as the eye can see. But then the splashdown reveals this otherworldly landscape is far from fantasy. As I dip below the surface of what some might say is the most refreshing pool of water imaginable, the cool and calming sensation is a travel moment – those minutes of elusive wonderment we all seek as we traverse the globe – and it feels like everything but an optical illusion. It's a glorious baptism.

Brazil's Parque Nacional dos Lençóis Maranhenses, a 1500 sq km expanse of cinematic sandscapes, is a natural treasure. Located in the far northeastern state of Maranhão, it is the kind of place travel dreams are made of, a transcendental protected park of blanketing white sand dunes only broken up by the inviting cerulean lagoons that pepper the sandy hills between March and September (there is almost no vegetation whatsoever). From the air, the sweeping landscape gives the appearance of rolling bed sheets (*lençóis* in Portuguese), pitching across the world's most picturesque bed. From the ground, a no-filters-required desertscape unravels into the horizon in every direction.

Lençóis Maranhenses is

reached from the nearby town of Barreirinhas, a five-hour drive from the Unesco World Heritage–listed city of São Luís, from where open-sided 4WD bus tours routinely hit some of the park's biggest lagoons, Lagoa Azul (Blue Lagoon) and Lagoa Bonita (Beautiful Lagoon). Needless to say, this is not the best way to experience the park. I have opted instead for a private tour with Buna, a gentle beast of a character who owns and operates Rancho da Buna in the charming sand village of Atins, a 90-minute boat ride along the Rio Preguiças from Barreirinhas, the park's most picturesque village to bed down in.

Everywhere you look, the landscape is alarmingly similar, yet Buna knows the park backwards and forwards (a trusted guide is a must for navigating within the park). Thus it is Buna who has carted me off to a series of secluded lagoons, far, far away from the tour buses and tourists on day trips from Barreirinhus, and afforded me the opportunity to immerse myself in this aquatic Eden once mistaken for a mirage. When I re-surface, I'm lost, surrounded by nothing and no one. Paradise found. By Kevin Raub

Cisne Branco runs buses from Saõ Luís to Barreirinhas, the gateway to the park (www.cisnebrancoturismo.com.br).

Icelandic Phallological Museum

'Stop your juvenile giggling, they'll deny you entry.' My then boyfriend, an Australian fond of innuendo, was directing a photo shoot: me with a casual arm around a gigantic sculpture of a penis in Húsavík, on Iceland's remote north coast. But neither of us could suppress tears of laughter as we entered the Phallological Museum and viewed the world's largest collection of penises (from hamster to blue whale), the phallic tribute to the Iceland Olympic handball team, and the 'waiting list' of human donors. The museum moved in 2011 to a less-secret location; it's now blatantly out and proud (sorry) in Reykjavík, and with its first human donation: the pickled penis of a 95-year-old Icelander.
By Karyn Noble

☞ The museum is on Reykjavík's main shopping street at 116 Laugavegur, and is open from 10am to 6pm daily. For further information, see www.phallus.is.

© ARCTIC IMAGES / Alamy

Ⓝ ⒺАR Ⓓ АКАR, Ⓢ ЕNEGAL. 14.8388 / −17.2341

LAC ROSE

Not far from Senegal's sprawling coastal capital, le Lac Rose (the Pink Lake) more than lives up to its name. On a hot, sun-drenched day in the dry season, this shimmering lake a mere 30km northeast of Dakar looks more like a Martian landscape than West African countryside. Every inch of its mirrored, gently rippling surface seems to glow with a richly saturated pink – the kind of jaw-dropping, flamingo-like shade that nearly makes you doubt your own eyes.

The source of this pink pomposity? The lake has an incredibly high salt content, making it the ideal setting for a type of cyanobacteria known as Dunaliella salina to flourish. In order to better absorb light from the sun, these microscopic salt feeders in turn produce a red pigment, which then gives the waters its vibrant, otherworldly hues. The landscape looks even more a figment of science fiction given its surroundings: towering, blindingly white mounds of salt piled along the shore (the work of toiling labourers who make their living harvesting the salt), with rolling sand dunes just beyond that narrowly separate the lakeside from the pounding waves of the Atlantic.

Much like in Jordan's Dead Sea or Utah's Great Salt Lake, swimmers can float effortlessly on the hypersaline waters of Lac Rose. Those who prefer a less immersive experience can hire a *pirogue* (wooden boat) for a row out on to the lake. Nearby guesthouses make fine settings for an overnight stay, and can arrange horse riding and other excursions around the lake.

☛ *The best time to visit is from November to May. Travel agencies in Dakar can arrange day trips to Lac Rose, or you can hire your own driver from around €60 per day.*

SENEGAL & GAMBIA, 13.6917 / -14.8731

SENEGAMBIAN STONE CIRCLES

Death is confusing and mysterious, and so are these stone circles and burial mounds found across Senegal and The Gambia. Eerie and beautiful, sitting quietly and unobtrusively amid the region's grasslands, the monuments consist of monolithic, laterite pillars arranged in a circle around a burial plot, with one or more frontal stones to the east. Although there are a lot of them – about 17,000 spread across 33,000 sq km – and although they were made continuously for about 2,000 years, surprisingly little is known about the circles' origins.

Archaeologists aren't sure when the first circles were made or who made them. They don't know what the arrangements mean, how the burial practices functioned in the culture, or how they fit in with Islam, which arrived in the region during the height of stone circle production. The burial style is a total conundrum: bones and skulls were arranged within the circles in elaborate patterns – a quasi-fence of bones set vertically in the earth, leg bones laid out in a design, a layer of jawbones covered with upside-down pots – and no one has any idea why. Oh, and locals say that stones occasionally light up at night. No big deal.

Maybe because of these mysteries (or maybe because it's a burial ground, where larger mysteries prevail), the fields of stones feel magical, as if they're a liminal place between worlds. And the sites are still living monuments: Gambians don't practice what we would call funerary or religious rituals there, but they visit – on their way to work, the market, home – to place a small stone or vegetable atop a monolith, take a moment to reflect, and make a wish.

☛ The Gambia's Wassu Stone Circles are the easiest to visit and have a museum on-site. Take a day trip from Janjanbureh, about 25km away; hotels can arrange tours.

SINTRA, PORTUGAL, 38.7961 / −9.3960

QUINTA DA REGALEIRA WELLS

The spiral staircases of these towers aren't just forbidding, they represent a journey from death to rebirth. Hints at dark alchemy are scattered around the Unesco-protected estate of Quinta da Regaleira – a flamboyant blend of Gothic, Moorish and Renaissance architectural styles – especially around its showy gardens. Beneath this lavish residence, commissioned by coffee tycoon António Carvalho Monteiro, burrow two wells. But there's no water: these hidden tunnels were once used in secretive Masonic initiation rites. One has nine moss-rimmed levels, hinting at Dante's nine circles of Hell and Heaven, across its 27m height. The other has straight staircases, with steps numbered according to Masonic principles, descending to a huge Knights Templar cross.

☞ *Quinta da Regaleira is open daily; it's located 700m west of central Sintra.*

© Vladimir Melnik / Getty Images

El Jadida, Morocco, 33.2562 / −8.5020

Citerne Portugaise

As I strolled in the condensed maze of crooked streets in the El Jadida's Cité Portugaise, I envisaged the scene 500 years ago when it was the Mazagan, one of Portugal's first West African fortified colonies. However, it wasn't until I descended into the Citerne Portugaise that I felt like I'd travelled back in time. With nothing but a brilliant shaft of light from the outside world of today, I was left to absorb this late-Gothic architectural marvel. And how absorbing it was. The thin film of water in this vaulted cistern may have multiplied the light, shadows and columns by a factor of two, but it amplified its grandeur no end. By Matt Phillips

🚌 There are numerous daily buses and trains that connect the city of El Jadida with Casablanca.

FEZ, MOROCCO, 34.06225 / -4.9827

Water Clock

Whenever I visit Fez's bustling souk to buy fresh produce, I admire this majestic building with its vital role in medieval times. I was once told that the Water Clock – or clepsydra – was designed by a magician whose secret of how it worked died with him. But that's a fanciful story. The weight-driven clock was completed in 1357 as part of the Bou Inania Medersa, and was home to a very important man: the muwaqqit (timekeeper), whose job was to maintain the clocks, so correct prayer times were given to the muezzin. There were similar ingenious clocks across the medieval Arab world, in Damascus, Toledo and Tlemcen in Algeria. There was even another in Fez, at the Karaouine Mosque.
By Helen Ranger

~~~~~~~~~~~~~~~~~~~~

🢒 The Water Clock is on Tala'a Kebira opposite the Bouanania Medersa, a few minutes' walk east from Bab Bou Jeloud.

NEAR LLANES, SPAIN, 43.4476 / -4.8860

PLAYA DE GULPIYURI

The fine sand and cool seawater are exactly what you'd expect of a beach on Spain's northern coast; the only difference is that Playa de Gulpiyuri is right in the middle of a field. This tiny beach in Llanes could almost have been designed by a surrealist artist. Its 50m of sand, backed by majestic crags of limestone, lies more than 100m from the sea shore. It's not a lake beach, nor an illusion: a tunnel beneath the rocks channels water from the Cantabrian Sea into a cove. Timid bathers can swim with confidence, knowing there's absolutely no risk of being swept out to sea.

~~~~~~~~~~~~~~~~~~~~

🢒 You'll need your own wheels to access the beach; it's off the A8 road between Santander and Oviedo, on Spain's northern coast. See www.playagulpiyuri.com.

⊕JENNÉ, ⊙MALI, 13.9052 / -4.5553

GRANDE MOSQUÉE

Even on market Monday, when Djenné's dirt streets and squares are thronged with thousands of Malians and all their colourful wares, it's hard to take your eyes off the Grande Mosquée. Somehow both graceful and imposing, it rises above the dust like a living creature, with its porcupine-like wooden support spars jutting out from its fleshy mud facade.

Constructed in 1907, and still the world's largest mud-brick structure, the Grande Mosquée is actually a faithful recreation of the mosque that was built here in 1280 after Koi Konboro – Djenné's 26th king – converted to Islam. The original stood for over 600 years as a symbol of the island city's cultural significance and wealth, only to fall into ruin

in the early 1800s after the jihad of fundamentalist Islamic warrior-king, Cheikhou Amadou.

Today's mosque, much like the original, requires annual maintenance to ensure its longevity, and every year at the end of rainy season up to 4000 locals volunteer to assist the skilled masons from the Boso ethnic group to complete the task. The structure's complicated wooden spine protrudes from the surface for this very reason – it is instrumental in allowing the craftspeople access during this re-rendering process.

Non-Muslims are not allowed inside this place of worship, but great views of it are possible from the Petit Marché and the roofs of the nearby houses.

☛ *Djenné sits on an island in the Bani River, 35km west of the Mopti–Bamako road. When security isn't an issue, the journey from Bamako takes around eight hours.*

DOGON COUNTRY, MALI.
14.1617 / -3.5641

CLIFF DWELLINGS OF THE DOGON PEOPLE

Mali's Dogon Country looks as if it could be inhabited by hobbits, so otherworldly is the architecture of its people. Built from rock and mud, these strange dwellings cling beehive-like to the cliffs and upper slopes of the Bandiagara Escarpment, the steep-walled cliff that closes off Dogon lands from the rest of Mali – such isolation was very much the idea, and remains a bulwark against invasion in these newly troubled times. To spend days walking from one village to the next – marvelling at the elaborately carved doors, enjoying the playfulness of the conical straw-roofed granaries, sitting with the elders in the togunas or open-walled meeting places – is to wander into some dreamy African fairytale.

☛ Access Dogon Country via Bandiagara or Douentza, but check the security situation first.

© Timothy Allen / Getty Images

© imageBROKER / Alamy

FALKIRK, SCOTLAND. 56.0198 / -3.7555

THE KELPIES

The giant horses of Scotland's Forth and Clyde Canal toss their heads in a display of equine strength – or rather, the strength of Scotland's waterways.

In Scottish folklore, kelpies are water-dwelling spirits in the shape of horses, who carry humans on their backs before drowning them. Occasionally they take the form of comely young men or women, who lure virgins into the spirit world. Fortunately this glittering steel sculpture, towering 30m above The Helix parklands, has no such malign intent. Clydesdale horses once tugged barges along Scotland's canals, and artist Andy Scott considered kelpies an apt symbol of the might of the country's waterways and its industrial heritage.

☛ You can glimpse the sculptures from the M9 between Falkirk and Grangemouth, or take a guided tour and step inside; see www.thehelix.co.uk.

ITALIAN CHAPEL

An ornate Italian-style chapel, which was built by prisoners of war, is now a symbol of reconciliation on the wind-blasted island of Lamb Holm, one of Scotland's Orkney Islands.

In 1942, Italian prisoners of war were brought to work on causeways linking Orkney to the southern islands. When Italy capitulated in 1943, they were prisoners no more. They lobbied for a place of worship, and were soon using every spare hour to line the chapel's walls, paint frescoes, and mould a font out of concrete. The chapel's elaborate decorations are all the more remarkable considering wartime constraints on building materials. Its interior has a womb-like ambience, with a rosy brick vault framing an altar decorated with the Virgin Mary and cherubs.

☞ Lamb Holm is a short drive from Orkney's capital, Kirkwall. The chapel is open daily, but hours vary. Call ahead before visiting (+44 (0)1856 781580).

Koro, Mali. 14.0747 / -3.0827

ANTOGO FISHING FRENZY

Fishermen can be a superstitious lot, but the good fisherfolk of Koro in Mali surely win the prize. On a day chosen by the village elders in the dry season every year, the men of the village – a woman discovered the fish, legend holds, but women may not participate, go figure – surround the shrinking lake. Six, seven, eight deep they stand, jostling for position. Then, on the appointed signal, this concentrated mass of humanity storms the lake, each and every man hoping to grab a fish with his bare hands. The fish don't even stand a chance in this frenetic ritual that – on its serious side – reaffirms the local belief in ancestor worship.

☛ *Koro is in Dogon Country; buses pass through en route from Sévaré to Ouahigouya in Burkina Faso. Dry season runs from November to March or April.*

epa european pressphoto agency b.v./ Alamy

ⒷORJA. ⓈPAIN. 41.8548 / −1.5755

ECCE HOMO

No botched piece of art has captivated the world like Borja's *Ecce Homo*. When a well-meaning local amateur artist attempted to restore a weathered fresco of Jesus in the church of Santuario de Misericordia, the comical result was captured in news outlets across the globe.

In 2012, hapless artist Cecilia Giménez attempted to rejuvenate a weathered fresco of a pensive Christ crowned with thorns, originally painted in the 1930s by Elías García Martínez. Unfortunately the makeover went awry, and the untrained Giménez turned *Ecce Homo* into a cartoonish smudge with beady, misaligned eyes, and a halo of hair bearing an unfortunate resemblance to a chimp.

Split-screens of the mural before and after the 'restoration' tickled the funny bone of people worldwide, who dubbed it 'Ecce Mono' (behold the monkey) and 'the Beast Christ'. The well-meaning attempt to improve the artwork, only to damage it further, had an irresistible irony.

The fresco failure went from being an online meme to a real-life tourist attraction. Today, visitors queue to take selfies with *Ecce Homo*. Proceeds from the small admission fee are directed to a local nursing home, while a range of *Ecce Homo* souvenirs has kept this sleepy Spanish town afloat in a testing economic climate. Meanwhile Cecilia Giménez has emerged from being a global embarrassment to the toast of her hometown.

 It takes less than an hour to drive from Zaragoza to Borja, although irregular buses also connect these destinations. Plan your visit and find out more information on www.borja.es.

Accra, Ghana, 5.6037 / -0.1870

KANE KWEI COFFINS

Dying to spend eternity inside an enormous beer bottle? Want your final resting place to be a large wooden chicken? Head down to Kane Kwei Coffins, a blink-and-you'll-miss-it workshop tucked away in a dusty corner of Accra, where a group of hardworking young artists create colourful fantasy coffins for the great and the good of Ghana – as well as fans, collectors and galleries across the world. Dreamed up in the 1950s by carpenter Seth Kane Kwei, and continued today by his son and grandson, the coffins – known as *abebuu adekai* in the local Ga dialect – traditionally represent the lives, loves and aspirations of those that they carry to the grave: a giant pen for a writer, for example, or a guitar for a musician. More bizarre offerings have included a mobile phone, a hairdryer and even an ample bosom. If you fancy coff-in up the cash for one, you'll spend anything from US$600 to several thousand. In 2014, a coffin in the shape of a Porsche made by a former Kane Kwei apprentice, Paa Joe, sold for a record US$9,200 at London auction house Bonhams.

The Kane Kwei workshop is situated in the district of Teshie, in eastern Accra. A taxi ride to here from the city centre should cost around 15 cedis (US$5).

10

TOP 10

LONDON'S STRANGEST SIGHTS

LONDON, ENGLAND, 51.5209 / -0.0777

① Dennis Severs House

Curiosities from across London's long history could fill several volumes. One of the most immersive oddities is Dennis Severs' House. The artist arranged the 10 rooms of this Georgian townhouse as a 'still-life drama' of London life in the 18th and 19th centuries. Discarded clothing and lingering smoke give visitors the uncanny impression that the house's fictional aristocratic residents are only steps ahead of them.

☛ *The closest station is Shoreditch High Street. See www.dennissevershouse.co.uk.*

LONDON, ENGLAND, 51.5068 / -0.1287

② Soho Noses

From 1996 to 2005, artist Rick Buckley secreted up to 35 plaster noses, casts of his own, around Soho. The project is thought to be a statement about the nosiness of London's widespread CCTV cameras.

☛ *Find the noses in the West End. See www. london-walking-tours.co.uk/the-seven-noses-of-soho.*

WONDERFUL MAGA

Dennis Severs
will hold
A Smoking Room Meeting
In the Liberty of Norton Folgate
Spitalfields

Carriages

London E.

10 TOP

---

① LONDON, ENGLAND, 51.5314 / −0.0803

③ Hoxton Street Monster Supplies

Forget Buckingham Palace fridge magnets, the ideal London souvenir is a tin of mortal terror or cubed earwax from this East London curiosity shop.

The closest station is Hoxton; open afternoons from Tuesday to Saturday. monstersupplies.org.

---

① LONDON, ENGLAND, 51.5138 / −0.0979

④ Plague Pit of St Paul's

London's plague pandemic resulted in mass graves at Old Street, Islington Green and Golden Square. One of the largest, at St Paul's, was created after crowded East London was hit by 1664's Great Plague.

As you gaze at St Paul's Cathedral, try not to picture the plague pit below.

---

① LONDON, ENGLAND, 51.5207 / −0.1335

⑤ Eisenhower Air Raid Shelter

Eight London Tube stations had deep air raid shelters during WWII, including this pillbox-shaped building, used by US Army Signal Corps in the run-up to D-Day.

Find it on Chenies St near Goodge Street Underground Station.

---

① LONDON, ENGLAND, 51.5120 / −0.1724

⑥ Pet Cemetery

This pint-sized cemetery, established in Hyde Park in 1881, is the final resting place of beloved Buddys and Fidos. The first stone laid here is engraved with 'Poor Cherry', in memory of a terrier.

The cemetery is behind Victoria Gate Lodge, off Bayswater Rd.

---

① LONDON, ENGLAND, 51.5135 / −0.1837

⑦ Fake Houses of Leinster Gardens

These Bayswater houses are not as they seem. Walk around the back and you'll see they're just a facade, formerly a secret entrance to the Underground.

To get to Leinster Gardens, walk roughly 600m southwest from Paddington Station.

---

① LONDON, ENGLAND, 51.5039 / −0.0935

⑧ Cross Bones Graveyard

Corpses considered too unseemly for holy ground were buried here, including prostitutes. This resting place is now a monument to London's outsiders.

From Borough station, walk north up Redcross Way to find the graveyard.

---

① LONDON, ENGLAND, 51.5134 / −0.1366

⑨ Broad Street Water Pump

An 1854 cholera epidemic was halted simply by turning off a tap. A replica pump marks where John Snow traced the outbreak and removed the handle.

The pump is on the corner of Lexington St and Broadwick St in Soho.

---

① LONDON, ENGLAND, 51.5126 / −0.0916

⑩ Temple of Mithras

In 1954, the remains of a Temple of Mithras were discovered in the heart of London's financial district. Town planners were undeterred and simply relocated the ruins close to Queen Victoria St.

The ruin is a five-minute walk from London's Millennium Bridge on the north side of the Thames.

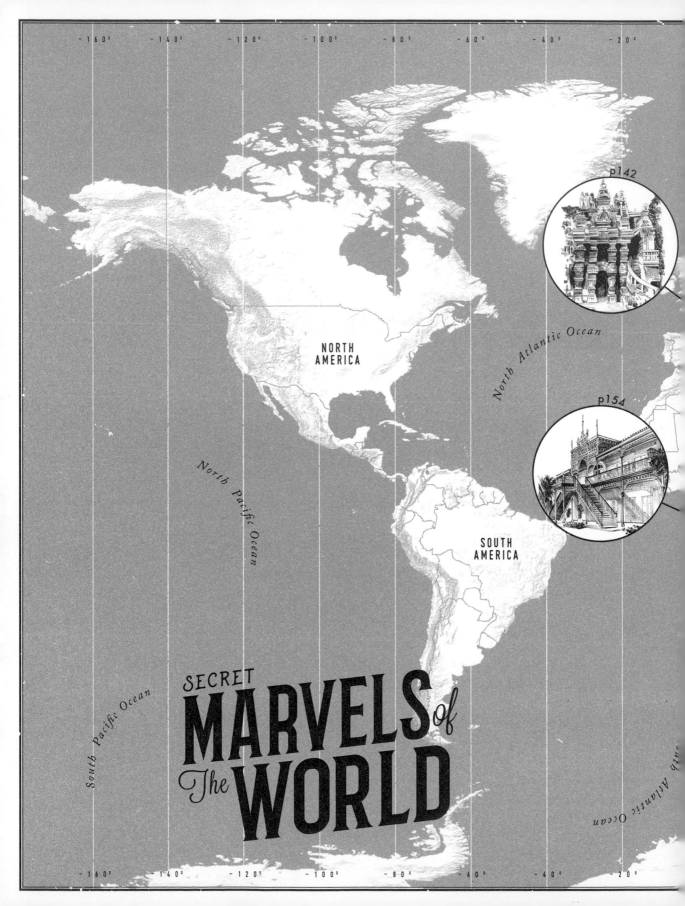

p142

p154

North Atlantic Ocean

NORTH
AMERICA

North Pacific Ocean

SOUTH
AMERICA

South Pacific Ocean

South Atlantic Ocean

SECRET
MARVELS of
The WORLD

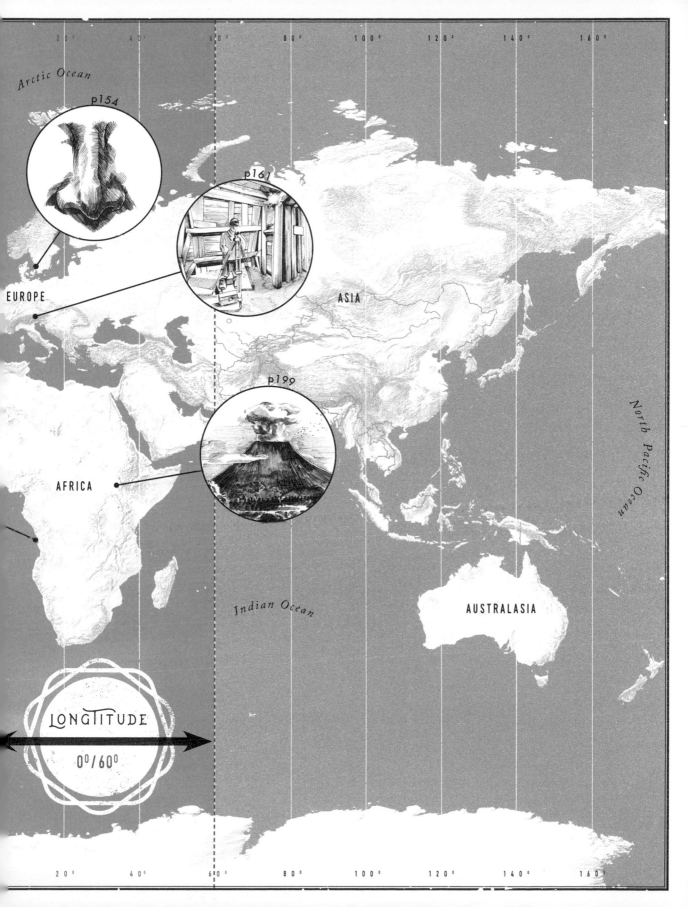

Arctic Ocean

p154

p161

EUROPE

ASIA

p199

AFRICA

North Pacific Ocean

Indian Ocean

AUSTRALASIA

LONGITUDE

0⁰/60⁰

20°   40°   60°   80°   100°   120°   140°   160°

20°   40°   60°   80°   100°   120°   140°   160°

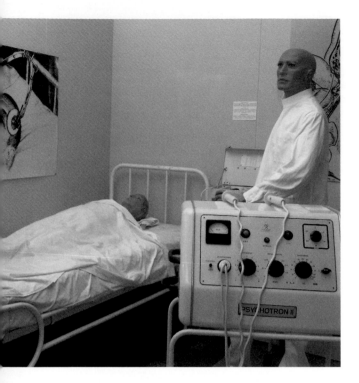

© BSIP/SA / Alamy

GHENT, BELGIUM, 51.067 / 1.0327

MUSEUM DR GUISLAIN

Due to its brick arches and cathedral windows, the Museum Dr Guislain in Ghent is an impressive, if ominous, sight. Belgium's first psychiatric hospital, dating to 1857, houses a museum that is both gruesome and uplifting. It leads visitors on a journey through the history of mental health. Freezing water and spinning chambers were among the unpleasant methods of scaring people sane during the late 18th and early 19th century. Repress a shudder as you sidle past straightjackets, cages, shackles and radiographic equipment dating to the turn of the 20th century. Then allow your faith to be restored: Joseph Guislain, who established the original hospice here, was a healthcare reformer who helped phase out brutish treatments and pioneered humane, patient-focused care.

🐾 *This neo-Gothic complex is located 2km north of Ghent's old town (www.museumdrguis-lain.be; Jozef Guislainstraat 43). Hop aboard tram number 1 to Guislainstraat.*

THE LOIRE, FRANCE, 47.3458 / 0.5314

LES GROTTES PETRIFIANTES

You can't rush art, especially when the artist is a cave system in France's Loire. Place any object, from a doll to a vase (but maybe not your iPhone), in the waters of Savonnières caves and within the space of a year it will be entirely coated in limestone. Water rich in minerals trickles slowly across the grotto's interior, and any objects in its way obtain a glistening coat. Still, nature needs a helping hand: items need to be turned roughly every three weeks to ensure the resulting 'sculpture' won't be lopsided. Fortunately for impatient souvenir-hunters, the caves have a shop with a few they prepared earlier.

This subterranean system was mostly formed during the Middle Ages. The local limestone, *tuffeau*, has marvellous applications beyond the sculptures. It is the source material for France's famous Loire Valley castles, including world-famous Château de Chambord.

Inside the caves, you can explore a goblin kingdom of dangling stalactites, overhanging ledges, and tiered rock formations resembling church organs, all of them formed over centuries. These cool caverns also have exactly the right humidity levels to store wine. The final chamber even offers wine tasting – and what better way to heighten your enjoyment of this geological marvel than a few sips of crisp Sauvignon Blanc?

🐾 *Visits to the caves are by hour-long guided tour (www.grottes-savonnieres.com) Jan to Nov. Les Grottes Petrifiantes are 16km west of Tours.*

CHAUTE-VIENNE, FRANCE, 45.9292 / 1.0355

THE MARTYRED VILLAGE OF ORADOUR-SUR-GLANE

Not a single burned-out car was removed after the massacre of Oradour-sur-Glane. The remains of this French village, where 642 inhabitants were murdered during World War II, are memorialised as a warning to future generations.

On 10 June 1944, Nazi soldiers entered Oradour-sur-Glane. They divided the villagers between barns and the church, then murdered them. The few surviving eyewitnesses recall that men's legs were shot to prevent escape before they were slaughtered. Women and children were barred inside a church, which was then set on fire, and they were shot as they tried to escape. An American navigator who witnessed the aftermath even reported a scene of crucifixion. It was WWII's worst Nazi massacre of French civilians, and historians still wonder why Oradour was targeted. Retaliation for partisan attacks was common, but little Oradour was no hotbed of the French Resistance.

After the war, Charles De Gaulle announced the rebuilding of Oradour-sur-Glane northwest of the original village. The charred rubble of the martyred town would be preserved, making it unique among destroyed villages in Europe, most of which were rebuilt on the same spot or marked with memorials. A sign at the entrance reads simply 'Souviens-Toi' ('Remember'). But remembrance doesn't come easy, especially as the site begins to decay.

🖝 *Oradour-sur-Glane's memorial centre (www.oradour.org) and village is 20km northwest of Limoges.*

'The dancers throw themselves about with abandon while villagers call out requests and favours of their dead ancestors'

COVE, BENIN, 7.2189 / 2.3394

Egungun Voodoo Ceremony

The drums begin at dawn, drawing people from across the valley. The dancers materialise wraith-like from the forest, where they have spent the night fasting and praying, adjusting their costumes that will allow them to summon deceased ancestors. Voodoo is the official religion of Benin and more than half of its citizens practice it in some form. Six thousand years ago, African Voodoo began its evolution near this village of Cove in Benin, where today, the Egungun ceremony will open a portal for the return of the dead.

Elaborate costumes, layered with esoteric meaning, hide the identity of the dancer who opens his soul to the drumming, and his body to those who came before him, allowing them to see through his eyes how their descendants are faring without them. Drums intensify as the dancers twirl themselves into a dervish-like trance. They twist and jerk as the dead, no longer used to a physical existence, adjust to human form once again. During this vulnerable time both evil and good spirits may arrive, so everyone is wary. The dancers throw themselves about with abandon while villagers call out requests and favours of their dead ancestors. Assistants with long poles keep the spectators from touching the dancers, because to do so would drag them into the spirit world.

I am photographing this transformation when the robes of a dancer brush against me, and a hush falls over the assembled crowd. One of the presiding witch doctors rushes to my side, carrying a lion femur inlaid with cowry shells, his talisman of power. His eyes roll back and he chants while passing the lion bone over my body like an airport security screener. I am being exorcised. The village closes in, to see if I am transported away. When the witch doctor's power is spent from pulling the bad spirits from my body into the bone, he collapses, clutching the bone that now must be purified in a ceremony all its own.

As I leave the village, the people surround me, touching me, pushing their children forward for me to lay hands on them. I am now special as one who has gone to the edge of the spirit world and returned, and so I too will enter their legends and myths. *By James Dorsey*

☞ *Cove is in south Central Benin around 80km from the coast and halfway between Abomey and Ketou. Local safari companies offer tours to Cove, but you can also just show up in the village and ask. They are very visitor friendly.*

PARIS, FRANCE, 48.83383 / 2.33242

CATACOMBES DE PARIS

The City of Light's boulevards and manicured gardens are ruled by chic locals, but below them is a kingdom of the dead. The bones of an estimated six million people are piled along dank passageways that snake beneath Paris.

As Paris' population grew, cemeteries teemed with corpses. A basement wall near Les Innocents cemetery collapsed under pressure from a mass grave. From the 1780s, bodies were exhumed and placed in what is now the catacombs. Today, around 1km of tunnels – marked with signs announcing entry to an 'empire of death' – form the official section, easy to visit without risking more than a bout of claustrophobia.

The full network, an estimated 280km, was eked out gradually, starting with the centuries-old carrières de Paris (quarries). It's irresistible to urban explorers despite the perils (and the law). Many cataphiles, as the most obsessive are known, act as caretakers: clearing tunnels or painting murals. But unsurprisingly, the catacombs also claim new victims. Philibert Aspairt, an 18th-century doorkeeper, descended into the catacombs and wasn't found for 11 years, identified by the keys rusting on his belt.

Some tunnels were used by the French Resistance; elsewhere is 'Le Bunker', a former Nazi stronghold still with German-language signs that urge silence and forbid smoking. But the grim highlight for cataphiles is Le Carrefour des Morts ('the crossroads of the dead'), where you crawl along a low tunnel piled with yellowing bones.

☞ **The entry to the catacombs (www.catacombes.paris.fr) is close to Denfert-Rochereau metro station.**

© Pete Seaward / Lonely Planet Images

℗ÚBOL. ⚓SPAIN. 42.0149 / 2 9833

CASTELL DE PÚBOL

Referring to Gala Dalí merely as the wife of Salvador Dalí doesn't do justice to the formidable Russian socialite and muse of some of the 20th century's greatest artists. The Castell de Púbol was her retreat from Salvador's whirlwind existence, and it offers teasing insights into the shared life of surrealism's most famous couple.

Russian-born Gala married literary giant Paul Éluard and took Dadaist artist Max Ernst as a lover, before moving on to Salvador Dalí. They married, though Gala's dalliances didn't stop. In fact, the prospect of his charismatic wife playing away was thrilling to Salvador. Besotted with Gala, he was delighted by the idea of giving her a place to 'reign

like an absolute sovereign'. In 1969, he bought a medieval castle in Púbol, decorating it according to Gala's tastes. Ornamenting the Gothic-meets-Renaissance chateau with antiques and hand-painted ceilings was a labour of love. Velvet drapes and candelabra still decorate its walls, while a lip-shaped sofa and fountains with angler-fish statues add dashes of surreality. Gala would only allow Salvador permission to visit Castell de Púbol if he submitted a hand-written request.

The palace eventually became Gala's tomb. After her burial in its basement, Salvador used the castle as an artist's studio, hoping to channel his muse from the beyond.

☞ *Open mid-March to December; www.salvador-dali.org. Visit by car or tour, or via a bus to La Pera.*

ROTTERDAM, NETHERLANDS,
51.5288 / 4.3013

KIJK-KUBUS
MUSEUM-HOUSE

Rotterdam is dotted with innovative architectural design but one building stands out – the higgledy-piggledy tilted yellow-and-grey cubes of the Overblaak Development, designed by Piet Blom. Each of these 'cube houses' was built to resemble a tree, so the collective effect is that of a forest. Visitors can tour one of the buildings at the Kijk-Kubus Museum-House. You might expect your head to spin with disorientation as you are led upside down or at odd inclines, but the 45-degree angles you see outside the building are completely at odds with the logical interior. However, there is a need for customised angular furniture to fit the quirky dimensions.

Open 11am-5pm daily opposite Rotterdam Blaak station. (www.kubuswoning.nl).

© PNovarc Images./ Alamy. Designed by Piet Blom

ⒽALSTEREN, ⓃETHERLANDS.
51.5288 / 4.3013

LOOPGRAAFBRUG

It's easy to imagine that you are parting the waves as you stride along the 'Moses Bridge' near Halsteren. Walking the length of the sunken pedestrian pathway, also known as the Loopgraafbrug (trench bridge), you'll see that the water rises almost to head height on each side. The walkway descends down a muddy bank before crossing the moat of Fort de Roovere, an entrenchment that fell to the French during the Austrian War of Succession in the 18th century. RO&AD Architecten masterminded this wooden bridge to retain the fortress' austere, isolated air. These days the fort is an under-loved tourist destination, although the bridge itself attracts plenty of curious visitors.

🐾 *Fort de Roovere is a 100km drive west from Eindhoven, along the A58.*

© Barcroft / Getty Images

Ⓞ SHOGBO, ⓃIGERIA.
7.7592 / 4.5569

OSUN SACRED FOREST

Ever imagined wandering through a beautiful rainforest in West Africa to find numerous sculptures by a renowned artist? Didn't think so; it's a bit beyond the realm of most people's realities. But the Osun Sacred Forest is just that – another reality. The site of the Shrine of Oshun (the Yoruba fertility goddess), this forest captured the imagination of Austrian painter and sculptor Susanne Wenger when she moved to Oshogbo in southeastern Nigeria during the 1950s. She adopted and promoted the Yoruba religion, and became known locally as Adunni Olosa (the 'Adored One'). In addition to her works, many other sculptures now call the forest home, after a 21st-century renaissance by local artists.

🐾 *The forest is on the outskirts of Oshogbo. Minibuses connect the town with Lagos (three hours).*

© Art Directors & TRIP / Alamy

HAUTERIVES, FRANCE. 45.2561 / 5.0276
LE PALAIS IDÉAL

Resembling the most extravagant of Hindu temples, the 'ideal palace' was built by postman-cum-artist Ferdinand Cheval over a period of 33 years. When Cheval's foot struck a pebble on a spring day in 1879, he was inspired by the shape of the rock and pocketed it for safekeeping. A collection of unusual pebbles became the building materials for a fairytale palace. Drawing inspiration from a range of eras, Cheval crafted gargoyles, gateways, stairs, turrets and elaborate columns using rocks he found along his 29km postal route. The palace was completed in 1912 but it was decades later, long after Cheval's death, that visitors began to come to this temple to human patience.

☞ *The palace (www.facteurcheval.com) is in Hauterives, 55km south of Lyon.*

© Raimund Linke / Getty Images

NORANGSDAL VALLEY, NORWAY. 62.1756 / 6.7292
LYNGSTØYLVATNET

Travellers to Norway are usually hypnotised by soaring cliffs and glassy fjords. But there are wonders beneath the water, too: an entire town lurks beneath Lyngstøylvatnet. In 1908, an avalanche from Mt Keipen set rocky rubble in motion to create a natural dam. The resulting lake, Lyngstøylvatnet, swallowed up huts, bridges, part of a forest and a section of old road. Today, skilled divers don their thickest wetsuits to plunge into the chilly waters, where they can somersault among old stone walls and duck beneath a short bridge, now hemmed by clouds of algae.

☞ *The lake is only for experienced divers and most easily visited by car. A trip is best teamed with a visit to Sunnylven Church and Hellesylt Waterfalls, 35km southeast by road.*

THE ALPS, SWITZERLAND. 46.6942 / 8.3575
TRIFTBRÜCKE

Don't look down: you're walking along one of the Swiss Alps' longest and highest pedestrian bridges, and it's beginning to tremble in a sudden high wind. Even the cable-car ascent to the Triftbrücke seems designed to make your stomach lurch. Built in 2009, the Triftbrücke was modelled after the Nepalese-style triple-rope bridge, a simple but durable design seen across the country's mountain passes. For walkers, this crossing seems much longer than 170m, dangling above the cliffs of the Trift Gorge and dropping to the teal waters of Triftsee. To avoid glancing down, fix your gaze on the glacier and mountain panorama ahead.

☞ *Take the cable car at Nessental Triftbahn bus stop, then a 90-minute hike each way. June to October only.*

Ⓔ ESBJERG, Ⓓ ENMARK. 55.48776 / 8.41119

MAN MEETS THE SEA

As you sail into Esbjerg harbour, you won't fail to notice four seated figures by the harbourside who rather look as if they've been expecting you. These 9m-high statues comprise the arresting Man Meets the Sea installation. On a clear day, these gleaming white figures are visible from the deck of a boat some 10km away. The brainchild of Svend Wiig Hansen, this sizeable artwork was first unveiled in 1995 to celebrate Esbjerg municipality's centenary of independence. The artist intended the sculptures to evoke a pure sense of uniformity and timelessness, capturing a meeting between humanity and nature before the former lost its way. Faced with these impassive figures, it's hard not to wonder what they might see as they gaze way out to the North Sea.

🖝 The sculptures are on Sædding Strand, 4km south of Esbjerg. Catch bus 3 from the train station.

TOP 10

NERVE-WRACKING ROCKS

Near Tyssedal, Norway, 60.1242 / 6.7401

① Trolltunga

The tongue of rock jutting above the water at Ringedalsvatnet is one of Norway's most spectacular photo ops. Hikers embark on a tough, 12-hour circuit from Skjeggedal to reach this panorama of sheer cliffs above water. The highlight is balancing on the 700m-high rock, one of several nerve-jangling outcrops you can pose on around the world.

🖝 Reach the rock via a 12-hour hiking circuit from the village of Skjeggedal, which is 5km east of Tyssedal in southern Norway.

Near Chennai, India, 12.6188 / 80.1922

② Balancing Rock of Mahabalipuram

It's a 250-tonne rock, 6m tall and on a 45-degree slope, but attempts to roll 'Krishna's Butterball' downhill have failed, and tourists safely pose beneath.

🖝 The rock is just off Madha Kovil Street in Mahabalipuram, 55km south of Chennai.

TIJUCA NATIONAL PARK, BRAZIL.
-22.9975 / -43.2859

③ Pedra da Gávea

For a death-defying holiday photo, head to this 844m-high Rio lookout. From the right angle, you'll appear to cling to a rock high above the beach; in reality, you're two feet from solid ground.

It's a tough, six-hour return hike through Tijuca National Park. Hire a guide: www.nattrip.com.br.

NEAR ØYGARDSTØL, NORWAY, 59.0337 / 6.5933

④ Kjeragbolten

The ultimate in daring poses is atop this boulder, gripped between two cliffs above a 984m drop. The block was deposited here by glacial movement and has become a vertigo-inducing spot for a photo.

The 9km hike to Kjeragbolten, some of the route assisted by chains, begins in Øygardstøl.

© Ron Nickel / Getty Images

⑤ Nature's Time Post

TIVERTON, CANADA, 44.3629 / -66.2243

Inspiring countless attempts at perspective trickery photos, the basalt column known as 'Nature's Time Post' appears to balance on its tip on the corner of a larger rock in the Bay of Fundy.

☛ Find the column via a 2.5km hike and 235 stairs; the route begins off Hwy 217, Tiverton.

NEAR PREIKESTOLHYTTA, NORWAY, 58.9863 / 6.1903

⑥ Preikestolen

Rising sharply 604m above the Lysefjord, 'Pulpit Rock' is the reward for an intense four-hour hike in Norway's Ryfylke fjord region – snap a photo near the edge, but not that near the edge!

☛ Take a bus from Stavanger ferry terminal to Preikestolhytta, the trailhead for Pulpit Rock.

NORTHERN TERRITORY, AUSTRALIA, -20.5612 / 134.2615

⑦ Devils Marbles

Granite globes are dotted around a parched valley in Australia's Northern Territory. To Aboriginal people, these weathered boulders have sacred significance. One pair seemingly defy gravity.

☛ The Devils Marbles reserve is on the Stuart Highway, 100km south of Tennant Creek.

UTAH, USA, 38.7009 / -109.5646

⑧ Balanced Rock

Balanced Rock roosts on a slender 39m column, looking ready to fall at any moment. Its twin rock formation did indeed tumble during the 1970s, so don't stand too close, just in case...

☛ A 20-minute hiking trail to the rock begins off the main road of Arches National Park in Utah.

ARIZONA, USA, 31.9988 / -109.3176

⑨ Chiricahua National Monument

Resembling a spinning top amid the creeks, volcanic formations and grottoes of this Arizona park, the Big Balanced Rock perches improbably at its narrow end.

☛ Various trails from Echo Canyon Trailhead in Chiricahua National Monument reach the rock.

RUOKOLAHTI, FINLAND, 61.4935 / 28.4294

⑩ Kummakivi

It's impossible to resist posing, arms raised, beneath this boulder in Finland. Performing a balancing act on a low mound, the 7m-wide rock was deposited by glacial movement, though folktales blame trolls.

☛ The forest concealing the rock is a 10km drive north from route 62 in southeastern Finland.

HAMBURG, GERMANY, 53.5438 / 9.9885

MINIATUR WUNDERLAND

Abandon yourself to train-spotting geekdom and unleash your inner child. Miniatur Wunderland has the largest model railway in the world, along with doll-sized Renaissance buildings, tiny stadiums with pin-sized people, and little trains rattling among fairy-sized forests. Miniatur Wunderland's Hamburg hometown is recreated down to the last detail, from its columned Kunsthalle to the Reeperbahn. There's also a Lilliputian Scandinavia, with boats bobbing in snow-rimmed lakes, and a recreation of Las Vegas by night. Started in 2000, the creation of this miniature world has taken 760,000 hours (and counting). Planned additions to Miniatur Wunderland include a Monaco Formula 1 circuit, slated for 2019.

Book tickets at www.miniatur-wunderland.com. Reach it from Baumwall on the U3 subway line.

◎NEAR AGADEZ, ◎NIGER, 17.7500 / 10.06667

TREE OF TÉNÉRÉ

The last one standing. Almost. Once the sole tree in the middle of the Sahara – the survivor of the ancient Saharan forests – this acacia was justifiably famous. Not only was it the only tree in Africa featured on the Michelin map, but more importantly the Tree of Ténéré marked the location of a critical well for water for those crossing the heart of this inhospitable desert. That was until 1973, when it was knocked down by a Libyan truck driver. What were the odds of that? Today the tree is a metal replica, which stands in the original's place, to honour it.

☞ *When the security situation permits, the Tree of Ténéré can be reached by a 4WD expedition from Agadez. In the meantime, remnants of the original are in the national museum in Niamey.*

© Arterra / Getty Imagess

AALBORG, DENMARK, 57.0430 / 9.91521

SINGING TREES

Plenty of gardeners sing to their plants, but in Aalborg the plants sing back. Trees in Kildeparken have their own individual soundtracks, often linked to the artist who planted them. This Danish city has been persuading stars to plant trees in Kildeparken since 1987, starting with Cliff Richard. A dazzling roll-call followed his example, including Sting, Beyoncé, Elton John, Shakira and ZZ Top. It seemed logical for the park to sing its gratitude, so in 2012, oak and cherry trees were wired to play music. Stroll through the park, press the 'play' buttons on the trees, and be serenaded by a choir of tree-hugging celebrities.

Listen to the Singing Trees year-round in Kildeparken, south of central Aalborg near the city's bus and train stations.

SOUTH TYROL, ITALY, 46.8037 / 10.5314

CAMPANILE DI CURON

With its backdrop of mountains and forested shores, Reschensee is a snapshot of pristine nature – until you notice a bell tower jutting from the water. This lake in Italy's South Tyrol was created artificially by the building of a dam in 1950, merging three lakes into one. Along with five square kilometres of farmland and dozens of homes, a 14th-century church was forever submerged by the water, except for its bell tower. In midwinter when the lake freezes over, it is possible to walk out to the tower. Arguably the church is even lovelier as an apparition rising silently from Reschensee.

Close to Italy's border with Switzerland and Austria, the lake is visitable from three countries; plan on www.suedtirolerland.it.

RÅBJERG MILE

In a slow, sandy suicide, this Danish dune is gradually drifting away from the conservation zone designed to protect it. Forty metres high and consisting of four million cubic metres of sand, the Råbjerg Mile is Denmark's largest dune. It bulldozes along northern Jutland, moving 15m each year.

For hundreds of years, sand dunes have bothered the Danes. Between the 15th and 18th centuries, shifting sands drove people out of their homes. The tower of a church swallowed up by sand in 1795 is still visible, now dubbed 'Den Tilsandede Kirke' (the buried church). In the 19th century, the Sand Drift Act was established to allow the government to buy dune-covered land and stabilise it by planting trees.

The Danish government bought the land enclosing the Råbjerg Mile in 1900. Instead of trying to halt its onward march, they decided to see what this mammoth dune would do, and demonstrate to future generations what happens when dunes are left to run amok. Trouble is, the Råbjerg Mile is speeding out of the protective zone. While officials scramble to adjust the paperwork protecting it, the dune is steadily growing in popularity among birdwatchers and hikers.

🖝 *From Skagen, cycle south along Gamle Landevej. Seek local advice, as some areas have quicksand.*

NIGER. 16.864930 / 11.953712

MEMORIAL TO UTA 772

It points in the direction of Paris, the city that was to be flight UTA 772's final destination. It sits near where the fuselage of the bombed DC10 fell into the Sahara on 19 September 1989. And it lives on as a remarkable tribute to all those who perished on the flight from Brazzaville. Built by the deceased's families and 140 Nigerians, the monument is constructed from 170 mirrors (one for each victim), rocks and vestiges of the plane itself. Seen from above, it is a life-sized DC10 silhouette, forming the needle of a giant compass. One of the original plane's wings stands upright from the north arrow, bearing a plaque with the victims' names.

Visible from the Brazzaville–Paris flight path, the memorial can be reached by 4WD from Agadez, if security permits.

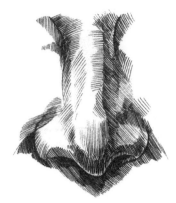

LUND. SWEDEN. 55.7055 / 13.1957

LUND NASOTHEK

It's not easy getting your hooter immortalised in a 'nasothek' – a collection of noses. These carefully curated repositories only admit the finest of human facial protuberances. Only the most distinguished of nostrils need apply. And the nasothek at Lund University in Sweden is the most extensive collection of its kind in Europe; since 1986 it has assembled more than 100 casts of noses. Each one is decided through a guarded process of nomination and debate. Authors, doctors and local legends have offered their noses to immortality, enduring a very public plaster-cast process. It's hoped that the noses will inspire younger members of the university.

This collection on Sandgatan 2 in Lund is open weekdays (term time), 9am–6pm. nasala.se.

LUANDA. ANGOLA. –8.8122 / 13.2357

PALÁCIO DE FERRO

Luanda's striking yellow Palácio de Ferro, which reopened as a cultural centre in 2016, is a beautiful building with a murky provenance. With its decorative iron balustrades and bold art nouveau parapets it looks distinctly Eiffel-esque – indeed, popular legend suggests it was built for an exposition in France in the 1890s on the designs of Gustave Eiffel. Subsequently dismantled, it was put on a ship bound for Madagascar. After the ship ran aground in storms off Angola's Skeleton Coast, however, the building ended up in Luanda. Despite its romantic history, no official documentation of the 'iron palace' exists. Instead, it sits like an unsolved mystery amid Luanda's 21st-century oil towers.

The Palácio is in Luanda's city centre, known as the baixa. Opening times vary; entry is free.

ROME. ITALY. 41.8194 / 12.5573

VIA APPIA ANTICA

The first great superhighway of the Roman world, Via Appia Antica was the most celebrated of Rome's consular roads. Named after Appius Claudius Caecus, who laid the first 90km section in 312 BC, it was completed in 190 BC and quickly became a key strategic artery, linking Rome with the southern port of Brindisi.

The ancients dubbed it the regina viarum (queen of roads) and today it's still a majestic sight. Monuments and milestones line the cobbled thoroughfare as it heads out of town, flanked by towering pine trees and lush fields littered with evocative ruins and hidden villas. It has long been one of Rome's most exclusive addresses,

but behind the beauty lies a dark history. This is where Spartacus and 6000 of his slave rebels were crucified in 71 BC, and where the ancients came to bury their dead. Well-to-do Romans built elaborate mausoleums whilst the early Christians went underground, creating a 300km network of subterranean burial chambers – the catacombs.

Legend also has it that St Peter met a vision of Jesus here. According to the story, Peter was fleeing Rome when he saw Christ on the site where the Chiesa del Domine Quo Vadis now stands. The two exchanged words and Peter decided to head back into town, where he was promptly arrested and crucified.

Take bus 660 from Colli Albani metro station (line A) or bus 118 from Circo Massimo (line B).

10 ⒯ ⒪ ⒫ BERLIN WALLS AROUND THE WORLD

Ⓑ ERLIN, Ⓖ ERMANY, 52.5045 / 13.4413

① East Side Gallery

The Berlin Wall divided East Germany from the west from 1961 until its destruction in 1989. The murals decorating Mühlenstrasse's surviving 1.3km of wall capture both the sorrow of separation and the joy that greeted the wall's demise. Parts of the wall were torn down, and some slabs were sent across the world. Many now stand as grim warnings in parks, museums and hotel lobbies.

☛ *View the Wall on Mühlenstrasse, west of Oberbaum Bridge. www.eastsidegallery-berlin.de.*

Ⓢ EOUL, Ⓢ OUTH Ⓚ OREA, 37.5664 / 126.9898

② Berlin Square

A corner of old Berlin tucked nonchalantly within Seoul's futuristic cityscape, 'Berlin Square' not only has a section of the Wall but also a blue Berlin bear and German-style street lamps.

☛ *Walk south and east from Jonggak station to reach the small plaza.*

Ⓚ INGSTON, Ⓙ AMAICA, 17.9940 / −76.7831

③ Jamaica Military Museum

A two-tonne slab gifted to Usain Bolt, after he broke records in Berlin, stands outside Kingston's Military Museum, decorated with a mural of the sprinter.

☛ *The museum is in Eden Gardens, open from Wednesday to Sunday.*

Ⓑ RUSSELS, Ⓑ ELGIUM, 50.8396 / 4.3762

④ European Parliament

A section of Wall that once loomed over Potsdamer Platz now stands near the EU's Parlamentarium. The 'New WR 9.85' inscription refers to the 100m sprint world record when it was painted.

☛ *Find the slab off Rue Wiertz, in Brussels' Quartier Européen.*

ⓈOFIA, ⒷULGARIA, 42.6856 / 23.3191

⑤ National Palace of Culture

Several memorials surround Sofia's Palace of Culture, including the 1300 Year Monument to victims of the Communist regime, and a section of the Berlin Wall.

The Palace of Culture is in the heart of town, near metro station NDK.

ⒹALLAS, USA, 32.8004 / -96.8304

⑥ Dallas Hilton Anatole

Two segments of the Berlin Wall are tastefully back-lit inside this luxurious Dallas hotel. Their screaming mouth designs were created by Berlin street artist Jürgen Grosse.

The hotel is just north of downtown Dallas, off the Stemmons Fwy.

ISRAEL, 32.7003 / 34.9827

⑦ Ein Hod

Ein Hod, an artistic enclave in northern Israel, has been home to a panel of the Berlin Wall since 1992, adding to the village's offbeat melange of outdoor art and micro-galleries.

Reach Ein Hod by car from Haifa along road 4. Take the eastbound turnoff to road 7111.

ⓋATICAN ⒸITY ⓈTATE, 41.9033 / 12.4504

⑧ Vatican Gardens

Given to the Pope by Formula 1 honcho Marco Piccinini, the hunk of Wall in the Vatican Gardens features a mural of Berlin's St Michael's Church, which was once obscured by the Wall.

Take metro line A to Ottaviano-San Pietro.

ⓃEW ⒸYORK ⒸITY, USA, 40.7040 / -74.0173

⑨ Battery Park

One of the 'big heads' by the French street artist Thierry Noir stares out from this section of the Wall, which found its way to New York City as a gift from the German Consulate.

Battery Park is on the southern tip of Lower Manhattan; find the wall on Kowsky Plaza.

ⒸAPE ⓉOWN, ⓈOUTH ⒶFRICA, -33.9217 / 18.4220

⑩ St George's Mall

A slice of the Wall that was originally gifted to Nelson Mandela by the city of Berlin now stands by St George's Mall, a busy pedestrianised street in the centre of Cape Town.

St George's Mall is 500m from Cape Town's main railway station.

10 TOP OUTSTANDING OSSUARIES

HALLSTATT, AUSTRIA. 47.5636 / 13.6487

① Beinhaus Hallstatt

In the Austrian Alps, skull painting is an enduring art form, and death comes in a rainbow of shades at Hallstatt's charnel house. Half of its 1200 skulls are painted with floral crowns, crucifixes and even calligraphy of their former owners' names. Some skulls date back 800 years, but a few of the colourful craniums were laid here during the last century.

☛ *The ossuary adjoins Hallstatt's parish church and is open from May to October.*

NEAR KUTNÁ HORA, CZECH REPUBLIC. 49.9614 / 15.2883

② Kostnice v Sedlci

Chandeliers, monstrances and coats of arms have been crafted from every bone in the human body at this creepy chapel. As a flourish, creator František Rint left a signature shaped from tiny bones.

☛ *The ossuary is located 2km east of Kutná Hora. It is open from April to October.*

ROME, ITALY. 41.9048 / 12.4886

③ Convento dei Cappuccini

Hooded skeletons lean against a skull altar at this crypt. From the 1500s to 1900s, praying monks knew one day their bones would join those of their brethren.

☛ *The church and convent complex in Rome is open daily. The nearest metro stop is Barberini.*

NIŠ, SERBIA. 43.3121 / 21.9238

④ Skull Tower

After an uprising in 1809, the ruling Turks built a 3m-high tower of skulls to deter future rebellions. Today, Niš' skull tower symbolises resistance, though the number of skulls has depleted from 952 to 54.

☛ *To get to the Skull Tower, take a bus from central Niš towards Niška Banja.*

ⒶNear Valladolid, Spain, 41.6762 / -4.9178

⑤ Church of Santa Maria

The mortal remains of half a millennium of Spanish monks are housed in the ossuary of this 12th-century church. Its walls are piled high with femurs, while 3000 skulls glare blankly at visitors.

🖝 The church is a 22km drive west of Valladolid. It's only open on weekends.

ⒸKudowa-Zdrój, Poland, 50.4515 / 16.2419

⑥ Kaplica Czaszek

More than 3000 skulls of victims of cholera, the Black Death and numerous wars slumber inside this 18th-century chapel in Czermna village. Another 20,000 bones are in the cellar beneath your feet.

🖝 The Czaszek chapel is about 1km north of the centre of Kudowa-Zdrój.

ⒼLima, Peru, -12.0453 / -77.0270

⑦ Monastery of San Francisco

Beneath the baroque towers of this monastery reside the bones of 70,000 people. They're carefully arranged, radiating out from a cluster of crania.

🖝 The pristine, white colonnaded convent is in Lima, 250m from Desamparados station.

④

⑥

⒱Verdun, France, 49.2069 / 5.4239

⑧ Douaumont Ossuary

The remains of 130,000 German and French soldiers mingle in this concrete charnel house. Bones regularly emerge from the ground in northern France, the scene of the 300-day Battle of Verdun in WWI.

🖝 Verdun's tourist office can arrange daytrips to Douaumont (en.verdun-tourisme.com).

⒦Kent, England, 51.0727 / 1.0841

⑨ St Leonard's Church

This Norman-era church guards 590 skulls and 8000 leg bones dating across hundreds of years, the oldest from the 1300s. They are thought to be remains that were reinterred after local cemeteries filled.

🖝 St Leonard's Church is in Hythe in Kent, some 17km west of Dover.

⒮Saint Catherine, Egypt, 28.5553 / 33.9759

⑩ St Catherine's Monastery

Glowing gold in the desert sun, St Catherine's is one of the oldest monasteries in the world. Former monks sleep peacefully in its small ossuary.

🖝 Guided excursions are available from Dahab. See www.sinaimonastery.com.

POSTOJNA CAVES

When unearthly amphibians were first seen in Postojna's caves in the 17th century, the obvious explanation was that they were infant dragons. But the truth about the newt-like proteus is almost as intriguing – this ghostly pale amphibian is found only in Postojna's 24km of caves. The hardy proteus can survive up to a decade without food and is completely blind, darting among the subterranean waterways using its ability to perceive weak electrical fields.

The caves and their slimy residents have been welcoming visitors for some time. Miniature trains have trundled into the grotto for more than 140 years: Empress Elisabeth of Austria even took a tour, though sadly the velvet sedan chairs used for her visit are no longer available. Today, the cave walls drip with multi-tentacled stalactites and pillars of limestone rise like the altar of a baroque cathedral. The shiny 5m-tall stalagmite dubbed 'The Brilliant' inspires the clicking of cameras, though it's the tanks of proteus that steal the limelight. Biologists have high hopes for what these slippery creatures may contribute to science; their regenerative powers may hold keys to cancer therapies or even slowing down the ageing process in humans. Only in 2016 were scientists finally able to observe baby proteus hatching and growing. For now, the baby dragons are keeping their secrets under wraps.

☛ *Postojna (www.postojnska-jama.eu) is an hour from Ljubljana by bus.*

IDRIJA, SLOVENIA.
45.9997 / 14.0228

MERCURY MINE

The town of Idrija built its fortune from 500 years of poisonous liquid metal mining. For centuries, mercury was pivotal for technological innovations in thermometers and lamps. Idrija's abundant mercury was discovered in 1490, and the Slovenian town held the world's largest mercury mine for centuries. Down St Anthony's Mineshaft, the tunnels have been preserved and the walls still sparkle with beads of the toxic metal (mercifully contained behind glass). The mine is named after the patron saint of miners, and tours bypass a small chapel where workers once prayed before their shifts. Idrija is also famous for its intricate lace, which makes a much more suitable souvenir.

🦶 Tours of the mine last 90 minutes. Idrija is 60km east of Ljubljana. www.antonijevrov.si.

ZADAR, CROATIA.
44.1173 / 15.2199

SEA ORGAN

A lowly melody emanates from the shore in Zadar, trumpeted straight from the bottom of the sea. Here, in the centre of Croatia's glittering coast, a marble staircase conceals a set of 35 pipes and a submerged chamber. The movement of the waves pushes seawater into the pipes, expelling air tunefully, allowing a melody to waft along the promenade. This sea shanty harnesses the power of the tides. It can be solemn, harmonious or downright atonal depending on the weather conditions. This musical experiment, the brainchild of architect Nikola Bašić, has been piping out its seven different chords since 2005.

🦶 The sea organ bellows its melody on the western edge of Zadar's Riva, 500m northwest of the national museum.

ŽELÍZY, SLOVENIA.
45.9997 / 14.0228

ZELÍZY STONE DEVILS

If you go down to the woods today, these sinister statues might stop you in your tracks. Like a nightmarish Mount Rushmore, two stone 'devil heads' (Čertovy hlavy) lurk on the forested outskirts of Želízy, 35km north of Prague. The creator of these sculptures is Czech artist Václav Levý, a shoemaker's son who rose to prominence as a sculptor. He took his craft as far as Rome and Vienna, and decorated churches across the continent including the tympanum of mighty St Vitus in Prague. Still, it's a little surprising that a sculptor renowned for religious themes should have left two monstrous visages to gather moss in the Czech countryside.

🦶 The Devils sulk on a hillock south of Želízy village, visible from the main road. It's a 300m walk from the centre.

© Alen Ferina / Alamy

© Michal Boubin / Alamy

ITINERARY

EERIE NAMIBIA

Ⓝamib Ⓓesert, Ⓝamibia, −26.7022 / 15.2318

KOLMANSKOP

Some ghost towns remain frozen in time. Some rot unappealingly. Kolmanskop, on the other hand, is being spectacularly consumed by desert dunes, one grain of sand at a time. Built as Consolidated Diamond Mines' headquarters in the early 1900s, it boasted a bowling alley, theatre and casino. However, after richer pickings were found at Oranjemund, Kolmanskop's time was up – it was completely abandoned by 1956. Clamber over the dunes in the buildings' surreal interiors.

Kolmanskop is a 15-minute drive from Lüderitz, just off the B4.

ⓁNAMIB ⒹESERT. ⓃNAMIBIA. –26.7022 / 15.2318
FAIRY CIRCLES

Radioactive soil, termites and plant toxins – they've all been considered as causes, but despite all the science, the fairy circles are still a mystery. Dotted randomly across the eastern fringes of the Namib Desert, these countless circular patches (2m-15m in diameter) are devoid of any vegetation, their red soils standing out in a sea of golden grass. From the seat of a moving vehicle, you might just fail to notice this remarkable phenomenon, especially if you didn't know to look for it. But take to the sky (or your 4WD's roof) and the fairy circles leap out at you. *The NamibRand Nature Reserve and remote Marienfluss Valley are great for fairy circles, but they occur widely.*

ⓁNAMIB ⒹESERT. ⓃNAMIBIA. –24.7593 / 15.2924
DEADVLEI

Walk among the skeletons and shadows of an ancient forest in surreal surroundings, namely Deadvei, a bleached, cracked clay pan enveloped by towering dunes of bright orange hues. *Deadvlei is a 1.5km walk from the end of the Sossusvlei access road in Namib-Naukluft National Park.*

ⓁNAMBI ⒹESERT. ⓃNAMIBIA. –21.8104 / 15.1760
ROCK ARCH, SPITZKOPPE

Defying gravity for millennia and providing what is perhaps the best frame for a night sky in the whole world, the rock arch near the mighty 1728m massif of Namibia's Spitzkoppe is nature's gift to every photographer. The sky is so clear here that the stars are just as bright and numerous on the horizon as they are above you – call it a celestial blanket. *Turn northwest off the B2 on to the D1918, towards Henties Bay. After an 18km drive, turn north on to the D3716.*

ⓁNAMIB ⒹESERT. ⓃNAMIBIA. –19.9715 / 13.0653
SINGING DUNES

Sure, nature can inspire you to sing. But how do you feel about nature belting out a note or two itself? The unique mineral composition of the Namib Desert's sand, particularly in areas along the Skeleton Coast, ensures that it resonates (usually in notes E, F or G) when disturbed. Slide on your backside down a dune's leeward side and listen to it roar. *The dunes behind remote Terrace Bay are particularly good singers. It's reachable on the D34/D2302 with a 4WD.*

'We gazed at the hissing steam, vertical jets of fire, thunderous explosions and the pitter–patter of sizzling rocks rolling down the craters' flanks'

◌NEAR ⦾ICILY, ITALY, 38.8034 / 15.2326

Stromboli

Sitting astride the volcanic arc between Italy's Mt Vesuvius and Sicily's Mt Etna, the hyperactive fire-breathing island of Stromboli has captured human imaginations for eons. Ancient sailors dubbed it 'lighthouse of the Mediterranean' for its constant eruptions, and the volcano-lover in me had long felt drawn to this perfect cone floating in isolation at the Aeolian archipelago's eastern edge. So, on a sunny mid-May afternoon, with a full moon forecast, I cruised over for a visit.

My small group set off at 4.30pm from San Vincenzo church. A steady climb through yellow broom and wild capers brought us above the tree line, revealing bird's eye views of whitewashed Stromboli village and the sparkling Mediterranean. Above us, a zigzag line of fellow hikers slogged summit-wards across bare ashen expanses.

Two hours later, we emerged into the otherworldly landscape of Stromboli's summit: smoking craters juxtaposed against a ruddy twilight sky, with the setting sun and its reflection tracing a giant upside-down exclamation mark across the sea. For the next 60 minutes, bundled against the cold, we enjoyed front-row views of the volcano's fireworks. From our exhilarating vantage point above the craters, we gazed in wonder at the steadily hissing steam, punctuated at unpredictable intervals by vertical jets of fire, thunderous explosions and the pitter-patter of sizzling rocks rolling down the craters' flanks. As the skies darkened, the eruptions morphed from red-freckled billows of grey smoke to vivid fountains of red-orange light – each unique, all beautiful.

What goes up must come down. Eventually our headlamp-clad crew stepped single-file on to the talus-strewn wasteland of Stromboli's eastern slope and began our steep descent, with the moonlit sea spread out at our feet, stretching to the twinkling lights of Italy's mainland.

Once was not enough. The mountain had gotten under my skin, and I felt compelled to linger. At dusk the next night I hopped on a boat to observe the eruptions from the sea, and before sunrise the following morning I hiked up to the Sciara del Fuoco, the desolate grey expanse below Stromboli's craters where you can watch molten rocks careen down the slopes and crash into the Mediterranean 900m below. A decade later, I'm as obsessed as ever; I've returned almost every year since, and Stromboli's magic still hasn't worn thin.
By Gregor Clark

 Access Stromboli by daily hydrofoil from Milazzo (Sicily) or twice-weekly ferry from Naples. The summit's off-limits to under-7s.

ᎦVALBARD, ◯NORWAY, 78.2357 / 15.4932

GLOBAL SEED VAULT

If you've ever mulled over how humankind could begin anew after a global disaster – say, crop failure or a zombie apocalypse – then you will be heartened to hear about Norway's Global Seed Vault. Squirrelled away on the northerly archipelago of Svalbard, the bank's mission is to store enough seeds to ensure genetic diversity among crops around the globe.

Around 1700 agricultural outposts across the world already carry their own stocks of seeds. Diverse varieties of crops, resistant to disease or hardy in droughts, are stored quietly for a rainy day (or rather, a not-so-rainy one). Their fragile contents would be easily lost in power outages or manmade

disasters, so the Global Seed Bank's vaults provide the ultimate back-up plan: 860,000 samples of around 4000 plant species, safely stashed in sealed baggies in a far-flung Arctic safehouse.

It doesn't get much safer, or more remote, than halfway between northern Norway and the North Pole. The site even has James Bond-esque safeguards in place: in the event of a power failure, the seldom-opened vault will remain sealed. The permafrost will keep stocks cold. And security measures stipulate that the stored seeds can only be retrieved by the nation that placed them here, ensuring no one can capitalise on another country's agricultural crisis.

 Svalbard's airport is served by flights from Oslo and Tromsø. Book tours at www.svalbardscience.com.

© Richard Wareham Fotografie / Alamy

NOWE CZARNOWO, POLAND,
53.2139 / 14.4757

CROOKED FOREST

Hansel and Gretel would run in the opposite direction from this unsettling forest, where trees snake out of the ground at an unnatural angle. In the witchy woodland of *Krzywy Las* – 'Crooked Forest' – more than 400 pine trees have a peculiar C-shaped bend. Theories are wide-ranging: some suggest unusually heavy snowfall could have crushed the trees in this grove while they were saplings; others have said that wartime tanks may have rumbled through and distorted their growth. Inventive farming methods are the most likely culprit, however. Curved logs would have been awfully handy for shipbuilding, so experimental farmers may have intervened with the trees' natural growth, though no one has admitted to it.

This wacky glade is 2km north of Nowe Czarnowo, itself 33km south of Szczecin, a lively port in western Poland.

SARAJEVO, BOSNIA & HERCEGOVINA, 43.8563 / 18.4131

SARAJEVO ROSES

Sorrow and hope blossom out of the concrete in Bosnia & Hercegovina's capital, Sarajevo. Scars left by deadly mortar strikes during the Siege of Sarajevo have been filled with red resin, creating street-level memorials to the lost. Between 1992 and 1996, more than 300 bombs per day hit Sarajevo, launched by Republika Srpska army tanks squatting in the surrounding hills. Over the course of 1425 bloody days, 11,541 civilians were killed in Sarajevo.

When a mortar shell hits a hard surface such as concrete, it creates a central crater surrounded by smaller dents. When filled with red resin, these markings resemble vivid red blooms, or pools of blood, on the surface of Sarajevo's streets. No single person or group claims to have created Sarajevo's roses, so they are deemed to belong to the people who lived through the siege. But as a result, these rose-shaped memorials are bereft of an authority to preserve them. As years pass and sections of road have been replaced, many roses have disappeared. Still, in recent years, groups of volunteers have painstakingly repainted the roses to protect them from footfall and weather damage.

With so many locals carrying physical and psychological scars from the war, the roses' resemblance to open wounds is apt. Though some have mixed feelings about the attention the roses receive from visitors to the city, many more see them as an embodiment of grief and even hope sprouting around Sarajevo.

Sarajevo Roses can be seen around the city. Look for them at Markale Market, Ferhadija Promenade and Grand Park.

© Maciej Bledowski / Alamy

CROATIA. 44.8654 / 15.5820

PLITVICE LAKES NATIONAL PARK

War-torn history is washed away by Plitvice's ever-changing landscape of pools and terraces. As you step along wooden walkways over cerulean pools, it's hard to imagine that landmines once dotted this slice of Eden. Waterfalls feed the park's 16 crystalline lakes, and butterflies gather near the spray. The tallest waterfall, Veliki Slap, tumbles from 70m high. But Unesco-listed Plitvice Lakes National Park was also among the first battle sites between Croatia and Serbia during the Balkan Wars of the 1990s, with 'Plitvice Bloody Easter' in 1991 the first fatal armed confrontation of the Croatian War of Independence. The last of the remaining landmines are thought to have now been weeded out, but in the more untrodden depths of the park, it's impossible to be sure.

In a place touched by war, it's cathartic to know that Plitvice Lakes is constantly renewing itself. Its lakes form as water washes over the chalk and limestone, creating travertine barriers. As sediment is deposited and washed away, the lake system moves as well (even if you might have to wait hundreds of years to observe the effects). The names of different lakes hint at regional history; Kaluđerovo Jezero takes its name from a monk who lived in a grotto at the canyon's edge, harking back to times when this landscape was used as a spiritual refuge.

 Buses connect the lakes (www.np-plitvicka-jezera.hr) with Split, Zadar and Zagreb. Admission fees vary.

© Martin Harvey / Getty Images

© Marcus Lindstrom / Getty Images

NAMIBIA. -26.6090 / 16.1075

Wild Horses of the Namib Desert

It's not often that you sit in a bleak desert waiting for a wild stallion or two. After all, desert-dwelling horses are a rare sight on this planet of ours. Yet that's exactly what I was doing at Garup Pan. To pass the time I considered the theories of their origin... Descendants of cavalry horses abandoned by the Schutztruppe (German Imperial Army) in 1915? Relations of horses shipwrecked en route to Australia from Europe? Offspring of the stud stock of Baron Captain Hans-Heinrich von Wolf, who built Duwisib Castle 150km north of here in 1909? My thoughts were interrupted by dots appearing in the heat haze, and within minutes a dozen of the mystical horses paraded past me. Incredible. By Matt Phillips

☛ Garub Pan is 1500m north of the road to Lüderitz in southern Namibia; the turn off is 20km west of Aus.

VIENNA. AUSTRIA. 48.2073 / 16.3943

HUNDERTWASSERHAUS

Leafy roofs, uneven floors, and a tapestry of powder blue, coral and gold... This apartment block, designed with Expressionist panache by Friedensreich Hundertwasser, couldn't be more different from Vienna's stately baroque churches and grey multistorey blocks. Never a man to colour within the lines – much less to draw them straight – artist and architect Hundertwasser created a fairytale complex of flowing, organic shapes, where tree branches billow from the windows. Best of all, Hundertwasser decreed that every tenant had the right to personalise the area outside their window, following their own unique tastes: another way for the artist's irrepressible spirit (and distaste for uniformity) to live on after his death.

☛ The house is at Kegelgasse 37-39. There's a museum of the architect's work nearby. www.hundertwasser-haus.info.

CENTRAL CEDERBERG, SOUTH AFRICA, -32.4433 / 19.2538

WOLFBERG ARCH

A triumphant hiker stands, solo, beneath the ochre-hued sandstone arch, gazing dumbfounded. Dumbfounded at this magnificent natural rock sculpture, dumbfounded at the view, and perhaps more than a little surprised that they managed to complete the hike to get here.

Leaving from Sanddrif Holiday Resort, the four-hour trek to the Wolfberg Arch first passes through the Wolfberg Cracks, a series of crevices and caverns carved into the cliff face. Once you've scrambled, balanced, crawled and squeezed through the Cracks, the landscape flattens and soon enough the majesty of the Arch is before you.

The path is easy to follow, but that doesn't mean it's easy to hike. Unpeopled beauty like this doesn't come without a little hard work. After the vertiginous climb through the Cracks, the mildly undulating wander to the Arch might seem a breeze, but though the route is largely flat, it is also largely devoid of shade – and it can get stiflingly hot in the Cederberg. The Arch itself provides respite, as you crane your neck to admire this gaping gateway sculpted out of the rock face. The return hike follows the same path, but to truly acquaint yourself with the arch, pack a tent and split the hike over two days. The nights are notoriously chilly but the ceiling of stars and the chance to have the glowing dawn Arch to yourself makes every shiver worthwhile.

🔫 *A well-maintained gravel road leads from the N7, 30km north of Citrusdal, to Sanddrif Holiday Resort (www.sanddrif.com). Buy hiking permits here and stay the night before setting off at sunrise on the hike.*

Bajina Basta, Bosnia & Hercegovina.
43.9844 / 19.5666

DRINA RIVER HOUSE

Ever grumbled about noisy neighbours or dreamed of having river views? This tiny house is marooned on a rocky islet on the Drina River, the watery seam that separates Bosnia & Hercegovina and Serbia. Built in the 1960s by locals yearning for some blissful isolation, the photogenic chalet seems to defy gravity on its rocky perch, with barely enough shore space to moor a kayak. Vulnerable to flooding, this pocket-sized hideaway has been rebuilt more than once. These days it's much photographed by visitors to tranquil Bajina Basta village, and remains a curiosity for canoeists wending their way down the river.

🛶 Bajina Basta is quiet spot; you'll need private transport. It's a three-hour drive from Belgrade.

Slovenský Raj National Park, Slovakia.
48.8633 / 20.3116

DOBSINSKÁ ICE CAVE

There is a dark majesty to Slovenský Raj National Park, where bats flutter between limestone cliffs and perilous sinkholes dot the plateaus. Within this Slovakian nature reserve, the phenomenon most guaranteed to elicit a shiver (literally) is Dobšinská Ice Cave. This Unesco-listed cave enjoys perpetual winter, as cold air sinks in and warm air can't penetrate its depths, ensuring the temperature never exceeds 0.5°C. This perma-freeze has allowed more than 110,100 cubic metres of ice to amass: frozen walls gleam blue and silver, frosty stalactites sparkle from the ceiling, and thick pillars of ice seem plucked from a Snow Queen's ballroom.

🛶 From the car park, it's a 20-minute walk to the entrance (guided tours only). See www.ssj.sk.

'Sliding in through the narrow sniper hole, I found the interior pristine, save for evidence of a few birds that had nested here'

ALBANIA, 41.1533 / 20.1683

Albania's Concrete Bunkers

Nothing sums up Albania's bizarre 20th-century history more than its famous bunkers. When I first arrived at the country's only airport more than 15 years ago, these remnants of Communist-era paranoia were everywhere, dotting the landscape like some kind of naturally occurring life form. Their domed concrete roofs and narrow eye slits crouched suggestively on either side of the road to Tirana, ready for an invasion that never came.

Getting to see one up close would prove far trickier than I thought, however, as my Albanian friends reacted with something approaching disgust when I said I wanted to go inside one. During Albania's difficult times the bunkers had been repurposed in various ways – as makeshift toilets, winter stables for goats, and as secluded spots favoured by unmarried couples. Some were even inhabited during Albania's darkest days.

On top of that, the bunkers weren't built in towns but in remote, hillside locations, and so I didn't get close to one on that first trip. When I returned again a decade later it was fascinating to see how many had disappeared. They were no longer ubiquitous and, while not rare, were definitely not the semi-geological feature they had been on my first trip. Those that had survived were generally in terrible condition: roofs collapsed, covered in graffiti and long forgotten.

A few years ago, however, I stumbled across the perfect bunker and went inside for the first time. I was stunned to find it in mint condition, defending a bridge over a wide gorge on a backwater road in southern Albania. With not even a village nearby, this beauty had weathered the storms of Albania's various political incarnations since the 1970s almost totally untouched. I slid in

through the narrow sniper hole and found the interior pristine, save for evidence of a few birds that had nested there. It was damp inside, a cool refuge from the summer heat, though I didn't find myself envying the soldier who had been billeted there.

Legend has it that Albania's Communist dictator Enver Hoxha made the designer of the bunker stand inside the prototype while a tank drove over it, and when the bunker's roof survived the manoeuvre intact, the dictator gave the order to cover the entire country in them. They may be becoming rarer and rarer these days, but they were built in such sheer numbers that they will arguably never be entirely absent from Albania's rugged hillsides.
By Tom Masters

The bunkers can be found country-wide, though those in a decent state tend to be in remote areas. It's best to ask the locals.

Carpathian Mountains, Slovakia, 49.3301 / 21.6238

WOODEN CHURCHES

The wooden churches of Slovakia's Carpathian Mountains are marvels of craftsmanship. The majority were built between the 17th and 19th centuries, when they were lovingly carved and filled with painted icons. Most were constructed without using a single nail.

Discovering them is part of the fun: drive among the patchwork of meadows that covers eastern Slovakia, pull over in a sleepy village, and knock on the door of a gingerbread-esque church. Some of the oldest are Gothic in style, such as Hervartov's church, with its distinctive witch's hat shape; others resemble grand farmhouses with whitewashed walls and wooden eaves, as in Kežmarok.

These sedate villages see few tourists, so you'll have to wait for – or indeed, wake – a caretaker to grant you access (their phone numbers are sometimes posted on the doors). Once you strike it lucky and gain entry to one of these intimate shrines, the beauty within is staggering: one of the loveliest is Greek Catholic Jedlinka church (built in 1736), harbouring a gloriously gilded iconostasis.

The churches also bear witness to intriguing moments of history. Several were enclaves of peace and tolerance during the anti-Hapsburg revolutions. The denominations represented, including Greek Catholic and Lutheran, are testament to the variety of Christian faiths practised across this region.

 Experience the wooden churches as part of a road trip. Plan your route on www.drevenechramy.sk.

KAILO, FINLAND, 60.4733 / 22.0053

MOOMIN WORLD

Mouthless, magical trolls have proved an enduring feature of Scandinavian children's fiction. Finnish writer and illustrator Tove Jansson captivated generations of readers with the adventures of these whimsical hippo-shaped pixies. Accompanied by a magical cast of characters including silent, electricity-channelling Hattifatteners and the lonely phantom Groke, the Moomins now have their very own theme park on Kailo island near Naantali in Finland. Immerse yourself in the surreal by peeping into neon-lit caves, seeking out the resident witch, and watching Moomin-costumed dancers sway on stage. It's best to leave reality at the gate of this peculiar children's theme park.

🐾 The park is 16km west of Turku. A Moomin bus links Turku harbour to Moomin World (www.moominworld.fi).

© Jenni Virta Ilaine's Lifiari Oy

© Hemis / Alamy

CURONIAN SPIT, LITHUANIA, 55.5355 / 21.1172

WITCHES' HILL

If you do decide to go down to the woods today, you might see devils and warty witches glaring through the birch trees. On the Curonian Spit, the narrow tendril of land connecting Lithuania with the Russian territory of Kaliningrad, sinister folkloric wood carvings speckle a forested sand dune. Raganų Kalnas (Witches' Hill) is an open-air sculpture gallery comprising 71 charmingly creepy figures from the Neringa region, whittled from wood between 1979 and the early 2000s. This enigmatic glade, an easy 20km drive south from the port town of Klaipėda, has hosted midsummer folk celebrations for centuries. You'll find satanic totem poles, toothy dragons and a tiny playground where you can slide down a crone's tongue.

🐾 The Witches' Hill gallery is clearly signposted from the main road in Juodkrantė.

ITINERARY
MYSTICAL METEORA

Kalampaka, Greece, 39.7214 / 21.6336

METEORA

The World Heritage-listed site of Meteora is hardly a secret – it's one of Greece's most popular destinations – but it still holds many surprises. The series of soaring pinnacles were formed over 11 million years ago, when sedimentary rock was pushed upwards from the earth's core, and subsequent millennia of erosion created the mind-boggling towering outcrops you see on postcards across Greece (the word meteora derives from Greek meteoros, meaning 'suspended in the air'). The ancient monasteries that perch atop these jutting formations were built as safe havens following the incursions of the Turks in the 14th century. Of the 24 monasteries that survive, six are still active and can be visited. (Look out for the baskets and ropes that were used to hoist monks hundreds of metres heavenwards!) But there's more to Meteora than its remarkable rocks and monasteries. The region also offers spiritual highs of another kind.

☞ *Meteora is best reached from the local villages of Kalambaka and Kastraki. Buses go to Trikala (22km southeast of Kalambaka); from here, there are regular services to Kalambaka.*

KALAMPAKA, GREECE, 39.8815 / 20.7065
MONOPATIA & CAVES
From the 11th century, before the construction of the monasteries, hermits lived in isolation in caves scattered throughout Meteora, linked by a spiderweb-like network of *monopatia* (old monks' trails). Follow these ancient, off-piste tracks and you'll discover former monasteries, plus cave hermitages hidden in vertical rock faces (from below, they resemble pigeon holes).

KALAMPAKA, GREECE, VARIOUS
HERMIT-LIKE CLIMBS
Visitors can tackle an adrenaline-boosting 'scrambling' tour – clip yourself on to a rope and say your prayers. You'll traverse narrow rock ledges, following routes once taken by intrepid hermits.

KALAMPAKA, GREECE, 39.6813 / 21.6807
THEOPETRA CAVE
Completely camouflaged in the hillside, the fascinating Theopetra Cave dates back to the time of the Neanderthals. A wall in front of the cave is believed to be one of the oldest known structures built by humans. You can tour the cave with a guide and rub shoulders with ghosts of the region's past. Theopetra is 7km southeast of Kalambaka.

KALAMPAKA, GREECE, 39.4500 / 21.4833
PINDOS GORGE
The tiny, attractive village of Pyli is the gateway to the stunning, forested Pindos Gorge (an excellent day's circuitous drive). Pyli is also home to the quirky but very beautiful 13th-century Church of Porta Panagia. The fun here is being shown around by the elderly 'keeper of the key'; ask for him at the nearby cafe. Pyli is 46km south of Kalambaka – you'll need your own wheels.

KALAMPAKA, GREECE, 39.7103 / 21.6301
ALSOS HOUSE
No visit to Meteora is complete without a stay at Alsos House (www.alsoshouse.gr), owned by Yiannis Karakantas. Yiannis, seemingly Greece's answer to British humorist John Cleese, knows more about Meteora than the nuns do their vespers. If you're lucky, he might share some of his secrets about this stunning spot.

Ⓑelogradchik, Ⓑulgaria, 43.6219 / 22.6800

KALETO FORTRESS

It's hard to tell where the citadel ends and boulders begin at Belogradchik's fortress, stealthily camouflaged amid rocks on the northerly slopes of the Balkan Mountains. With walls 2m thick and 12m high, this sturdy stronghold was a key lookout during Bulgaria's Second Empire. Climbing ladders access some of the site's most vertiginous outcrops, allowing you to imagine surveying the hills for medieval armies on the move. The rocks whisper their own secrets, too; some have strangely humanoid shapes, giving rise to folk tales about their origins. One story describes a beautiful nun who fell pregnant but was saved from disgrace by being turned to stone – little comfort perhaps.

☛ The Kaleto fortress is signposted from the town of Belogradchik in northwestern Bulgaria; it looms 1km southwest of the centre. See www.muzeibelogradchik.com.

RILA, BULGARIA, 42.0930 / 23.1136

STOB PYRAMIDS

As you step among spindles of sandstone and kick up orange dust on this hiking trail, you'll feel as if you're roving another planet. In Stob village, Bulgaria's green meadowlands give way to sandstone towers and pyramids, rising 40m above jagged rock. Geologists explain this Martian landscape was created by the onslaught of snow and wind. Folk wisdom, however, claims these statuesque pillars are the petrified remains of a wedding party who froze in shock when the best man kissed the bride-to-be. Scoff if you like, but as you hike through this forest of russet stone, don't be surprised if old fairytales exert a compelling grip...

🔫 *Stob is a five-minute drive from Rila, one of Bulgaria's best-known tourist destinations. Alternatively, it's a scenic hour-long hike between the two villages.*

KALAHARI DESERT, BOTSWANA, -20.0227 / 21.3551

DROTSKY'S CAVE

Known only to the indigenous San people until well into the 20th century, and reputed to be the hiding place for the fabulous treasure of picaresque 19th-century South African Hendrik Matthys van Zyl, Drotsky's Cave carries all the romance of the deliciously remote. The spot is known as Gcwihaba in the San tongue, meaning 'hyena's hole'. Hidden far from the nearest paved road in northwestern Botswana, the cave is a cathedral of 10m-long stalagmites and stalactites, not to mention bats with long wings and long ears. Most wonderfully of all, the sense of isolation, the silence and the complete absence of tourist infrastructure all create a feeling that you've stumbled upon one of the earth's last unknown corners.

🔫 *The only way to reach the cave is by 4WD expedition. Take food, water, maps, torches...*

THE KAROO, SOUTH AFRICA, -32.2547 / 24.5480

THE GIANT FLAG

This ambitious project will carpet a barren patch of the Karoo with the world's largest flag – a South African flag the size of 66 soccer fields, comprised of 2.5 million desert cacti and succulents, and a four-megawatt solar field. The crowdfunded US$13 million installation will generate electricity to power 4000 homes, as well as bringing tourists and 700 environmental 'green-collar' jobs to the deprived region. It will ultimately be visible from space, but for now you can watch the project taking shape from the viewing platform among the Valley of Desolation's dolerite pillars, in Camdeboo National Park. At time of writing, US$1.8 million has been donated, with supporters adopting plants (US$7), roads (US$72) and solar panels (US$180).

🔫 *The Valley of Desolation opens 7am to 6pm. Hire a car or join a tour in nearby Graaff-Reinet. www.giantflag.co.za.*

© Vladimir Alexeev / Alamy

- 183 -

Near Šiauliai, Lithuania. 56.0153 / 23.4167

HILL OF CROSSES

Lithuania's crucifix-covered mound is no humble pilgrimage spot. The Hill of Crosses (Kryžių kalnas) forms a defiant, spiky silhouette that grew from protests against Soviet oppression.

Locals have laid crosses here since the 19th century; it's thought that the first ones honoured those who died during an anti-tsarist uprising. A total of 130 were counted in 1900, and they continued to be laid for decades thereafter. Soviet authorities tried to stop this public display of devotion by bulldozing the site in 1961. Wooden crosses were burnt and metallic ones melted. But this only spurred on the faithful, who crept to the site under cloak of darkness to add more crosses. The KGB tried every trick in the book, from road blocks to marking the area as a quarantine zone. Nothing worked: the hill grew higher, crucifix by crucifix.

After 1989, when Lithuania struggled free from the Iron Curtain, the Hill became a symbol of victory. Crosses were laid here openly, from simple bound twigs to ornate silver ones and memorials honouring those deported to Siberia under the Soviets. Pope John Paul II's visit in 1993 solidified its status as a pilgrimage spot, and the hill bulged to 60m long and almost as wide. The current number of crosses is thought to be 100,000 and counting.

 The Hill of Crosses (www.kryziukalnas.lt) is 12km north of Šiauliai. Drive or take a Joniškis-bound bus.

⊙MARAMURES, ROMANIA, 47.9713 / 23.6928

Merry Cemetery

It's unusual to exit a graveyard with a smile on your face but that's what I did after visiting the Merry Cemetery in the village of Săpânța. I studied some of the 800 colourful wooden tombstones, each bearing a strange carved likeness of the deceased – a shepherd tending his flock, a mother cooking for her family, a barber shaving a customer – and guffawed. Yes, the dearly departed are much missed, but that shepherd was a bit of a drunk, the mother a nag and the barber drew more blood than a leech. It was Ioan Stan Pătraș, a woodcarver, who created the first tombstone in 1935, having looked death in the face and laughed. He still brings the house down. By Steve Fallon

🚌 Open daily, 8am to 6pm. Two or three buses per day go to Săpânța from Sighetu Marmației.

10

TOP 10

UNSETTLING HOTELS

TALLINN, ESTONIA, 59.4366 / 24.7551

① Hotel Viru

Foreign visitors weren't funnelled into the Hotel Viru for its views. Under Soviet rule, surveillance was rife in Tallinn, and each of the 60 rooms in the Hotel Viru was bugged. Today, the hotel has a KGB Museum in the former surveillance room, brimming with 1970s radio equipment and gas masks. However, the hidden microphones have long ago been removed from the rooms, we promise…

☞ Book online to stay at Hotel Viru (www.sokoshotels.fi/en/tallinn/sokos-hotel-viru).

PYONGYANG, NORTH KOREA, 39.0360 / 125.7313

② Ryugyong Hotel

Don't try to stay at this 105-storey hotel in the world's most secretive country. Rumours are rife about why this vast triangle is unfinished after 30 years of construction and $750 million invested.

☞ Admire, but don't enter. The closest stop on Pyongyang's metro is Konsol.

LIEPĀJA, LATVIA, 56.546355 / 21.021008

③ Karosta Prison

Test your masochistic side at a century-old ex-military prison in Liepāja (below), complete with bullying staff and a rusty door slamming shut. Try not to dream of the Nazi and Soviet prisoners locked in this very cell.

☛ Book prison accommodation, tours and spy games online at www.karostascietums.lv.

COLORADO, USA, 40.383036 / -105.519304

④ The Stanley Hotel

This 1909 hotel (right), near Rocky Mountains National Park, inspired Stephen King to write his masterpiece *The Shining*. It's also the location of repeated sightings of its long-dead owners.

☛ Book ahead (www.stanleyhotel.com) and resist the urge to write macabre messages on the doors.

HAMPSHIRE, ENGLAND, 50.739873 / -1.095296

⑤ No Man's Fort

The threat of attacks by Napoleon III stirred the British to fortify their sea defences, building No Man's Fort with a team of divers. Showered by gunfire during two World Wars, it now hosts a luxurious hotel.

☛ Boats link Gunwharf Quays in Portsmouth to the hotel (www.solentforts.com).

MAINE, USA, 44.094956 / -70.212674

⑥ Hotel Crypt

Awaking in a coffin is a nightmare, but you pay for the privilege in Lewiston, Maine. The former resident of the crypt, Father Wallace, lay here for more than a century; now it's your turn. The pine coffin sleeps two.

☛ Book on www.hotelcrypt.com; cheerier rooms are available at parent hotel, Inn at the Agora.

STEKENE, BELGIUM, 51.2279 / 4.0545

⑦ CasAnus

Snuggle up in a bulging, 10m-long bowel, 20km west of Antwerp. This realistic replica of a large intestine, created by artist Joep Van Lieshout, sleeps two people in the spare bedroom inside.

☛ Book into an intestine for the night via www.verbekefoundation.com.

NAGASAKI, JAPAN, 33.0899 / 129.7876

⑧ Henn na Hotel

This automated hotel is either unsettling or efficient, depending on how you feel about mechanical receptionists, a robot porter and facial recognition. Oh, and two of the reception robots are dinosaurs.

☛ The hotel is in Sasebo, Nagasaki, across the river from Huis Ten Bosch station. www.h-n-h.jp.

CALIFORNIA, USA, 34.0443 / -118.2508

⑨ Hotel Cecil

Inspiring TV's *American Horror Story*, this hotel was the site of three murders and many suicides, a former residence of serial killer Richard Ramirez, and where student Elisa Lam met her unexplained death in 2013.

☛ To escape its reputation, the hotel rebranded as Stay on Main (www.stayonmain.com).

FLORENCE, ITALY, 43.7744 / 11.2521

⑩ Albergo Burchianti

Even guests who are sceptics at check-in emerge the next morning with tales of ghostly maids and poltergeist groping. At least sleepless nights allow time to admire the ceiling frescoes and four-posters.

☛ The hotel (www.hotelburchianti.it) is 400m from Florence's Santa Maria del Fiore Cathedral.

ITINERARY
THE REAL DRACULA TRAIL

SIGHIȘOARA, ROMANIA.
46.2195 / 24.7928
Casa Dracula

Dracula, or Vlad Țepeș, protected Wallachia against Turkish attacks, though he's gone down in history as Vlad the Impaler. While he never guzzled blood (to our knowledge), his brutal deeds eclipse those of any fictional count. Die-hard Dracula fans go to Vlad Țepeș' birthplace, although far from being a shadowy lair, this flower-wreathed medieval building now houses a restaurant. *The house is in the pretty town of Sighișoara. Enjoy a bite (to eat) at the restaurant (www.casavladdracul. ro) and see the room where Vlad was born.*

BRAȘOV, ROMANIA. 45.6387 / 25.5935
MT TÂMPA

These days, the forested peak rising above Brașov is adorned with a Hollywood-style sign. In 1459, however, the preferred hilltop decoration was 40 impaled merchants. Vlad Țepeș was fond of sending a clear message about the consequences of breaking his laws. Locals would joke that Brașov was an ideal place to lose your purse because people were so afraid of being accused of theft that any amount of money could lie untouched on the ground. *Walking trails lead up Mt Tâmpa, or take the cable car from Aleea Tiberiu Brediceanu.*

SNAGOV, ROMANIA.
44.7294 / 26.1757
SNAGOV ISLAND MONASTERY

Vlad Țepeș slumbers for all eternity in a stone church at this island monastery. His grave is situated towards the back of the church. Vlad was beheaded in 1476 during a battle with the Turks – presumably to ensure that he didn't rise from the grave – and it's thought that his headless body was returned to Snagov, though some historians say otherwise. During his life, Vlad was a great supporter of the monastery, fortifying its outbuildings and commissioning its church and – less conventionally – the on-site torture chamber. *SnagovTur (www.snagov.ro) runs guided half-day boat tours of Snagov's lake and monastery.*

BUCHAREST, ROMANIA. 44.4302 / 26.1008
PALATUL VOIEVODAL CURTEA VECHE

Vlad Țepeș established his princely court in Bucharest in 1459, and it remained his royal residence during the rare periods when he wasn't leading armies against the Turks or indulging in impalement. The palace was the centre of the city's thriving trade; amble around the chambers and snap a selfie with a fearsome bust of Vlad. *The site (Str Franceză 21-23) is only 100m from the northern edge of Bucharest's Parcul Unirii.*

ROMANIA. 45.3535 / 24.6351
POIENARI FORTRESS

Castles throughout Romania clamour to claim a link with Vlad Țepeș, but Poienari is the real deal. Wallachia's warlord chose this crag as a lookout over the pass between Wallachia and Transylvania. Ever thrifty, Vlad Țepeș relied on the cheap labour of captured Turks to built the hilltop citadel. Although now in ruins, these walls offer the most authentic glimpse of Dracula's fearsome military prowess. *The fortress is 25km north of Curtea de Argeș. If you don't have a car, get a bus from Curtea de Argeș to Căpățânenii and hike the remaining 4km.*

Ⓢ BOTSWANA. −20.8910 / 25.8220

KUBU ISLAND

Visiting Kubu Island is like stepping through the looking glass into an entirely different dimension. Rising from a remote corner of the world's largest network of salt flats, the Makgadikgadi pans of the Kalahari Desert in northern Botswana, Kubu is a magical world of epic baobabs and horizons that never seem to end, a hallucinatory place where the sense of scale and singular beauty can be a dizzying experience. And don't be fooled by the absence of water. Perhaps just five centuries ago, hippos wallowed in the shallows of what was once a vast inland sea (the word 'kubu' means hippopotamus in the local Setswana language).

More prosaically, the shorebirds of old bequeathed more than a mere name to this magical place – the white that stains the boulders overlooking the void is fossilised guano (bird shit) left by avian sentinels that rested here between fishing expeditions on what was once a real island. There's even a stone semi-circle and stone tools left by peoples now vanished from the earth, as if to deepen the mystery. To here find such unlikely connections to an otherwise forgotten past may seem incongruous. But when you sit with your back to a baobab and look out over the never-ending sweep of a world seemingly without end, time slips away into eternity.

 There's a community-run campsite (www.kubuisland.com) on Kubu. Get here by 4WD with reliable GPS.

THE KAROO, SOUTH AFRICA, -31.8652 / 24.5521

Owl House

In the unlikely setting of Nieu Bethesda, a secluded village in a remote corner of the Karoo semi-desert, is a striking piece of 'outsider' art, a surreal, poignant, and at times disturbing work by the late Helen Martins. Back in her isolated hometown after a failed marriage, she set about filling her house and garden with hundreds of concrete figures, painted or decorated with colourful glass and wirework. I roamed the silent rows of camels, mermaids, farmers, nativity scenes and trademark owls, feeling saddened by the story of Martins, who took her own life in 1976, yet uplifted by her creativity in the face of bad fortune. By James Bainbridge

🛥 Open 9am to 5pm daily, entry R60. Get to Nieu Bethesda by car, or join a tour in Graaff-Reinet, 55km south. www.theowlhouse.co.za.

ȘINCA, ROMANIA, 45.7540 / 25.1673

ȘINCA VECHE

A beam of sunlight pierces the gloom of the cave. A cluster of devotees, standing with eyes closed, palms outstretched, are bathed in light. They represent only a few of the spiritual seekers who journey to Șinca Veche's cave temple. Although it was established by monks in the 1700s, the site's spiritual significance is thought to date to much earlier. Its main chamber resembles a garden shed, with planks of wood and a cross marking a sandy entryway. Within, candles flicker around makeshift altars while light streams through an opening in the cave roof. Locals whisper that praying here heals fertility problems. From the cave mouth, paths lead to a small, immaculate hermitage and gardens.

🛥 The temple stands 1km south of Șinca Veche; you'll need private transport. It's an easy detour between Sibiu and Brașov. www.sincaveche.ro.

LOPĂTARI, ROMANIA, 45.534536 / 26.548821

LIVING FIRES

The plains of Lopătari are an infernal wasteland, where a sulphurous stench clouds the air and flames burst from the soil. Fortunately, the so-called 'living fire' (in Romanian, *focul viu*) only rises to 20cm in height. Natural gases, rather than demonic influence, produce the fires, which smoulder away within cracks in the dark earth. At night, when the plains are speckled with orange and blue fire, the land has a truly hellish air. But Romanian folklore's account of the living fires is rather cheering, explaining them as purifying flames that protect wildlife and bestow good fortune. Singed shoes aren't considered lucky, however, so watch your step.

🛥 Drive the 203K road for approximately 60km from Buzău towards Terca, ideally with a 4WD (the road is rough). Handwritten signs direct the final hike to the fires.

ITINERARY

BIZARRE BULGARIAN ROAD-TRIP

Central Mountains, Bulgaria. 42.7360 / 25.3936

BUZLUDZHA UFO

Glaring down from a 1441m peak, this concrete dome looks ready to beam up hikers in Bulgaria's Central Mountains. Dubbed 'Buzludzha UFO', this was once a Socialist assembly hall. Its mosaics of Soviet leaders are chipped, and the crowning red star shattered long ago. Those drawn to its dilapidated grandeur are gloomy about plans to renovate it into a museum; so visit now, while it remains a romantic wreck. From Shipka village, a potholed road zigzags 20km up to the UFO.

From Shipka village, a potholed road zigzags 20km up to the UFO.

SHIPKA, BULGARIA, 42.7481 / 25.3214
FREEDOM MONUMENT

Stretch your calf muscles before attempting the 1000 stairs to Shipka's Freedom Monument. This granite memorial is a lightning rod for Bulgarian national pride. More than 7000 Russian troops and Bulgarian volunteers saw off an Ottoman army of quadruple the size in 1877's Battle of Shipka Pass. Frostbite was rife, rocks served as ammunition when they ran out of firepower, and human bodies were used as weapons. *Hold on to your lunch for the hairpin bends en route from Shipka village to the monument, a 15km drive.*

KAZANLÂK, BULGARIA, 42.6899 / 25.3510
THRACIAN BURIAL MOUNDS

The unassuming hillocks in and around Kazanlâk guard Thracian tombs – and you can step right inside these ancient burial chambers. Fourth-century-BC Shushmanets Tomb, with its austere columns and crushed stone walls, is remarkably intact. Meanwhile, archaeologists continue to debate why a horse, but no human, skeleton was found within Ostrusha Tomb. *Thracian tombs are subtly signposted from the main E85 road between Kazanlâk and Shipka.*

ROZOVO, BULGARIA, 42.5642 / 25.4108
VALLEY OF THE ROSES

Between May and June, central Bulgaria is aflame with roses and the air heavy with their scent. In villages such as Rozovo, Kanchevo and Razhena, springtime brings petal-themed festivities unchanged for centuries. Tree branches dipped in rose water will be shaken at you, rose-scented liqueurs proffered, and perfumes wafted your way while villagers dance in circles. *There are several Valley of the Roses villages along the Buzovgrad-Yagoda road, south of Kazanlâk.*

ASENOVGRAD, BULGARIA 41.9865 / 24.8730
ASEN'S FORTRESS

Mountainous Bulgaria has no shortage of rugged panoramas, but it's hard to beat the views from Asen's Fortress. The citadel roosts above thickly forested valleys. Inside, a chapel with peeling frescoes is home to swooping magpies, and crumbling lookout posts survey the moun-

tains. Thracians, Romans and Ottomans all seized on this fortress as the perfect spot to spy approaching enemies. *The fortress squats on a cliff 19km southeast of Plovdiv. Drive south to Asenovgrad along route 86, and follow 'Asenova Krepost' road signs.*

PERUSHTITSA, BULGARIA, 42.0741 / 24.5561
RED CHURCH

The skeletal remains of a late Roman church stand silently above wildflower meadows near the town of Perushtitsa. This enigmatic ruin once housed saintly relics; if you peer closely you'll see faded frescoes on its inner walls. Allow yourself time to discover another of Perushtitsa's ruined churches, Sveti Arhangeli Mihael, which bore witness to a frenzied massacre by the Ottomans. *Perushtitsa is an easy 22km drive south and west of Bulgaria's second city, Plovdiv. There are also frequent buses that run from the city.*

Ⓜ MINSK, BELARUS, 53.9313 / 27.6460

NATIONAL LIBRARY OF BELARUS

A gem of the Minsk skyline in the most literal sense, this diamond-shaped library glints above a forest of apartment blocks. Housing 3.5 million documents, this 72m-high cyborg of a library has grown into an unexpected favourite among Belarusian couples on dates. Its popularity is largely thanks to an observation deck that gazes over Minsk's ever-sprawling cityscape. From the top you can admire multistorey apartment blocks, many of them bedecked with vast Soviet-era murals. It isn't a classic sunset view; but when night falls and this rhombicuboctahedron (that's a shape with eight triangular and 18 square faces) glitters over Minsk, space-age romance never looked so good.

☛ *The National Library of Belarus (www.nlb.by) is a 400m walk from Minsk's Uschod metro station, which is on the blue line. Graf Cafe at the top serves a great cappuccino.*

Ⓥirunga Ⓜountains, Ⓓemocratic Ⓡepublic of the Ⓒongo, –1.5220 / 29.2495

Nyiragongo

The ascent started easily enough, as a gentle walk through the forest, but quickly became hotter as the lush vegetation shrunk back and the soft muddy floor gave way to the cracked black lava field that dates from Nyiragongo's last eruption in 2002. The gradient got steeper as we scrambled up the volcanic cone to the collection of tiny mountain shelters just below the rim, our home for the night. The volcano's rumble was clearly audible above us, and soon we saw the famous lava lake in all its terrible glory: violent eruptions happening within it sent plumes of lava shooting from the pit below and a red-hued smoke rose into the clear sky. Nature's terrifying scale had never been more apparent. By Tom Masters

☛ Book an ascent (and get a DRC visa) through www.virunga.org, which can also book accommodation.

ZIMBABWE. -20.5572 / 28.5125

MATOBO NATIONAL PARK

With its surreal dreamscape of boulders improbably stacked upon one another, rainbow-coloured lizards, bright psychedelic lichen and hair-like vegetation that's more animal than plant, the only thing missing from atop Matobo National Park is one of Salvador Dalí's melting clocks. Here at World's View you'll experience the raw power of the African wilderness; a stillness and timelessness that is almost transcendental. No wonder it's sacred to the indigenous Ndebele, and why Cecil Rhodes (Rhodesia's founder), chose it as his burial place. This World Heritage-listed park also contains ancient San rock art, black and white rhino, and the highest density of leopard in Africa.

The park is 30km south of Bulawayo. Entry is US$15, and there are wonderful lodges inside and out of the park.

KASANKA NATIONAL PARK, ZAMBIA.
-12.5833 / 30.2010

BAT MIGRATION

Do you think Africa's greatest migration involves wildebeest plodding across the open plains of the Serengeti and Masai Mara? You are not alone. But some nine million more mammals are involved in this little-known migration in southern Africa each year. Between October and December, 10 million or so straw-coloured fruit bats descend into the tiny Mushitu swamp forest within northern Zambia's Kasanka National Park. The concentration of life above you (whether flying or perched) is truly astonishing. During daylight hours walk the forest floor beneath the hanging masses, and come sunset and sunrise climb up into the elevated canopy hides to join the massive bats as they take flight.

There are two airstrips in the park for chartered light aircraft. If driving, it's 91km from Serenje.

© Rick Strange / Alamy

PAMUKKALE-HIERAPOLIS

High above the village of Pamukkale (meaning Cotton Castle) lie the famous travertines, limpid pools of turquoise water in chalk-white trays of calcium carbonate shaped like giant water-lily leaves. *Sans* shoes, visitors tiptoe up through the pools to the plateau above. There, in the Pamukkale Termal, better-heeled swimmers can take to water the temperature of a soothing bath. Beneath them, the snapped-off trunks of ancient columns offer evocative testimony to the existence of a spa here since Graeco-Roman times.

So stunning are the travertines that they tend to overshadow the ruins of ancient Hierapolis straddling the hillside above them. Yet the ruins here can give even better-known Ephesus a run for its money. The huge theatre shows off the wealth and importance of the old city that once stood on the plateau – from its tiered stone seats visitors can all but see the actors of antiquity striding on to the stage. Nearby, the apostle St Philip was crucified upside down, a dastardly deed commemorated by an octagonal martyrium to which pilgrims used to flock. Flagstones still line Frontinus St where visitors can follow the ancients as far as a toilet block designed to accommodate multiple bottoms. A ruinous gate opens on to a necropolis of house-sized tombs that sprawls for two kilometres, silent but for the hoots of the owls.

 Visitors can stay the night in Pamukkale village and walk up to the travertines via one of three trails.

ABOUKIR, EGYPT. 31.4186 / 30.1569

THE LOST CITY OF THONIS-HERACLEION

Shaken and then stirred, this city of antiquity – once ancient Egypt's gateway to the Western world – was toppled into the depths of the Mediterranean Sea by liquefaction and subsidence after a series of earthquakes. There it languished for well over a millennium, the swirling currents blanketing its countless treasures under layers of silt – until 2000 when the lost city of Thonis-Heracleion was unearthed in the Bay of Aboukir by French divers.

You may not recognise it by name, but you'll certainly be familiar with the legendary characters that form part of its history – Heracles is believed to have taken his first footsteps in Africa here, and Paris of Troy and Helen sought refuge in Thonis-Heracleion during their famous flight from Sparta.

While many priceless relics have been raised from the sea floor, such as 5m-high statues of Egyptian gods, stele with pristine hieroglyphics and sections of impressive temples, less than five per cent of the city has been excavated. Such was the scale of Thonis-Heracleion's sprawl – built atop muddy sandbanks and interlinking islands (much like Venice in Italy) – that the underwater archaeologist credited with the find estimated it would take 200 years to fully exhume.

For non-archaeologist divers, the major sight in this vicinity is the wreck of *L'Orient*, Napoleon's flagship that was sunk near here in 1798.

Get to Aboukir by flagging down an east-bound microbus along the Corniche in Alexandria (E£2).

10

⊕op 10

MICRONATIONS

🜨 MOLDOVA, 46.8465 / 29.5998

① Transnistria

Breakaway Transnistria is not recognised by neighbouring Moldova and Ukraine, or indeed anywhere, though it has border control and currency (the Transnistrian ruble). Following its pro-independence referendum in 2006, Transnistria waits to spread its wings. In the meantime, lost-in-time Soviet buildings, impressive Bendery Fortress and local brandy Kvint are good reasons to pass through.

☞ *Twelve-hour trips here don't require paperwork; just bring your passport and register at the border.*

🜨 ENGLAND, 51.8906 / 1.4818

② Principality of Sealand

Sealand arguably kickstarted the new crop of micronations, many of them symbolic protests or vanity projects. Founded in 1967, Sealand occupies an offshore platform 12km from England's east coast.

☞ *Call ahead to confirm use of the helipad to visit Sealand (www.sealandgov.org).*

⑦

ITALY, 43.8298 / 7.6999

③ Principality of Seborga

A paperwork error gave this Italian province a stab at independence. Its sale in 1729 wasn't registered, and it wasn't mentioned in Italy's 1861 Unification Act, so local Giorgio Carbone stepped up as prince.

☞ *Seborga is near the France-Italy border. The closest airport is Nice.*

①LITHUANIA, 54.6806 / 25.2956

④ Republic of Užupis

Artists transformed Vilnius' previously shabby Užupis district into a thriving bohemian enclave and declared it a republic in 1997, complete with flag, president and an army of 11.

☞ *Walk straight into Užupis (www.umi.lt) from Vilnius, across the bridge on Išganytojo gatvė.*

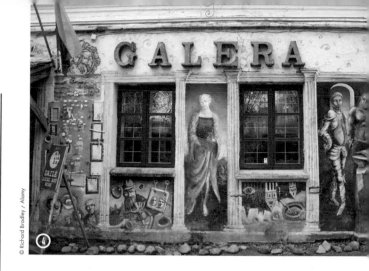

④

USA, 24.5637 / -81.7675

⑤ Conch Republic

Key West's semi-serious secession from the USA was originally a protest against border patrol roadblocks. Its passports and independence celebrations proved popular. It claims four 'conch-sulates' outside Florida.

🐚 Visit from Key West International Airport, or drive south from Miami (www.conch-republic.com).

AUSTRALIA, -28.2113 / 114.8240

⑥ Hutt River Principality

It's easier than you think to hobnob with royalty: Western Australia's Hutt River Principality offers tours are led daily by princes Leonard and Graeme. Read more about this micronation on page 251.

🐚 It costs A$4 to obtain a visa for the principality (www.principality-hutt-river.com).

DENMARK, 55.6746 / 12.6006

⑦ Freetown Christiania

Christiania broke free as a self-governing district when hippies occupied the old military barracks in 1971. It flourished as a free-thinking collective known for colourful murals and cannabis stalls.

🐚 Walk into Christiania, 2km east of Tivoli Gardens. Heed the 'no photography' signs.

SWEDEN, 56.2864 / 12.5410

⑧ Royal Republic of Ladonia

When the council managing Kullaberg nature reserve demanded artist Lars Vilks remove his driftwood and stone sculptures, he formed this micronation instead.

🐚 Ladonia is on Sweden's southwest coast. You can apply for citizenship online (www.ladonia.org).

USA, 39.3228 / -119.5396

⑨ Republic of Molossia

As much a vanity project as a micronation, Kevin Baugh – or rather 'His Excellency, the President of Molossia' – declared two properties and grounds to be an independent country in 1999.

🐚 Molossia (www.molossia.org) is a 55km drive southeast from Reno, Nevada.

FRANCE, 46.9902 / 6.4636

⑩ République du Saugeais

To bring in a few Euros, residents established the tongue-in-cheek Republic of Saugeais. It began as a joke, presidents are elected by 'applause meter', and the community shies away from full independence.

🐚 The republic is near Doubs, eastern France; customs regulations are flexible.

⑤

'Still uninhabited, Pripyat is a freeze-frame of Soviet Ukraine. Its Ferris wheel and playground stand as rusty symbols of lost innocence'

UKRAINE, 51.2802 / 30.2083

Chernobyl Exclusion Zone

'Don't touch the moss!' bellows our guide. He's not worried about the fragile ecosystem. We're standing in the Chernobyl Exclusion Zone, where background radiation is 10 times the normal level – and slow-growing plants such as moss absorb it like a sponge.

Even before entering the zone, a vivid picture forms in my mind: a Soviet landscape laid waste by nuclear disaster, devoid of wildlife, where people no longer dare to tread. But as I step over broken glass in the ghost town of Pripyat, nature appears to be thriving. Birdlife chatters from the trees, and catfish thrash in the river. Meadows have waist-high grass, and trees burst from abandoned buildings. Meanwhile a church in the zone, St Elijah's, has a recent coat of paint. The Chernobyl Exclusion Zone is not the monochrome wasteland I imagined.

On 26 April 1986, an attempted safety-system test at Chernobyl nuclear power plant unleashed the worst nuclear disaster ever seen, ranked 7 on the International Nuclear Event Scale (there is no 8). An explosion ripped through Reactor 4, releasing radioactive particles into the air that were swept as far as the UK and Scandinavia. Pripyat had been purpose-built for plant workers, and its population of some 50,000 were among those bussed away from their homes, never to return.

Still uninhabited, Pripyat is a freeze-frame of Soviet Ukraine. Its Ferris wheel and playground, built shortly before the accident, stand as rusty symbols of lost innocence. In apartment blocks, creeper plants drag at the walls and stairwells decay. As I step gingerly over the threshold of an old school, I can see mouldering schoolbooks, upturned desks and child-sized gas masks.

But describing Chernobyl as 'reclaimed by nature' might be an overstatement. Occasional bear sightings and birdsong don't make a wildlife reserve, and many scientists have concluded that contaminated areas have smaller than expected populations of fauna. The human population is also low – but it's there. The most famous residents are Chernobyl's 'grandmothers'.

These women returned to their condemned farmsteads, believing removal from their homes to be a worse fate than radiation. Catastrophic levels of depression among people displaced by the disaster lend support to this idea.

More than once, I kick an empty vodka bottle from my path as I walk around Pripyat. It turns out that the exclusion zone is a popular place for illicit parties. Truly, the exclusion zone is a place to party like it's the last day on Earth. *By Anita Isalska*

Tours depart from Kyiv; wear long clothing. Tour company www.chernobylwel.com operates photography trips in the zone.

10 TOP SPINE-CHILLING CORPSES

TEHRAN, IRAN, 35.6870 / 51.4146

① Salt men

Meeting the blank-eyed gaze of a corpse features in more nightmares than bucket lists. But mummies, from saints to serial killers, can be popular tourist attractions. Iran exhibits some of the most unusually preserved cadavers, found in the Chehrabad salt mines. Most famed is 3rd-century Zanjan Salt Man, whose bearded head and leg, still clad in a leather boot, have been conserved by the salty conditions.

☞ *Find Zanjan Salt Man in Tehran's National Museum (nationalmuseum.ichto.ir).*

NUUK, GREENLAND, 64.1770 / -51.7462

② Qilakitsoq Mummies

Dry, Arctic winds preserved the oldest mummies in Greenland. The most unnerving of these 500-year-old Inuits is the doll-like corpse of a six-month-old baby, buried alive with his mother.

☞ *Meet the mummies at Greenland's National Museum (www.natmus.gl) in Nuuk.*

GORNO-ALTAYSK, RUSSIA, 51.9565 / 85.9467

③ Ukok Princess

The arms of this Siberian woman are covered in detailed tattoos from her shoulders to her wrists – and they look surprisingly modish, considering she died two and a half millennia ago.

☞ *Siberia's 'ice princess' is displayed at the Anokhin Museum in Gorno-Altaysk.*

BANGKOK, THAILAND, 13.75877 / 100.4852

④ See Uey Sae Ung

The private repose of death was deemed too pleasant a fate for cannibal killer See Uey Sae Ung. After he was executed, his body was preserved with paraffin and put on permanent display.

☞ *Creep up to the tar-black cadaver at Bangkok's Siriraj Medical Museum.*

①

GUANAJUATO, MEXICO, 21.0201 / -101.2662

⑤ Guanajuato Mummies

More than 100 mummies line the Museo de las Momias (left), from cholera victims to women buried alive. Creepiest of all is the room of babies dressed as saints to ease their passage to the afterlife.

☞ *The museum in Guanajuato is open daily. www.momiasdeguanajuato.gob.mx.*

BOLZANO, ITALY, 46.4999 / 11.3495

⑥ Iceman Ötzi

The grandfather of European mummies, this Tyrolean, preserved in a glacier since 3300BC, is older than Stonehenge. Named after the Ötztal Alps where he was found, Ötzi is thought to have been murdered.

☞ *Ötzi's leathery form is displayed at Bolzano's archaeology museum. See www.iceman.it.*

SALTA, ARGENTINA, -24.7890 / -65.4110

⑦ Llullaillaco Children

Offered as sacrifices to mediate between gods and the living, these eerily well-preserved Inca children met their end on top of Llullaillaco volcano on the border between Argentina and Chile.

☞ *Visit these bodies at the Museum of High Altitude Archaeology (www.maam.gob.ar) in Salta.*

SIENA, ITALY, 43.3197 / 11.3265

⑧ St Catherine of Siena

The head of St Catherine of Siena is framed by a Gothic-style silver reliquary (below left). The holy head was smuggled back to Catherine's hometown after her death in 1380. Her thumb is also displayed.

☞ *The Basilica of San Domenico is 300m from Piazza del Campo (www.basilicacateriniana.com).*

PALERMO, ITALY, 38.111755 / 13.3395

⑨ Palermo's Sleeping Beauty

An embalmer outdid himself with Rosalia Lombardo (above), who died of pneumonia in 1920. She's one of the youngest corpses in the Capuchin Crypts.

☞ *There are thousands of bodies in Palermo's catacombs (www.palermocatacombs.com).*

VARBERG, SWEDEN, 57.1056 / 12.2395

⑩ Bocksten Man

Still sporting strawberry blond hair, the skeletal remains of the Bocksten Man were dug from a swamp in 1936. The medieval man had been skewered with an oak spear, pinning him to a lake bed.

☞ *Admire handsome reconstructions at the Halland Museum (www.museumhalland.se).*

© Mazzzur / Getty Images

IRAN. 32.6747 / 51.6787

PIGEON TOWERS

If you've ever defended a picnic from pestering pigeons, it might seem baffling that generations of Iranians built towers to attract flocks of these birds. But pigeon poop was big business in 17th-century Iran. It was used as fertilizer, and in an area such as Isfahan, where melon-farming was widespread, enormous quantities of pigeon guano was required to keep dinner tables laden with fruit. To meet the huge demand, farmers needed pigeons to excrete en masse in a location where their nitrogen-rich droppings could be collected – without spilling a single, precious splatter.

The solution was to build huge dovecotes – towers designed for pigeons to land, rest and deposit their droppings. These brick towers resemble skyscrapers scaled to bird size, pitted with hundreds of pigeonholes and overlaid with plaster: a stylish, multistorey bathroom block. This innovation was not unique to Iran, though its pigeon towers might be the most impressive. There is evidence of industrial-scale dovecotes in ancient Egypt, and they endured for centuries in Scotland, France and the Baltics, and right across the Middle East.

Iran's stocky structures were so successful at gathering organic pigeon-processed fertiliser that thousands were built across the countryside. The availability of synthetic fertiliser led them to fall out of fashion; now they're simply roadside curiosities.

☛ *A few hundred pigeon towers remain in Iran, several visible from roads leading out of Isfahan.*

© De Agostini / Getty Images

⊙YAZD, IRAN, 31.8229 / 54.3541

YAZD TOWERS OF SILENCE

It has been generations since the last sky burial took place in the Towers of Silence at Yazd in central Iran, but vultures still circle ominously overhead in the thermal currents. The modern age has scattered the traditions of Zoroastrianism – one of the world's most ancient religions – to the desert winds, but the hills around Yazd preserve traces of one of its most enigmatic customs. Rising from a silent plain, the eerie stone towers, known as *dakhmas*, were once alive with carrion feeders, as the dead were laid out in tidy rows and slowly picked clean beneath the cloudless skies.

The story of Yazd is the story of a vanished civilisation. Untold thousands of men, women and children passed into eternity in the *dakhmas* of Yazd while Islamic empires waxed and waned and the Zoroastrian community dwindled to just 0.03 per cent of the Iranian population.

These days, all that remains here are the low stone houses where the dead were ritually bathed, the concentric circles where their bodies were laid out, and the central ossuaries where the bones were gathered. Combined with a visit to the Atashkadeh fire temple in central Yazd – where a sacred flame has been burning since at least AD 470 – it provides a tantalising glimpse into a culture that was old when Christianity and Islam were still young.

 Local buses shuttle from central Yazd to 'Dakhme', but it's easier to visit by taxi.

IBRI. OMAN. 23.26824 / 56.74753

TOMBS OF BAT

Prehistoric brick structures litter the deserts of northern Oman. The only snag with the so-called beehive tombs is their lack of bodily remains.

Around 24km east of Ibri in northern Oman, chambers of carefully stacked bricks rise from the desert dust. They form a striking silhouette, almost mimicking the corrugated rock face of Jebel Misht, the 'Comb Mountain', behind them. For all the grandeur of their location, the Tombs of Bat look almost as though they could have been hurriedly assembled yesterday, so their true age – around 5000 years young – was overlooked for centuries. Only in the 1970s did archaeologists begin to investigate these mystery mounds in earnest.

Unesco has praised the Tombs of Bat as the world's most complete 3rd millennium BC settlements and necropolises – if indeed that's what they are. Not a trace of human remains has been found inside the brick chambers, though time and reuse might be the reason why. It's theorised that these were temporary tombs intended for repeated use, which might explain why no ancient bones have been found within.

This archaeological site covers a large area. Bat has the largest number of beehives while Al Ayn, a further 30km drive, has some of the finest preserved examples.

☛ *You'll need a guide and driver, or a 4WD. From Ibri take route 9 to Ad Dreez, then east towards Bat.*

LE MORNE BRABANT

There aren't many things that can pull your feet from the sand and your gaze away from the sublime turquoise seas of Mauritius – but the dramatic, hulking mass of Le Morne Brabant is certainly one of them. Its sheer cliffs and squared top look so out of place on what is otherwise a very flat peninsula that you'd be forgiven for thinking it had been dropped from space. The best part? The view of Mauritius' seductive waters is even better from Le Morne Brabant's upper reaches.

A trail snakes up the back side of this monolith, and in just a couple of hours you'll be looking out over the spellbinding 360-degree view. The lower sections of the path wander gently through grasslands and indigenous forest before being interrupted by steep sections of rocky slopes – ropes and advice from the guides will ease your way up the latter.

At the very top of the hike you will come across a large cross, which is dedicated to a group of escaped slaves who are believed to have thrown themselves to their death from here. They'd seen colonial soldiers marching up the mountain and mistakenly believed slavery was calling again. In fact, they were about to be told that the trade had been abolished and that they were officially free. It's this history that led to the mountain's name – it means The Mournful One.

 Yanature (www.trekkingmauritius.com) is the only operator permitted to bring visitors up the mountain.

Karakum Desert, Turkmenistan, 40.1678 / 58.4105

DARVAZA CRATER

It's not easy getting to the Darvaza Crater, which is set in a vast desert in one of the most isolated countries of the world, but, boy, when you get there you will certainly know about it. Seemingly an entrance to the underworld, its boiling mud and blazing rock walls create such an intense, scorching heat you'll have to shield your face just standing on the rim. You'll also need to watch your step – there's no safety barrier to stop you from dropping right into this giant desert furnace.

The story goes that in 1971, Soviet engineers were looking for oil in the bleak Karakum Desert when their rig collapsed into a gas pocket below them. Fearful the methane would be dangerous, they set it alight, believing it would burn off in a couple of days. Forty years later it's still raging.

Roughly the size of an American football field and about 30m deep, the crater has been nicknamed the 'Door to Hell' by locals. The ferocity of the blaze and the enormity of its bleak surroundings make it an incredibly eerie spot. It's best seen at night, when the light drops, the darkness amplifies the noise of the blazing gas and the sky is illuminated by its glow.

☞ An organised tour to the crater is the easiest option; otherwise, take a shared taxi to Derweze and hitch a ride, or walk for two hours across the desert.

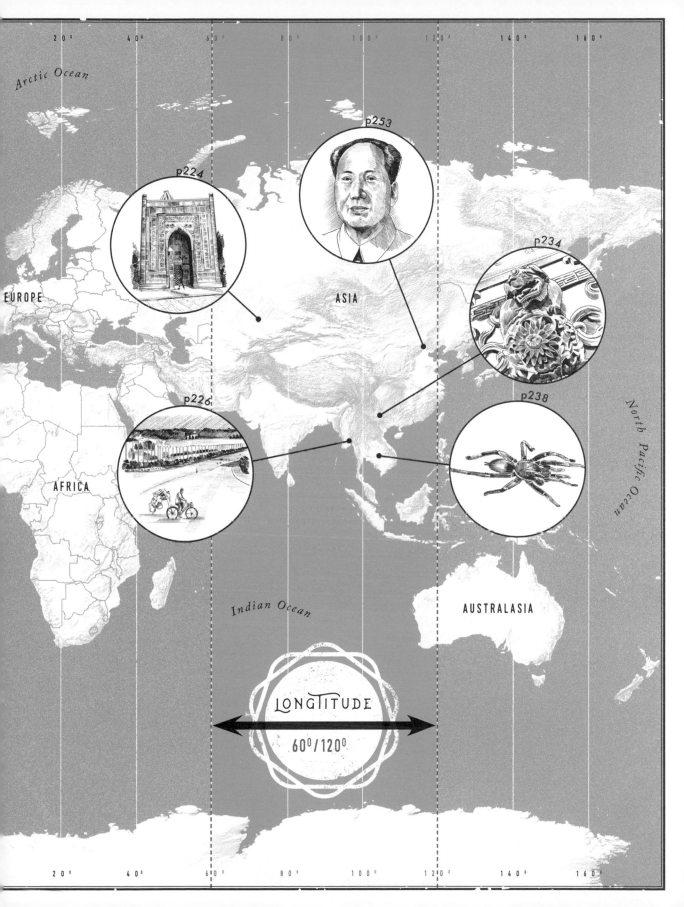

20°   40°   60°   80°   100°   120°   140°   160°

Arctic Ocean

EUROPE

p224

p253

ASIA

p234

AFRICA

p226

p238

Indian Ocean

AUSTRALASIA

North Pacific Ocean

LONGTITUDE

60°/120°

20°   40°   60°   80°   100°   120°   140°   160°

HINGOL NATIONAL PARK, PAKISTAN. 25.4332 / 65.2998

PRINCESS OF HOPE

Hingol National Park, the largest in Pakistan, has sweeping deserts scattered with sandstone crags, all melting into an estuary of the Hingol River. But one sight impresses above the others: the Princess of Hope. It's difficult to believe that this regal rock figure was created by the chaotic forces of wind and rain. The naturally formed stone tower resembles a woman in a flowing dress and cap, her arms bent at the elbow. Befitting the Princess' stately silhouette, there's an A-list origin to her nickname: upon visiting Pakistan's largest national park, Angelina Jolie was so inspired by the figure that she named her the 'Princess of Hope'.

🔛 *This desert anomaly is visible from Pakistan's coastal highway, the N10. She's a four-hour drive west of Karachi, at the southwestern edge of Hingol National Park.*

BAMYAN PROVINCE, AFGHANISTAN. 34.84143 / 67.2238

BAND-E-AMIR LAKES

The six lakes of Afghanistan's first national park glow an unearthly sapphire hue. Local lore says the lakes were created by the Prophet Muhammad's son-in-law. The less wondrous explanation is that mineral-rich waters flowed through the hills, leaving mineral deposits that gradually solidified into natural dams. Waterfalls babble between the terraces, and only a few paddleboats interrupt the lakes' pristine blue. War brought a halt to foreign tourism here, though a curious few do arrive to admire this habitat of ibex, wolves and wild sheep, and to see the ruins of the Bamiyan Buddhas, 4th-century statues that were destroyed by the Taliban in 2001.

🔛 *The lakes are far from the beaten track, most easily visited from Bamiyan, 75km east; it's possible to hire a driver in town. Keep to marked trails as there are landmines in the area.*

ASTANA, KAZAKHSTAN, 51.1283 / 71.4305

BAYTEREK MONUMENT

A 97m-high tower topped with a glass orb soars above the skyline of Astana, Kazakhstan's capital since 1997. The Bayterek Monument might look futuristic, but the design was inspired by ancient Kazakh legends. According to myth, a golden egg containing the secret of human happiness was laid by the mighty bird Samuruk at the top of a poplar – the 'tree of life' – tantalisingly out of reach of mere mortals. But in this case, you can travel directly to the golden egg by elevator; though instead of the meaning of life you'll access views of Astana and a handprint of President Nazarbayev.

 The Bayterek Monument (www.astana-bayterek.kz) rises from Nurzhol Blvd in the centre of Astana.

'Everywhere, rats tumble over thresholds, skitter down handrails and wriggle through nooks and crannies. A living tide surges across the floor'

BIKANER, INDIA, 27.7910 / 73.3408

Karni Mata Temple

To be honest, I'm not an enthusiastic fan of rats. It could be the fleshy, hairless tails, or the times I've woken in dark, third-rate hotel rooms to find myself not entirely alone. But I can't claim I didn't know what I was getting into when visiting Bikaner's legendary rat temple.

Founded by priests from the Charan caste – a tribal people once worshipped as divine by the Rajput rulers of Rajasthan – the Karni Mata Mandir at Deshnok is literally crawling with rats, but that's rather the idea. The scurrying, squealing rodents are worshipped by Hindu devotees as the reincarnated children of Karni Mata, patron deity of the royal families of Jodhpur and Bikaner.

From outside, this could be just another Rajasthani temple, albeit a nice example, built in the late-Mughal style by the 19th century

Maharajah of Bikaner. Inside, though, rodents rule. Everywhere, rats tumble over thresholds, skitter down handrails and wriggle through narrow nooks and crannies. In the inner sanctum, a living tide surges across the marble floor, scuttling between the feet of pilgrims to gather in hunched rows around giant metal trays of milk and *prasad* (ceremonial food).

Entering Karni Mata could be marketed as a form of immersion therapy for musophobes. For one thing, you have to go barefoot, so there's a 99 per cent chance that rats are going to run across your feet at some point in the proceedings. Personally, I found this idea less alarming than the potential health risks of eating food 'blessed' by being nibbled by holy rodents. In the end, I braved a single piece of candy-style sweet *prasad*, reasoning

that my immune system was sufficiently honed after several months in India that I could survive almost anything.

Perhaps the most striking thing about the temple, however, was not the swarming rodents, or the nerve-jangling sound of some 15,000 rats squealing in unison, but the adulation shown to the tiny animals by visiting pilgrims. On all sides, you'll see visitors feeding rats choice morsels and even dishing out affectionate strokes and kisses.

This would be a nightmare to some, but to the faithful, these are *kabas* – 'little children' – and are treated as lovingly as human children in this family-obsessed society. *By Joe Bindloss*

 The Karni Mata Temple is open daily from 4am to 10pm. Buses run regularly to Deshnok from Bikaner.

JAMMU & KASHMIR, INDIA,
34.2160 / 75.5030

ICE PHALLUS OF AMARNATH CAVE

At the Amarnath cave-shrine, 3888m above sea level, a sub-zero stalagmite draws Hindu pilgrims. Situated in northerly Jammu and Kashmir state, this frosty phallus is believed to be the symbolic 'ice lingam' of the god Shiva. It's a seasonal phenomenon: access to the 40m cave is nigh on impossible in winter; but in the late spring thaw, meltwater trickles into the cave and refreezes into the lingam.

The cave is believed to be where Shiva explained the universe's secrets to Parvati, goddess of love and fertility. But the ice lingam is shy around visitors: it melts more quickly when the body heat of groups of pilgrims raises the cave temperature.

Pilgrims ply a five-day route from Pahalgam, which is reachable by bus or taxi from Jammu. A shorter, more perilous route begins in Baltal.

NEAR TALAS, KYRGYZSTAN, 42.5268 / 72.3817

GUMBEZ OF MANAS

A mausoleum covered in intricate terracotta tiles pays tribute to Kyrgyzstan's most legendary warrior. Tales of Manas' heroic battles and his unification of tribes have been passed down orally for centuries, gathering mythic embellishment along the way. By the 19th century, the stories were collected into the *Epic of Manas*; its descriptions of Manas' noble heritage and battles against the Afghans are still chanted at festivals. Manas' highly ornamented tomb, commissioned by his wife, was labelled as the mausoleum of a young girl to prevent Manas' enemies from plundering it. The ruse worked and this 11m-tall tomb, complete with elaborate Arabic inscriptions and a Kyrgyz-style dome, is still intact. A museum dedicated to Manas' life is nearby.

The tomb is about 20km east of Talas; drive there or catch a taxi from the centre of town.

Ⓣian Ⓢhan Ⓜountains, Ⓚazakhstan. 42.9841 / 78.4674

LAKE KAINDY

Spears of spruce rise up from the water at this pristine lake, where a forest was drowned after an earthquake. The Kebin earthquake in 1911 triggered a landslide in the Tian Shan mountains, creating a natural dam that eventually brought this glassy, 400m lake into existence, submerging part of the forest. The lake occupies an ear-popping location at 2000m of altitude, close to Kazakhstan's border with Kyrgyzstan. Glowing an unearthly shade of turquoise and backed by forest-clad mountains, the sunken forest adds to the mystique of this tranquil place and has made it a hit among divers.

🛶 *Reach Lake Kaindy by car. On paved roads from Almaty it's about a 280km drive, east on the A351 then southwest.*

Ⓤⓥa Ⓟrovince, Ⓢri Ⓛanka. 6.7654 / 80.9526

HAPUTALE

Lofty Haputale is the perfect place to enjoy brews with views, all infused with the flavour of Britain's faded glory. Stretched across a steep mountain ridge, Haputale feels frozen in time: blanketing the misty hillsides are countless tea plantations, relics of British governance in Sri Lanka. In numerous colonial outposts, the Brits were quick to establish high-altitude hill stations where they could escape the heat. Places like Haputale, with an ideal tea-growing climate, allowed the British tea industry to flourish. The hillsides are still sprinkled with British-style bungalows, there's a tea factory where you can sip various styles of cuppa, and a 1970m lookout is named after Scottish tea mogul Thomas Lipton.

🚌 *Buses from Colombo take six hours to reach Haputale. The town is walkable.*

⌖ MYANMAR, 18.3765 / 96.4207

MANDALAY-YANGON EXPRESSWAY

Compliments are in short supply when it comes to the Mandalay–Yangon Expressway. Slicing north to south through half of Myanmar, the hurriedly built highway cut travel times in half, but has design flaws that cause several accidents per day. Grimly nicknamed the 'highway of death', roadside signs warn: 'Life is a Journey, complete it'. The most bizarre sections are at the halfway point, en route to Myanmar's purpose-built capital, Naypyidaw. In places the road is 20 lanes wide, most of them empty (as is the eerily underpopulated city). Locals murmur that this was cleverly contrived: an aircraft could land on this broad expressway, should an anti-government protest need dispersing in a hurry.

☛ *Driving the entire expressway takes around eight hours; go very carefully.*

⋔ANA, ⒷHUTAN, 27.5271 / 89.8781
CHIMI LHAKHANG

The raunchy teaching methods of a Buddhist sage are immortalised at this monastery in Punakha in Bhutan; and you might be struck with a lucky phallus. The temple was built in honour of Lama Drukpa Kunley, who supposedly vanquished a demoness with a thunderbolt. A model of the righteous thunderbolt is here, along with prayer wheels and fertility shrines. Lama Drukpa Kunley, dubbed the 'Divine Madman', was a fan of thinking outside the box, so his teaching methods were allusive and rich in penis symbolism. Unsurprisingly, Chimi Lhakhang has become a favourite pilgrimage place for couples with fertility problems, who seek blessings, sometimes in the form of being struck on the head with a wooden member.

🎏 *The shrine is in Pana village, accessed by a pathway from Sopsokha through rice fields before an uphill climb.*

⋔AWSYNRAM & ⒸHERRAPUNJI, INDIA, 25.2189 / 91.6618
MEGHALAYA TREE BRIDGES

Pinched between Bangladesh and Burma in India's far east, two regions are vying for the title of wettest place on Earth. Mawsynram and Cherrapunji, both in Meghalaya state, harness this heroic rainfall into 'living bridges', walkways plaited together from rubber tree roots. Weaving almost a kilometre of roots into a natural bridge takes skill. Hollow tree trunks are positioned strategically to guide their growth, and it can take more than a decade for tree roots to strengthen in their unnatural new pose. The result is breathtaking: knotted root bridges blend into the lush Meghalaya forest, able to support the weight of up to 50 people. One of the longest bridges, at 50m, is 20km east of Cherrapunji in Pynursla.

🎏 *The famous 'double-decker root bridge' is walkable from Cherrapunji Holiday Resort (www.cherrapunjee.com).*

①MON ⑤TATE. ②MYANMAR. 17.4819 / 97.0986

KYAIKTIYO PAGODA

A single strand of the Buddha's hair prevents this boulder from toppling from its rocky ledge – or so the stories say. In any case, the 'Golden Rock', atop Mount Kyaiktiyo in Mon State, appears to defy gravity. A 7m-tall boulder leans towards the edge of its perch; confoundingly, only a small surface area appears to touch the bedrock.

One of Myanmar's most sacred pilgrimage places, the entire surface of the boulder has been lovingly pasted with gold leaf, and a golden stupa (dome-shaped Buddhist shrine) crowns the top. Kyaiktiyo Pagoda's shimmering coat is constantly being renewed. Buddhist pilgrims (male only) cross a bridge to the rock to daub their own glittering

contribution on its surface; visiting the rock three times in a single year is thought to be particularly auspicious. But the most enthralling time to visit is the pilgrimage season from November to March. A hypnotic atmosphere takes hold: candles are lit, devotees make offerings of fruit, and the chanting of monks vibrates through the night air.

Pilgrims remove their sandals before the challenging 11km trail from Kinpun to the rock. More casual visitors rely on a bone-rattling uphill journey by trucks, which leave when full of pilgrims. Visits at sunset are spectacular, but trucks heading downhill from the rock stop at sundown, so you may need to stay in a guesthouse near the pagoda.

🐾 *The bus journey from Yangon to Kyaiktiyo can take up to five hours.*

ZHANGYE. ⓒHINA. 38.9164 / 100.1298

ZHANGYE DANXIÁ NATIONAL GEOPARK

Bands of colour from vermilion to pale green cover a mountainous 500 sq km site in Gansu province, where more than 20 million years of geological movement have pressed the sandstone into a multicoloured layer cake. Over centuries, the sandstone was weathered into pillars, while extreme desert temperatures split the rock to form creeks and cliff faces hundreds of metres high.

The name given to this kind of Martian landscape is 'danxia', and it can be found elsewhere in China, such as at the Binggou Danxia Park. There, too, is a landscape of towering rock columns and sheer cliffs, but its colours don't come close to matching the geopark, where the hills blaze in shades of yellow and red.

The park is threaded with walking trails and sightseeing cars trundle through, allowing access to lookout points over the spindly rock formations and tiger-striped hills. Most arresting is the 'Seven-Colour Mountain', which can be admired from the

park's fourth and largest viewing platform (easily reached by the park's sightseeing cars). The hills flame scarlet and gold during sunrise and sunset, so photographers should rise early. A spot of rain also makes the colours of the rainbow hills pop, so time your visit for between May and September.

© Sino Images / Getty Images

🐾 *Take a train to Zhangye (30km from the information centre) or fly via Xi'an. Plan on www.zydanxia.com.*

ⒸOCOS ⒾSLANDS, ⒶUSTRALIA,
-11.8257 / 96.8232

Cocos Islands Golf Club

It's an unusual location for a golf course, laid out as it is along an airport runway on a coral atoll in the middle of the Indian Ocean. I'm with a group of locals, pushing our carts along the Tarmac. There's friendly banter when yet another ball disappears into the lagoon. Then the siren goes and we wait at the edge of the runway. Cold drinks emerge from golf bags. A heavy military aircraft approaches, lands, taxis to the terminal. American soldiers from an oceanic base are stopping on their way to R&R in Australia. Their astonished faces peer through windows as amused golfers, raising a glass to the new arrivals, peer back. By Virginia Jealous

🐦 *The Golf Club is on West Island. Flights to the islands depart from Perth.*

ⓂELAKA, ⓂALAYSIA,
2.1838 / 102.2669

PORTUGUESE SETTLEMENT

Portugal's mastery of the seas – and hunger for trade and conquest – built a global empire with outposts across Asia during the 16th century. One was Melaka, a thriving port city on peninsula Malaysia's southwest coast. Melaka was a Portuguese colony for 130 years, until the Dutch seized it in 1641. There are few remnants of Melaka's once-formidable Portuguese fortress, aside from a gate. But the building of a wooden fishing village in 1933 reunited the local Portuguese community. The settlement, 2.5km east of Chinatown, is Porto with a dash of Malay flavour: Portuguese-style houses, Christian shrines, custard tarts, and seafood – though it comes with a spicy side of *sambal* (chilli sauce).

🐦 *It takes half an hour to walk from central Dutch Square to the Portuguese Settlement.*

ⒷANGKOK, ⓉHAILAND,
13.7483 / 100.5464

Chao Mae Tuptim Shrine

It's rare I feel bashful asking for directions, but seeking out Bangkok's penis shrine would make anyone shy. To reach the fertility shrine, a sanctuary of tree spirit Chao Mae Tuptim, I sidle past bouquets of phalluses: hulking wooden members tower 3m tall, while granite sculptures have more realistic proportions. Some are neatly tied with ribbons or wreathed in jasmine. But the atmosphere is far from bawdy: a young couple quietly watch smoke rise from sticks of incense, while nearby a gentleman binds his phallus – a wooden one, I hasten to add – in pink gauze. Serenity can be found in the strangest of places. By Anita Isalska

🐦 *The shrine is behind Bangkok's Swissô-tel Nai Lert Park; staff can direct you.*

℗HENSAVAN. ⒼAOS. 19.4306 / 103.1541

PLAIN OF JARS

Funeral urns, or convenient storage for rice wine? Historians hesitate over the meaning of these 2000-year-old granite and sandstone jars, some 3m in height, scattered southwest of Phonsavan.

Archaeology is a daredevil pursuit in these meadows, which are strewn with landmines. Cluster bombs were dropped here in the 1960s, mainly by US forces during the Laotian Civil War. Unexploded submunitions are still studded in the soil. Picking carefully through this former war zone, archaeologists have been able to pin down the jars' age to around 500BC. They were initially thought to be brewing barrels for alcohol, while larger urns were found to contain tools, jewellery and bones,

lending credence to the theory that at least some were funerary urns. They may have been used for 'primary burials', in which bodies are left to dry out before cremation; a cave nearby is thought to be the crematorium. Carvings of animals on the jar lids are not yet understood.

The region has 60 jar-spotting sites, and three of them have been completely cleared of landmines. Even so, it's important to stay on marked trails. Site One is the easiest to navigate and also the closest to the information centre. Sites Two and Three aren't as well maintained; independent travellers are best off visiting by motorbike; otherwise, consider joining a guided tour.

 Buses connect Vientiane with Phonsavan; from here, hire a bike or car, or take a guided tour.

10 TOP EYE-POPPING ASIAN FESTIVALS

BATU CAVES, MALAYSIA, 3.2378 / 101.6843

① Thaipusam

Want to follow a phallic procession, watch grappling wrestlers or take part in a divine paint fight? Over centuries, Asian countries have celebrated seasons, divine battles and artistic prowess through uproarious, radiant festivals. Guaranteed to remain seared in your memory is Thaipusam, where processions of worshippers pierce and skewer their bodies in dedication to Hindu god Murugan.

☞ Watch processions on the full moon day of Jan or Feb at Batu Caves, 15km north of Kuala Lumpur.

© Gavin Hellier / Getty Images

INDIA, 28.6461 / 77.2144

② Holi

Want to celebrate spring with a rainbow-streaked battle? In homage to Krishna's penchant for pranks, devotees in India throw colourful dyes to honour the victory of good over evil. Don't wear your best T-shirt.

☞ Holi hits the streets the day after March's full moon. Delhi's celebrations are particularly wild.

KAWASAKI, JAPAN, 35.5308 / 139.6974

③ Kanamara Matsuri

Watch a penis-shaped altar carried aloft by waves of revellers. This phallic festival (below right) celebrates a folk tale in which a woman was cured of vagina dentata when a blacksmith forged her a metal dildo.

☞ Join locals celebrating fertility every April in Kawasaki, 20km south of Tokyo.

CEBU, PHILIPPINES, 10.2940 / 123.9007

④ Sinulog

The Santo Niño dance (above right), to a backdrop of hypnotic drumming, is the unmistakable hallmark of Cebu's glittering carnival, a pagan-turned-Christian festival dating back more than 500 years.

☞ Parades kick off on the third Sunday of January, with Cebu City the heart of the action.

© Lim_Jessica / Getty Images

MONGOLIA. 47.8546 / 106.7838

⑤ Naadam

Gasp at Mongolia's centuries-old military arts – wrestling, archery, horse-racing and spear-throwing – at this nomads' Olympics, held in midsummer with pomp, costumed parades and breathtaking skill.

Festivities unfold mid-July (naadamfestival.com). Ulaanbaatar's stadium hosts the biggest events.

HARBIN. CHINA. 45.7777 / 126.6224

⑥ Harbin Ice Sculpture Festival

Palaces hewn from ice (left) are illuminated against the sky, while snow sculptures of beasts and Buddhas are lined on the banks of the frozen Songhua River.

The festival runs December to February across Harbin locations like Sun Island and Zhaolin parks.

HUE. VIETNAM. 16.4690 / 107.5858

⑦ Hue Festival

Kite-flying, boat racing and talent shows unfurl next to traditional crafts such as calligraphy and dance at this biennial carnival of culture in Hue. Entertainment ranges from historic carnivals to high-tech light shows.

Hue is in central Vietnam, connected to Ho Chi Minh City by daily flights. See www.huefestival.com.

NEPAL. 28.2238 / 83.9902

⑧ Dashain

Fifteen intense days of ritual acts, from blessings to the symbolic chasing of demons, lead to a gory climax of animal slaughter. The spilled blood represents battles between good and evil.

Dashain usually falls in September or October. Pokhara is a lively place to observe the rituals.

MYANMAR. 16.7982 / 96.1496

⑨ Tazaungdaing Festival

The night sky blazes with floating lanterns for this festival marking the end of Myanmar's rainy season. At Shwedagon Pagoda, locals compete to weave monks' robes ahead of the festival.

The festival is held during the full moon in the eighth month of the Burmese calendar.

RUSSIA. 55.7522 / 37.6232

⑩ Maslenitsa

Across Russia, floral headdresses and garlands of bagels are worn for a *bliny* (pancake) binge, to celebrate the end of winter. It's the last knees-up before Lent so overindulgence is encouraged.

Pancake vendors and effigy-burning are set up in many Russian towns in the last week before Lent.

○YUNNAN ℗ROVINCE. ℃HINA.
24.5617 / 102.8745

FUXIAN LAKE

After years of folk stories about a city under the water, the lichen-strewn remains of an ancient town were discovered by divers in China's third-deepest freshwater lake. First, flagstones and low walls furred with moss were detected; soon archaeologists were mapping a site measuring 2.5 sq km. Thanks to carbon dating, scientists pinpointed the age of the ruins to AD 260, dashing hopes that the site could be a lost city of Yunnan's Dian Kingdom. Still, the truth is equally interesting: examination of carved stones found on the lake floor has revealed mystical images including fertility symbols, ritual objects engraved with the sun and moon, and even animal-like masks.

☞ *Archaeological investigations continue, so you may be restricted to the lake shore.*

© Alex Linghorn / Getty Images

ⒼURVAN ⓈAIKHAN ⓃATIONAL ℗ARK. ⓂONGOLIA.
43.4960 / 104.0880

YOLYN AM

In the middle of the Gobi Desert's 'Valley of Vultures', an ice field lies cocooned by a steep gorge. Thanks to the shade of this canyon in Gurvan Saikhan National Park, the ice of Yolyn Am sometimes lasts into the summer. In winter, the frosty mantle covers several kilometres. Layers of bluish ice, streaked with desert dust, create interesting natural sculptures as well as perilous crevasses; watch your step if you plan to hike the bed of the gorge. Tragically, the year-round ice field may soon be a fleeting beauty, as locals report it getting thinner by the year.

☞ *You'll need your own wheels (and robust ones at that) to reach Yolyn Am. By road, it's 45km west of Dalanzadgad, a thinly spread mining and tourist town. You can reach Dalanzadgad by bus from Ulaanbaatar.*

JOHOR BAHRU, MALAYSIA, 1.4927 / 103.7414

ARULMIGU SRI RAJAKALIAMMAN TEMPLE

Shield your eyes as you step into this sanctuary of twinkling beads and glass mosaics. A stray beam of light provided the inspiration for Malaysia's first and only glass temple: while pondering how to rebuild one of Johor Bahru's oldest temples, a ray of light struck the eyes of Guru Bhagawan Sittar. Learning that the light source was a reflection from a glass icon more than a mile away, Sittar was inspired to create a temple of glass to draw believers into its light. Inside, crystal chandeliers set light bouncing off glass icons, and the walls are spangled with beads, each one engraved with a prayer. Most impressive is the multicoloured mosaic, made from more than 300,000 pieces of glass.

The temple is 1km north of JB Sentral station. Tourists are permitted to visit in the afternoon.

'I was unprepared for the nightmarish whimsy on display on the winding walkways: a crab with a man's head; a girl with a snail's body...'

◎INGAPORE. 1.2836 / 103.7818

Haw Par Villa

When Hercules made his journey to the underworld to dognap the demon pooch Cerberus, he had to wrestle ghosts and monsters. Visiting the underworld in Singapore was a little bit easier. All I had to do was jump off the Mass Rapid Transport train, stroll across Pasir Panjang Road, and step into the bowels of hell...

Haw Par Villa, a sculpture garden created by eccentric brothers Aw Boon Haw and Aw Boon Par (best known for inventing Tiger Balm), ranks as one of the world's most surreal tourist attractions. Sprawling over 3.2 hectares of prime Singapore real estate, and coated in untold gallons of primary-colour gloss paint, are more than a thousand statues of demons and deities from Chinese and Buddhist mythology. Many are arranged in gruesome dioramas of torture as a warning to anyone thinking of carrying out evil deeds in this lifetime.

I had encountered some wacky visions of the afterlife on my travels – Hieronymus Bosch's nightmares at Madrid's Museo del Prado, the concrete pumpkin-from-hell in Laos' Xieng Khuan Buddha Park – but Haw Par Villa held a special appeal. I think it was the hallucinogenic colours in the pictures I'd seen before visiting. Having been raised on Hendrix and Tom Wolfe's *The Electric Kool-Aid Acid Test*, seeing psychedelia in three living dimensions was much too alluring to resist.

Stepping through the innocent-looking Chinese gates, I was nevertheless unprepared for the nightmarish whimsy that was on display on the winding walkways. What was that? A crab with a man's head. And there? A girl with a snail's body. Nearby, the damned writhed in agony as they were crushed beneath grindstones and impaled on spikes, drenched in red-

paint gore as if part of an early Hammer horror film.

The lack of attendants and general scarcity of visitors – a situation which has bought the gardens close to closure on several occasions – only added to the sense of being transported into a freakish parallel universe.

In fact, it's not all doom and gloom here. For every sawing demon, there's an uplifting scene of Buddhist meditation or a magnificent Chinese dragon as large as a subway train. For the lay person, it's a mesmerising introduction to the rainbow world of Chinese and Buddhist mythology, and despite the patchy signage, the symbology – do bad deeds, get speared by devils – transcends the language divide. *By Joe Bindloss*

☞ *The sculpture park is open daily from 9am to 7pm. MRT trains run regularly to Haw Par Villa station.*

'For those who prefer their bugs cooked, vats of boiling peanut oil stand ready to add to them a deep fried, crispy, crunchy texture'

SIEM REAP, CAMBODIA, 13.3671 / 103.845

Creepy Crawly Market

Bugs for dinner? Before you turn up your nose at the idea, consider that entomophagy – the human use of insects as food – can be traced back to the earliest days of man. Many anthropologists believe that before the advent of agriculture, some 10,000 years ago, bugs were a staple feature in our diets. And in Siem Reap, at what the locals call the Creepy Crawly Market, diners can return to their roots.

The market is a moveable feast that relocates to a different part of the city each day, offering insects, reptiles and just about any living thing that can be found underneath a rock. Both locals and tourists line up at the stalls to ingest all manner of multi-legged, slithery critters. Local children even earn extra money by capturing the crawly critters and selling them to the vendors.

It is a simple outdoor market, offering generous-sized bowls filled with crickets, moth larvae, water bugs and tarantulas. Larger critters, like snakes, sit drying in the sun. Some people offer even more exotic fare under the table or from the trunk of their cars, such as bottles of so-called scorpion whiskey that actually includes the venomous creatures right there in the bottle! Granted, most diners prefer that their meals are not moving around on their plate, or looking you in the eye as you consume them, but that is all part of the exotic allure of the market. It is the old world merged with the new.

Most visitors treat the place like a walk-away cafe, grabbing a quick snack on the move. While some people prefer to eat their bugs au naturel, for those who prefer them cooked (which seems to be the majority), vats of boiling peanut oil stand ready to add to them a deep fried, crispy, crunchy texture, as well as an extra layer of flavour.

Siem Reap, the gateway to Angkor Wat, sits amongst deep jungle that provides an endless supply of tasty tidbits. In the past few months, the nomadic market has become so popular that one industrious entrepreneur has opened a permanent Bug Cafe – a clean, modern restaurant that advertises insect tapas and cocktails, where you can feast on a scorpion salad and tarantula ice cream.

By James Dorsey

☞ *The Creepy Crawly market pops up in a different spot every day; contact the tourist information office on Route 6 for that day's location. Otherwise, most locals will happily tell you where to find it.*

Near Siem Reap, Cambodia. 13.6862 / 104.0156

KBAL SPEAN

Fertility symbols are carved above and below the spray of a rushing waterway in Cambodia's Kulen Hills, often referred to as the 'River of 1000 Lingas'. Around 45km from Siem Reap's world-famous Angkor Wat complex, this 150m stretch of the Stung Kbal Spean River is lined with phallic symbols, along with carvings of the god Vishnu, monkey-headed Hanuman, and numerous other Hindu deities. The setting is as exhilarating as the art, with waterfalls tumbling down mythic scenes: in one, Vishnu reclines with Lakshmi by his feet; in another, Brahma sits majestically on a lotus flower. Reaching the site requires you to wend through the forest, occasionally hanging on to branches and tree roots as you scramble uphill.

It is thought that hermits began sculpting sacred forms in the riverbed during the 11th century, though some historians argue that the first lingas appeared 200 years earlier. The site was rediscovered in 1969 by an ethnologist, Jean Boulbet, guided here by a local hermit. Cambodia's Civil War prevented this archeological site from attracting much attention until the 1990s.

With overhanging trees and rushing water, it's all too easy to miss some of the most interesting carvings, so it's handy to go with a guide. Aim to visit between July and December, when water flows merrily over the rock.

 Kbal Spean is 50km north of Siem Reap by road. It's a slippery, uphill trek; wear hiking shoes.

ℭHRISTMAS ℐSLAND, ℐUSTRALIA, −10.4871 / 105.6294

RED CRAB MIGRATION

If you're on Christmas Island at the start of the rainy season, be sure to drive very, very carefully. It's the time of the annual red crab migration and these little fellas have just one thing in mind. Cars, trucks, bicycles – all become insignificant compared to the overwhelming urge to procreate.

Triggered by the first droplets of rain, crabs crawl from underground burrows deep in the forest and start their slow sideways creep to the beaches over five miles away. Within hours the trickle becomes a rolling red tide of tens of millions of grumpy-faced crabs, driven on by their deep-rooted impulse to mate, hell-bent on their tip-toe scuttle to the sea. It's an instinctive but tight schedule: migration, burrow digging, wooing and mating must all be done in time for the turn of the high tide of the last quarter of the moon. Only then will the females shimmy in the surf, spawning precious eggs into the ocean.

So, it's no wonder that nothing stands in their way. Scaling steep cliff faces, clinging to jagged rocks, fighting swarms of crazy yellow ants, the crabs lurch inexorably onwards. Despite road closures, crab fences and purpose-built underpasses, hordes of crabs play chicken with local traffic – rangers armed with plastic rakes patrol the streets, scooping the little critters out of harm's way. Drivers should be thankful for this: the crabs' shells are so tough they can cause punctures.

 Christmas Island can be reached by air from Perth (Australia) and Jakarta (Indonesia).

*'It's a small, shallow, clear pool of bright turquoise water,
sublit by sand that's soft and white as talcum powder'*

CHRISTMAS ISLAND, AUSTRALIA, −10.4270 / 105.7031

The Grotto

A narrow sealed road skirts the ocean between Flying Fish Cove and the golf course. It's a beautiful morning ride, past a mosque and a Chinese temple, past houses and shops in various stages of decay and renewal, followed by a series of cemeteries that fringe the limestone cliffs and forest of the shoreline on the way to the golf course. The sight and sound of the ocean is my constant companion, as are low-flying golden bosuns – elegant tropical birds that, as their name suggests, glow in the early sunlight.

I didn't notice the walking track into the Grotto during my first rides; it's easy to miss if you don't look out for it. It would be just as easy to pass by without bothering to turn off, unless you know what lies at the end. Stopping there is second nature to me now, though. The path is narrow

and overhung with rainforest vegetation; after a few metres it becomes rocky and descends, slightly, to a cave in the cliff wall. I hear the water before I see it; in calm weather it breathes gently in and out, but if the swell's up then the gulping ocean surges can, quite frankly, sound terrifying.

The appearance of the Grotto always amazes me. It's a small, shallow, clear pool of bright turquoise water, sublit by sand that's soft and white as talcum powder. Stalactites and stalagmites emerge from the smooth floor and roof. The shooshing water comes and goes from a small aperture at the back of the cave; serious cave divers occasionally navigate it, but – happily! – casual swimmers have never been sucked out to sea. I whip my clothes off and submerge, then float quietly, looking out and up into daylight

filtered through the trees. Shoals of tiny translucent fish mirror my movements.

There are informal local conventions about approaching the Grotto. My pile of clothes is visible and any new arrivals will coo-ee from the path, giving me time to grab a towel. On evening visits, a line of candles marking the entrance, along with evidence of champagne corks and silence from within, might mean that a couple is enjoying some 'private' time. Alternatively, sounds of conversation and laughter mean the Grotto is being shared by any comers. This morning, as most mornings, I have the place to myself and emerge relaxed and ready to absorb the coming day.
By Virginia Jealous

 Christmas Island can be reached by air from Perth (Australia) and Jakarta (Indonesia).

KARYAMUKTI, INDONESIA.
-6.9936 / 107.0563

GUNUNG PADANG

These ancient stone columns occupy a serene location, scattered across a terrace in the fragrant hills of Cianjur; but they have ignited an archaeological controversy that continues to rage. There is little solid evidence that this megalithic site in West Java was left behind by a 20,000-year-old civilisation. But some geologists continue to claim that these hunks of volcanic rock crown a man-made pyramid – an idea popular with the Indonesian government, as it would herald the discovery of the most advanced civilisation ever known. Most academics are sceptical, suggesting that the site is a dormant volcano, and that its columns of rock probably date to 1200BC.

Gunung Padang is a 24km drive southeast from Sukabumi.

WEST JAVA, INDONESIA. −6.8738 / 107.6846

WEEPING ROCKS

Toffee-coloured streams gush from a cliff face near Cimenyan in West Java. Curug Batu Templek's uncommon waterfalls are known as 'Indonesia's weeping rocks'. Their tears flow most abundantly between June and September, when the soil has been fed with plenty of rain; groundwater, rather than a river, is the source of these caramel cascades. There are few witnesses to these endless tears. The rocks are framed by thick forest north of Bandung, the main town of this volcanic region, and it's challenging to find. Beyond the main Nasution highway, roads are narrow, gravelly and not always suitable for cars. Expect some surprised stares when you ask villagers for directions (which you will almost certainly need to do).

By road, the rocks lie 12km northeast of Bandung. Consider going by bike or motorbike, or hire a local guide.

NEAR HOI AN, VIETNAM.
15.7907 / 108.1078

MY SON

Scattered beneath Cat's Tooth Mountain are the spellbinding ruins of the Kingdom of Champa. From the 4th to 13th centuries, this kingdom thrived along the coast of modern Vietnam. It's believed that monarchs were buried at My Son, where 18 temples still stand. Scenes from Hindu legends are visible, though tufts of grass now burst from the fired-brick walls. Nature has been nibbling away at these ruins since their abandonment in 1832. The French rediscovered the site later in the 19th century, but the temples suffered badly during US bombings in 1969. Dodge the tour groups by arriving in the early morning, or in the mid-afternoon.

By road, the ruins of My Son are an hour west of Hoi An. Browse the on-site museum before you explore the temples.

© Reciprocity Images / Alamy

'Our guide explains the spiritual significance of every rock, cliff, lone tree, all backed by Baikal vistas in shades of blue you never knew existed'

SIBERIA, RUSSIA, 53.1567 / 107.3836

Olkhon Island

'So this is Siberia?' I think to myself as I lie on the sun-warmed grass of Olkhon Island, gazing out across shimmering Lake Baikal. As I had discovered, Lake Baikal's biggest island is a place that quickly dispels all the stereotypes of Siberia as a place of icy Slavic cruelty.

Olkhon is a must-see on the trans-Siberia trail, but it keeps its secrets remote – it's a dusty, seven-hour road trip from Irkutsk, Eastern Siberia's de-facto capital. Wheezing buses spit travellers out in the tiny island capital of Khuzhir, a timber Soviet smudge and the only place to stay. This fly-blown village is an unlikely spot for a backpacker hostel, but Nikita's Homestead is more than a dusty flat with a few bunks. This Siberian retreat is a village within a village, its cabins celebrating the region's shamanist traditions.

The island is a special place for both adventurous travellers and the local Buryats – ethnic Mongolians who inhabit Siberia's east. Eerie, peaceful and almost otherworldly, it's home to a horde of shamanist spirits but mostly uninhabited by humans. Dramatically barren in the south, the north is a place of thick sandy-floored larch forest where the spirits dwell. Every rock, spring or oddly shaped tree is hung in colourful, wind-ragged cloth signifying the place as an *oboo*, home to a benevolent spirit.

Recuperated from the long ride from Irkutsk, the next day I take a minivan tour with a local Buryat guide. Paved roads peter out just metres from the village and we are soon treated to some extreme Siberian driving, our burly Buryat pounding an immortal Soviet-era 4x4 van across the dunes. As we hang onto our pant-polished leatherette seats, we spot more *oboos*, the ground around them carpeted in kopeck coins. When we stop, our guide explains the spiritual significance of every rock, cliff, lone tree, all backed by Baikal vistas in shades of blue you never knew existed, snow-capped mountains floating above the mist in on the far shore. It's little wonder the Buryats chose this as the home for their pantheon of gods and spirits.

Dusted and road weary, back in Khuzhir I find myself resting on that grass, listening to Siberia's silence – ethereal Olkhon, an unexpected island of exotic Asian tranquillity in Russia's vast expanse. *By Marc di Duca*

☛ *Olkhon Island is a seven-hour bus ride from Irkutsk.*

© Mak08 / Getty Images

⑥DALAT. VIETNAM. 11.9347 / 108.4307
HANG NGA GUESTHOUSE

Resembling a melted candle, this guesthouse in Dalat was inspired by the surreal art of Salvador Dalí. 'Crazy House' is different from every angle: on one side, warped walls seem menacing and windows glare like eye sockets; from another, traditional Vietnamese designs adorn the eaves. Architect and owner, Mrs Dang Viet Nga, sculpted jungle vines and ragged stairs to give Crazy House an organic feel. Beds are cradled in cauldron-like chambers, latticed windows look like spider's webs, while fittings are decorated with giraffe-skin patterns or camouflaged as tree stumps. This place aims to unleash guests' repressed feeling of freedom; stay the night and let your heart soar.

🕿 *Dalat is in Vietnam's Central Highlands. Book a night's stay at www. crazyhouse.vn.*

⑦NEAR HOI AN. VIETNAM. 16.0027 / 108.2633
AM PHU CAVE

Welcome to Hell. This cavern carries a stern moral warning, allowing visitors to experience the Buddhist concepts of purgatory and punishment across 10 vivid levels. The gruesomely decorated chambers in this 302m-long cave certainly make a persuasive case for renouncing evil. Its pathways are deliberately disorienting, and visitors will find a spiritual scale where one's actions in this life are weighed. If that doesn't perturb you, maybe the fanged demons and dioramas of women and men being beaten bloody will do the trick. The hellish chambers are beneath Thuy Son, one of the so-called 'Marble Mountains'; the lofty crag rising above the cave represents the heavens. Clamber up a steep stairwell towards the light (how apt) to escape.

🕿 *Thuy Son is 15km north of Hoi An.*

© Zhukov Oleg / Getty Images

© Barcroft Media / Getty Images

ⓃEAR ⓂAGELANG, ⒾNDONESIA, −7.6057 / 110.1805

GEREJA AYAM

As a universal symbol of peace, the dove is a fitting emblem for a place of worship. So it's a shame that the grand designs of Daniel Alamsjah now look so fowl. Alamsjah felt a divine calling to build a dove-shaped house of prayer for all faiths, roosting in central Java's Magelang hills. Its design falls somewhat short of a graceful dove, however: the hall's tower, shaped like a bird's head, has a gaping red beak, while its crown resembles a cock's comb. Nonetheless, it did operate successfully as a multi-faith place of worship and rehabilitation centre for drug abusers. But construction costs of the bird-shaped sanctuary

began to spiral, and it was left unfinished in 2000.

Now abandoned, it's affectionately dubbed the 'Chicken Church'. The moss gathering on its body forms a feathery coat, and chunks of masonry have tumbled from its tail, exposing a bare brick behind. Inside, pillars are dangerously weathered and it's mostly bare of furnishings. Some whisper that graffiti and discarded 'items' in the lower chambers suggest it's now being used for less-than-holy purposes. Dilapidation has increased interest in the Chicken Church, and locals enjoy a trickle of revenue from curious tourists. But its collapse can't be far away; go before it squawks its last.

🐾 *By road, Gereja Ayam is 20km south of Magelang town. It is unmaintained and so best admired from outside. Extreme caution is advised if you enter.*

ⒽONG ⒸONG. 22.2691 / 113.9987

BUFFALO BEACH

If you go for a sunset stroll on the shore of Lantau Island, you might attract the haughty stares of a buffalo. The beaches of this Hong Kong isle have become an unlikely spot for bulky mammals to idle. Buffalo are a remnant of Lantau's agricultural past and a point of friction between would-be developers, who claim the cattle are a nuisance to traffic and tourists, and conservationists seeking to preserve the population of buffalo. The Lantau Buffalo Association was founded to manage the animals and their habitat, but it's a losing battle, as development continues to encroach on the island's wetlands.

🐃 *Reach the island from central Hong Kong via the Tung Chung MTR line, or by ferry.*

Ⓑ RUNEI. 4.6159 / 114.3174

BILLIONTH BARREL MONUMENT

The Sultanate of Brunei commemorated its billionth barrel of crude oil, churned up at the onshore Seria oil fields, with this monument. Leading up to the slate-grey triumphal arches on the beach is a path flanked with placards embossed with Shell logos throughout the ages, in an affectionate tribute to the oil multinational. As Southeast Asia's third-largest oil producer, Brunei is extraordinarily wealthy for its small size. To continue a black-gold themed tour of Brunei, hop along to the Oil and Gas Discovery Centre (www.ogdc brunei.com), whose kid-friendly exhibitions seem designed to inspire Brunei's next generation of oil and gas engineers.

🐃 *Buses travel from the capital several times a day, but it's easier to hire a car.*

WA, AUSTRALIA, –28 0738 / 114.4712

PRINCIPALITY OF HUTT RIVER

Leonard George Casley became an overnight folk hero in Australia when, in 1970, he declared himself Prince Leonard and renamed his 7500-hectare property the Principality of Hutt River, as part of an agricultural protest writ large. This sovereign state (technically a self-proclaimed micronation) now occupies a chunk of Western Australia that's about the same size as Hong Kong with a population of just 23, when you don't include its 14,000 'worldwide citizens'. Foreigners crossing over the border from Australia must first get their passports stamped for a fee of A$4 at the Government Offices, located in the capital city of Nain. While in town you can meet Prince Leonard and the rest of the royal clan, learn about Hutt River's place on the world's stage, and pay your respects at the educational shrine of Princess Shirley, who died in 2013.

Prince Leonard considers himself a patron of the arts, so there is an impressive Royal Art Collection with more than 300 works from Australian and international artists. Other tourist attractions include the royal family's very own miniature golf course, the Royal Hutt River Golf Club. Trade up your Aussie dollars for the Principality's coins, stamps and trinkets, and BYO food and gear to stay overnight in a tent or caravan at the rustic campground by Hutt River.

 The Principality is 90km north of Geraldton and open daily from 9am to 4pm.

WA, AUSTRALIA, −34.3750 / 115.1363
CAPE LEEUWIN

This rugged headland, overseen by its 1895 lighthouse, is the most south-westerly point on the Australian mainland. To its south lie the wild waters of the Southern Ocean; next landfall is Antarctica. To its west the equally wild, if less frigid, waters of the Indian Ocean link Australia with Africa. The Cape is the spot where these two mighty oceans meet.

If the vagaries of light, weather, tide and swell allow, it's possible for a lucky visitor to see this merging of the waters. A distinct line becomes visible offshore, marking the point where the two oceans reach this end of their journeys. Standing near the cliff edge at the edge of the continent, it's an elemental experience.

🐾 *The closest township, Augusta, is 320km by road from Perth.*

© Australian Scenics / Getty Images

WA, AUSTRALIA, −33.4648 / 115.9104
GNOMESVILLE

It may be little more than a humble roundabout, but for 5000 gnomes, Gnomesville is the capital of the great Gnoman Empire with gnomes in planes, gnomes in trains and even one gnome riding a rocket! A local is said to have placed a solitary garden gnome in the hollow of a tree here in the 1990s. Fearing it was lonely, other townspeople followed suit. The population has grown exponentially ever since as visitors from around the world flock to Western Australia to drop off their beloved gnomes. Locals say Gnomesville's success as a tourist attraction has been so phe-gnome-nal that the population is slowly creeping onto private land. Consequently, they've built a detention centre for all displaced gnomes seeking asylum.

🐾 *Gnomesville is in the Ferguson Valley of WA, 35km inland from Bunbury by car. See www.gnomesville.com.*

WA. AUSTRALIA −34.4505 / 116.0533

Gloucester Tree

I always loved Enid Blyton's The Magic Faraway Tree, where adventures awaited at the top of an enchanted tree. But there's no whimsy about climbing the 60-odd metres up this fire lookout tree – it's a distinctly precarious experience. Vicious-looking metal spikes driven into the tree trunk spiral upwards and it's a hand-over-hand climb, with only a flimsy bit of wire netting for reassurance. Having tried skydiving and abseiling, I reckon I'm up for a bit of exhilaration, but with nothing to stop me slipping between the spokes I freeze halfway up with sheer heart-hammering terror. So, sorry, I can't tell you if magical folk live at the top of the tree. Do let me know if you see them.
By Tracy Whitmey

☛ The Gloucester Tree is close to Pemberton in WA.

BEIJING, CHINA, 39.9026 / 116.3978

MAUSOLEUM OF MAO ZEDONG

Few travellers dream of laying a marigold before the bloated body of Chairman Mao. But despite dying in 1976, Mao Zedong still pulls crowds of visitors to his stately mausoleum in Beijing's Tiān'ānmén Square. The mausoleum is so high-security (bags and cameras aren't allowed) that it's almost like visiting a living head of state. Visitors file past flower stalls that overflow with marigolds, popular offerings to the founding father of modern China. Mao's embalmed body is behind glass, and visitors are ushered past so quickly that many wonder if it is truly the communist leader's remains. Still, there's a range of Mao-themed souvenirs on sale, which last far longer than your fleeting glimpse.

☛ Mao's mausoleum and memorial hall are in Tiān'ānmén Square, walkable from Qianmen or Tiān'ānmén East stations.

'It's on quiet days when the romance of the wild Great Wall is conjured: miles of stone, crumbling and overgrown, epic beyond imagination'

Yan Mountains, China. 40.4546 / 116.5362

Zhengbei Tower

In the village of Xizhazi, nestled in the Yan Mountains, an unremarkable path winds upwards between terraced cornfields and mud-red farmhouses. Not much more than a shepherd's track, it climbs gently at first, past hens and snoozing dogs, then rises more steeply into a thickly wooded dell, leaving the village behind. Forty minutes later, through a clearing in the leaves, you get you first glimpse of stone. Then another – the crenelated crests of two watchtowers, peering over the tree line. Higher and higher the path climbs, tree roots becoming steps, branches becoming handholds. Then finally, hamstrings protesting, your destination looms into view: a sheer, inward-sloping wall of brick and white dolomite stone.

A stack of bricks has been fashioned into a precarious stairway; you're now inside a

© Andrius Aleksandravicius / Getty Images

Ming Dynasty watchtower. The ash of an old campfire darkens the worn stone floor. Beside it, a second set of stone steps rises all the way to the top. Now you're back in open air, standing on the upper battlement of the Zhengbei Tower, the highest point of the Jiankou section of Great Wall.

And all around you the world drops away. To the west, the crests of mountains plummet like a rollercoaster, then rise again, the Great Wall flowing across the ridgeline into the hazy distance. Sixty miles to the south, far out of sight, is Beijing. From up here it might as well be centuries away.

Jiankou means 'arrow notch', named for the way the mountains hook around the flat-floored valley. It's also surely a reference to the weapon that proved so lethal in the hands of the warriors from beyond the Great Wall – the very reason for its existence in the first place. It's on quiet days in places like Jiankou when the romance of the wild Great Wall is conjured: miles of brick and stone, crumbling and overgrown, epic beyond imagination. A testament to the rise and fall of empires, of threats long vanished and military technologies long since superseded.

To journey west along the Wall from here, one would need climbing equipment and comprehensive insurance cover.

Gravity-defying stretches with names like 'Soaring Eagle' and 'Sky Stair' beg the question: how did they build this, all those centuries ago? Hiking eastwards, the Great Wall tapers gently down mountains, and some hours later the wild battlements meet the upper reaches of the restored Mutianyu section. Climbing over a barricade onto smooth, recently laid cobbles, you're greeted by looks of astonishment from puffed-out tourists, who can only wonder at what discoveries lie beyond.

Jiankou is 1½ hours from Beijing. Take bus 916 from Dongzhimen to Huairou, then transfer to a taxi for the final stretch.

ᴢʜᴇᴊɪᴀɴɢ Pʀᴏᴠɪɴᴄᴇ, Cʜɪɴᴀ, 29.0641 / 119.1900

LONGYOU CAVES

Generations of locals thought Longyou's ponds were bottomless, but discoveries in 1992 revealed something far more interesting: 36 hand-carved caves. More than 30,000 sq m of manmade grottoes have been discovered so far. Floor to ceiling, each is roughly 30m, and every chamber is decorated with the same repetitive pattern of parallel lines, hand-chiseled in sandstone. Archaeologists' best guess is that the caves date to just before the Qin Dynasty, approximately 200BC, though no written record of their construction or meaning has yet been unearthed.

Five chambers have been opened for tourism, allowing visitors to marvel at symbols etched in the stone – fish, birds and animals. Also puzzling is how the caves were constructed with such precision (some walls are barely 50cm thick) and over what period of time. Scientists have estimated that a million cubic metres of stone would have been removed to hollow out the cave system. The pattern of parallel markings throughout would also have required an enormous amount of time.

One theory is that the Longyou Caves are an earthly recreation of the cosmos: the distribution of seven of its chambers have been compared to the formation of 'The Plough', part of the Ursa Major constellation. But many years are likely to pass before Longyou's secrets are revealed.

☞ *Jinhua, 55km east of the caves, is an ideal springboard to visit Longyou. See www.longyoushiku.com.*

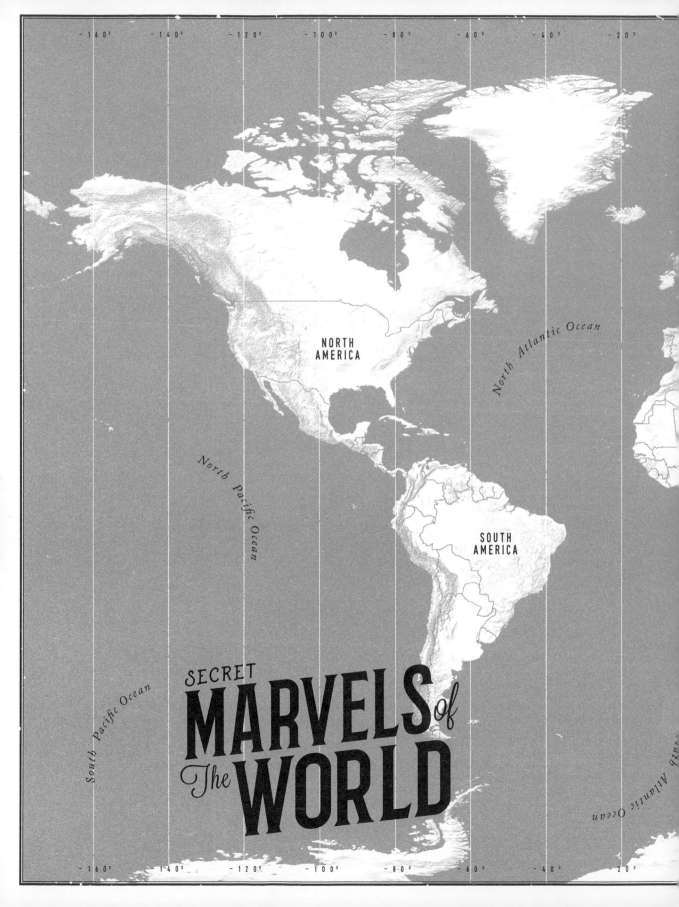

SECRET
MARVELS of
The WORLD

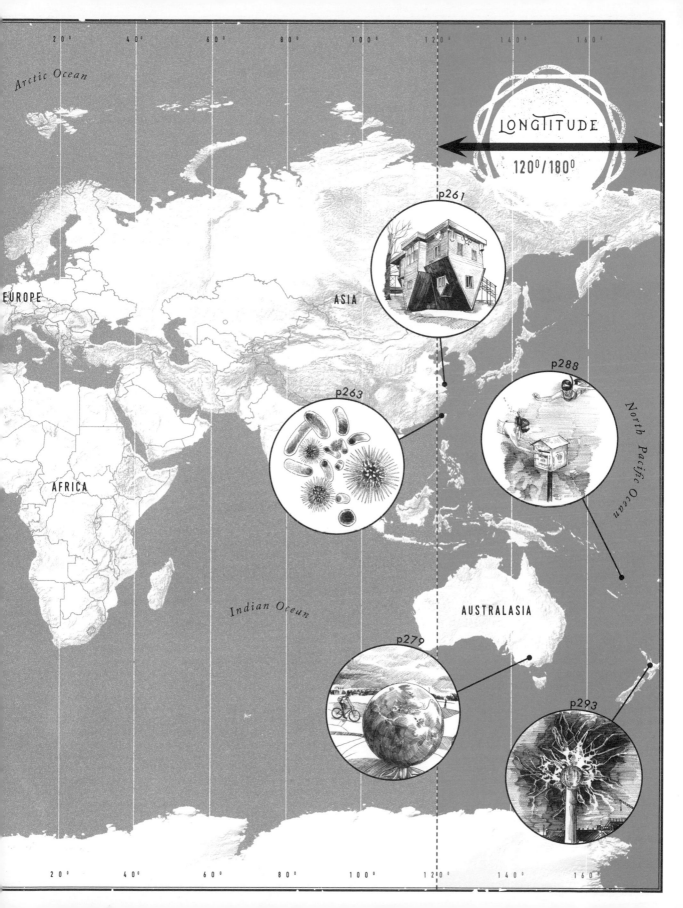

Arctic Ocean

EUROPE

AFRICA

Indian Ocean

AUSTRALASIA

North Pacific Ocean

NANTUN DISTRICT, TAIWAN,
24.1340 / 120.6114

RAINBOW VILLAGE

Former soldier Huang Yung-Fu breathed life into his fading village by painting it with birds, flowers and other riotously colourful designs. Almost a ghost town, this village near Taichung has turned into a local curiosity, growing ever-more kaleidoscopic with every lick of paint. Yung-Fu has been dubbed 'Grandpa Rainbow' because of his quest to brighten the village. Once home to military dependants, the village's population has all but departed; it's thought that Grandpa Rainbow is now the only permanent resident. He hoped that his work would save the village from destruction, but it's rumoured the government is biding its time before bulldozing it anyway. See this multi-coloured miracle while you still can.

☛ The rainbow village is in Nantun District, 8km west of central Taichung.

Near Shanghai, China.
30.8850 / 121.0154

UPSIDE-DOWN HOUSE

You can find out exactly what it feels like to dance on the ceiling like Lionel Richie at this unusual attraction. The weird and wacky Upside-Down House is a not-so-ideal home experience at the China Folk Painting Village, a tourist attraction in a historic canal town about an hour outside Shanghai. Designed to dizzy and disorientate, from the outside it looks like a passing tornado has scooped up a Scandinavian-style detached house and dumped it on its head. On the inside, sofas, appliances, cuddly toys and a fully-laid table dangle like furnished stalactites above your head. Even the toilet seat is up, which must mean an upside-down man lives there.

🐟 From Shanghai, take Metro Line 1 to Jinjiang Park Station, then taxi or bus to Fengjing Bus Station.

WA, Australia, −29.3640 / 120.6315

Lake Ballard

Lake Ballard is a salt lake, hazy as a mirage under outback sun. In this isolated landscape it's hard to tell if I'm looking at land or sky, or to imagine who or what made the tracks that meander between solitary figures dotted across the lake's surface. These 51 metal statues collectively form Inside Australia, British sculptor Antony Gormley's representation of the 51 residents of nearby township Menzies. Walking onto the lake, distance is deceptive. It's as if the figures are swimming in and out of focus, in and out of reach. Later I return at full moon, adding another perspective to this extraordinary place.
By Virginia Jealous

🐟 Lake Ballard is 51km from Menzies by road, and 200km from the nearest airport at Kalgoorlie.

© Alex Franklin / Alamy

⦿ SAGADA, ⦿ PHILIPPINES, 17.0818 / 120.9059

HANGING COFFINS

The hanging coffins of Sagada cradle their dead in a limbo between Heaven and Earth. At this vertiginous, open-air cemetery in Luzon's mountainous north, coffins are strapped to the side of steep cliffs. Following the traditions of indigenous Igorot peoples, the most honoured dead occupy higher parts of the cliff face, closer to the spirits of their ancestors. The tradition is practical, too: in hanging coffins, the dead are beyond reach of scavenging animals and floods. In past centuries, this burial rite was also a deterrent against rival tribes who might seek to grave-rob the heads of their enemies.

Igorot culture is at ease with the realities of death.

Some even fashion their own coffins, assisted by relatives if they are too frail. After death, a person's remains will be smoked, tightly wrapped in cloth, and carried to the cliffs. Along the way, relatives and well-wishers flock to touch the shrouded body, which is believed to bestow wisdom and luck. Coffins are designed to be snug: bodies are put in a foetal position, so the deceased's departure from life echoes their birth. Bones are sometimes broken to squeeze the body into its final resting pose. In modern Sagada, only elders follow these customs. Whether or not the practise endures, Sagada's hanging coffins are likely to loom over these misty valleys for centuries to come.

 See coffins in Echo Valley, a 30-minute hike (best taken with a guide) from Sagada's St Mary Church.

YILAN, TAIWAN, 24.7764 / 121.7352

BENEFICIAL MICROBES MUSEUM

No need to reach for the hand sanitiser. This Taiwanese museum intends to make visitors feel warm and fuzzy about bacteria, helping even germophobes to understand the microscopic organisms that inhabit our skin and guts. Visitors will learn about a host of friendly micro-organisms: there's *Lactobacillus johnsonii*, which helps humans to digest dairy; a suppressor of harmful bacteria named *Bifidobacterium longum*; and the bouncers of the bacteria world, *viridans streptococci*, which stand guard in human throats, preventing nastier microbes from entering. Expect fungus workshops, skin-care experiments and educational games for kids. You'll leave giving a silent salute to the colonies fighting the good fight in your body.

The museum is on Meizhou 1st Road in Yilan, 50km south of Taipei. See www bio-nin.com.tw.

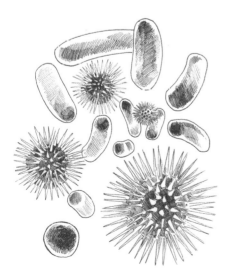

© Luca Tettoni / Getty Images

SAN JOAQUIN, PHILIPPINES, 10.5859 / 122.1410

SAN JOAQUIN CHURCH

This church in the Philippines is a sanctuary for contemplation, prayer and military might. The Roman Catholic parish in San Joaquin was built in 1869 from limestone and coral plucked from the Panay Gulf. Worshippers walking into church are greeted by a no-holds-barred battle scene – complete with soldiers on horseback and cocked rifles – carved in relief on the tympanum. This striking carving shows the Spanish victory over Moroccan troops in the Battle of Tetouan in 1860. Brawny soldiers might seem an unusual accompaniment to prayer, but coastal towns in the Philippines had suffered numerous Moorish raids, so the victory at Tetouan resonated deeply with local people.

Drive west from Iloilo City along the coastal road to reach San Joaquin.

SHENGSHAN ISLAND, CHINA.
30.7210 / 122.8221

HOUTOU WAN

Ghost towns are usually desolate places, but this fishing village on Shengshan Island, almost entirely carpeted in green, has a magical air. Many islands in the Zhoushan archipelago off China's east coast, have experienced ebbing populations as job-seekers flock to larger cities. Only a few dozen inhabitants remain in Houtou Wan. They are mostly elderly, loyal to their village but powerless to stop it from being slowly camouflaged by creepers and trees. Exploring the village is both eerie and uplifting: houses tumble haphazardly downhill to the sea, every stairwell and pathway choked with vines. Many houses lie empty, their dust-laden furnishings now a curiosity for tourists.

 Reach Shengshan Island from Shengsi, served by ferry services from Shanghai.

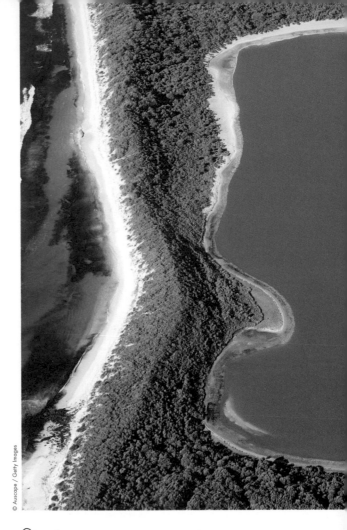

WA, AUSTRALIA. −34.0950 / 123.2028

LAKE HILLIER

Look at any map and chances are that all the bodies of water have been coloured blue. But if you were to draw Middle Island, part of Australia's little-known Recherche Archipelago, you'd need a pink crayon (preferably of a bubble-gum hue) to accurately depict its most striking landmark: Lake Hillier. Scientists aren't entirely sure how the lake got so pink. After all, it stands in stark contrast to the deep blue waves of the Southern Ocean just metres away. Unlike most coloured lakes, Hillier's hue is neither a reflection of the lakebed nor influenced by the dye of seasonal bacteria. As such, it retains its pink colour even when placed in a bottle.

Middle Island is part of a wilderness area that's off-limits to tourists, but you can still view Lake Hillier on a two-hour helicopter tour from Esperance, Western Australia.

IRIOMOTE, JAPAN, 24.4191 / 123.7995
STAR SAND BEACHES

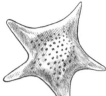

Scoop up the sand of Iriomote Island and you can hold entire constellations in your palm (if you look closely enough). Legends say that the star-shaped grains of sand on beaches around this tropical archipelago, closer to Taiwan than Japan's main islands, are the offspring of stars. In reality they are the prickly exoskeletons of tiny marine organisms, which amass in their millions on beaches along the northern coast of Iriomote Island. Starry sands are especially striking after storms churn up the sea bed, washing more miniature fossils ashore. Sadly, some local souvenir sellers are depleting the beaches of their unique sand by bottling it for tourists.

🕊 *Catch a ferry to Iriomote from Ishigaki Island, which is linked by flights from Tokyo.*

PANMUNJOM, SOUTH KOREA, 37.9557 / 126.6766
KOREAN DEMILITARIZED ZONE

A holiday on the edge of apocalypse might not be everyone's cup of Koryo (hangover-free ginseng liquor), but the 4km-wide, 240km-long buffer zone between North and South Korea is arguably the most famous sight on the whole Korean peninsula. And it has to be said, there's an undeniable frisson that comes from standing between gun-toting enemies surrounded by over a million landmines.

The place to come for a glimpse of Armageddon, and a peek across the razor wire into the secretive Democratic People's Republic of Korea, is Panmunjom, the tense 'truce village' in the Joint Security Area, just 55km from Seoul. Access is only via organised tour; ripped jeans, casual sportswear and T-shirts with provocative slogans are banned.

🕊 *Most people make arrangements in Seoul. Visits are permitted at 9.45am, 1.15pm and 3.15pm.*

JEJU, SOUTH KOREA, 33.5194 / 126.5241

HAENYEO

The women divers of Jeju island are known as Korea's mermaids. Since the 18th century, the haenyeo have plunged to incredible depths to retrieve octopus, abalone and sea urchins, passing their skills from mother to daughter. For many years, the economic clout that came with their diving skills made them heads of their households. While the tradition is slowly fading, Jeju still has many mermaids, some of them still diving at 80 years old.

Many haenyeo begin as children, scrabbling for seaweed in shallow waters before progressing to daring dives, ranking their skills by how deep they can go. Through years of experience, haenyeo train themselves to hold their breath for minutes at a time. For many, it's addictive: not just the rush of the dive and the thrill of seizing a catch with their own hands, but the economic independence that comes with it. The haenyeo divers have also become mournful observers of the effects of pollution on sea life, watching as the sea floor gradually empties of abalone.

Some locals still insist that male divers are too fragile to withstand cold waters, and that it would be scandalous for male and female divers to work together. While city jobs have lured many would-be haenyeo from the island, the Korean government still subsidises the diving equipment and healthcare of Jeju's mermaids.

 Jeju floats off Korea's southern coast. Numerous airlines fly to Jeju from Seoul and Busan.

ⓃEAR ⓈEOUL, ⓈOUTH ⓀORFA, 37.7519 / 128.8761

North Korean Submarine

The first thing that hits me is the metal smell. I dip my head through the studded doorway, seizing the handrail, which is rubbed bright and reeks of coins and saltwater. I clomp through the cramped stomach of the submarine and can't believe I'm standing in the spot where 26 North Korean crew spied on South Korea. The sub ran aground just near here in 1996, on a coast so remote that I'm the only tourist here today. The welded seams are exposed, as if no civilian was meant to witness this place. Yet I budge the cranks of a chunky machine to awaken it – nothing. In his panic, the commander burned his cache of secret documents; I touch the still-scorched wall, the stain like a dark speech bubble. Then I escape back into the daylight. By Phillip Tang

🛥 *Open daily 9am-4.30pm. Take the Seoul–Gang-neung bus, then a local bus to Unification Park.*

© Epa Euro:aean Pressphoto Agency B.V. / Alamy

ⒸHINA & ⓃORTH ⓀOREA, 42.0108 / 128.0661

HEAVEN LAKE

The caldera lake at the top of Mt Paektu may look serene, but it has associations with Loch Ness-style monsters and North Korean dictators. Straddling the border between China and North Korea at an altitude of 2189m, the crater lake is subject to persistent rumours about not one, but several watery beasts with long necks and horned heads. The 'Tianchi Lake Monsters' haven't been seen since some grainy footage emerged in 2007. But that's not to say that the lake has been silent: North Korea's state news agency declared that the lake's covering of winter ice cracked with grief when leader Kim Jong-Il died in 2011.

🛥 *Drive into the nature reserve through Erdaobaihezhen; the lake is 60km south.*

10 TOP TREMENDOUS TOILETS

SUWON, SOUTH KOREA, 37.3192 / 126.9780

① Mr Toilet House

Suppress your bashfulness at these monuments to the call of nature. From loos with views to sculptures that flush, these sights edify the humble toilet in all its forms. In Suwon, the 'Mr Toilet House' theme park turns humanity's most basic necessity into a family day out. Browse the toilet-shaped museum and snap photos of a big golden turd.

☛ *Local buses run from Sungkyunkwan University station to within 500m of the museum. See www.haewoojae.com.*

CHONGQING, CHINA, 29.6102 / 106.6015

② Porcelain Palace

Antoni Gaudí, who famously shaped Barcelona's skyline, probably didn't expect a toilet-themed tribute. But the world's largest toilet complex in Chongqing not only has 1000 urinals and toilets, it imitates the colours and tilework of the modernist architect.

☛ *Find it in the 'Foreigners' Street' area.*

LADAKH, INDIA, 34.0570 / 77.6672

③ Thiksey Gompa

Come for the Tibetan Buddhist art, linger for the loos. Urinals at this 3600m-altitude monastery overlook a valley panorama, allowing gents to spend a penny while contemplating the majesty of the mountains.

☛ *The monastery is 20km south of Leh, connected by local buses.*

SELÇUK, TURKEY, 37.9386 / 27.3423

④ Ephesus Toilets

There are no secrets in ancient bathhouses. These 1st-century AD municipal lavatories are a familiar sight, ovoid in shape and made of marble; except there are 36 of them laid out in long, sociable rows.

☛ *Ephesus archaeological site is near Selçuk in western Turkey.*

⑧

⑤ Toto Museum

KITAKYUSHU, JAPAN. 33.8722 / 130.8720

The high-tech toilets of Japan, with water jets, music and heated seats, are admired (and chuckled at) worldwide. Take the plunge and learn about their development at this museum of plumbing.

☞ Take the 21, 22 or 43 bus from Kokura station. See www.toto.co.jp.

⑥ Zero Aldwych

LONDON, ENGLAND. 51.5115 / -0.1193

Not keen on lingering all night in a lavatory? Cellar Door will change your mind. A public convenience once notorious in London's gay swinging scene has been transformed into a chic cocktail bar.

☞ Find the stairs to the bar between Aldwych and the Strand. See www.cellardoor.biz.

⑦ Manneken Pis

BRUSSELS, BELGIUM. 50.8450 / 4.3500

A cheeky 17th-century tribute to the joy of urination repeatedly ranks among Europe's most overrated sights. But this 60cm bronze of a boy peeing remains a symbol of Brussels' nonconformism and humour.

☞ Look for him between Rue du Chêne and Rue de l'Etuve.

⑧ Toilet Fountain

FOSHAN, CHINA. 23.0084 / 113.0819

Artist Shu Yong assembled 10,000 toilets, urinals and sinks into a 100m-long latrine-themed sculpture. This great wall took two months to create; visitors scramble to take pictures during its flushing cycles.

☞ It's on permanent display in Foshan's Shiwan Park, in central Guangdong.

⑨ Mumin Papa Cafe

AKASHI, JAPAN. 34.6506 / 134.9615

Answer the call of nature under the curious gaze of a sea turtle at this cafe in Akashi. The ladies' bathroom is enclosed by a huge aquarium, so you can scrutinise a marine scene through floor-to-ceiling glass.

☞ The cafe is at 60 Matsue, 500m from Akashi's Matsue Park.

⑩ Elvis Toilet

TENNESSEE, USA. 35.0474 / -90.0262

The porcelain throne in Elvis Presley's Memphis mansion is where the musical legend breathed (and strained) his last. Visitors to Graceland stand directly beneath the bathroom as they enter.

☞ Although the upper floor is cordoned off, superfans write to Elvis' descendants to request access.

⑦

© Shutterstock

'Vine–choked alleyways are strewn with rubble from the evocative, artful decay… I feel like I'm being escorted into a world of science fiction'

NAGASAKI, JAPAN, 32.6278 / 129.7386

Hashima

As the boat leaves Nagasaki Port, heading for the 'Ghost Island' of Hashima, I'm finding it hard to keep calm. I keep scanning the horizon for the unmistakable ship-like silhouette that gives the place its nickname: Battleship Island. We leave the shoreline, passing boats, barges, and uninhabited small islands, then someone calls: 'There it is!' Sure enough, just like a naval warship, the island seems to float on the surface of the water, faded yet unmistakeable against the azure sky.

Visiting Hashima had been on my bucket list for years, first while living in Japan in the '90s, then later again as photos of this wasteland cityscape began to surface in popular culture. Most famously, it was used as the villain's lair in the 2012 James Bond film, *Skyfall*.

Ironically, Hashima, owned by a coal company, was once the most densely populated place in Japan. When the coal mine closed in 1974, however, it took only four months for the island to be abandoned. Its dormitories, equipment, schools, clinics, and temples were all left behind like something out of a post-apocalyptic dream. Now buildings have sloughed away, revealing forgotten dolls, televisions, and kitchen appliances. Vine-choked alleyways are strewn with rubble from the evocative, artful decay. As we arrive and clamber out onto walkways, I feel like I'm being escorted into a world of science fiction. Rusted iron spikes are twisted into claw-like fingers. The mine shaft seems like a gaping mouth. I blink and see ghosts of miners coming up from the depths, blackened from head to toe.

We stop at a safe distance away from the structures, in case of sudden collapses. The group, a chatty bunch of mainly Japanese tourists, has fallen silent, sombre. I imagine spending a night on the island, watching as the sun soaks the cement. It's impressively bleak, devoid of not just human life, but any life at all. I'm hard-pressed to spot even a seagull wheeling around in the sky. As we return to the boat, I think of the Inca, the Maya, the Anasazi, the Egyptian Pharoahs. Will Tokyo and New York and Paris look like this someday? Who lived here? People will wonder, as they pass along marked paths. What caused them to leave? Where did they go? When the boat finally docks, the throngs of people around me seem more precious, and more fragile. It's a feeling that takes a long time to fade. *By Ray Bartlett*

☛ *Access is only via guided tour from Nagasaki's port; tours leave once or twice daily. See www.gunkanjima-concierge.com.*

ⒽIROSHIMA, ⒿAPAN, 34.3916 / 132.4532

HIROSHIMA SHADOWS

The ruined 'Atomic Bomb Dome' still stands by the Ota River, a silent witness to the 1945 bombing of Hiroshima. But the most haunting reminders of how human life can be destroyed in milliseconds are the Hiroshima shadows. Thermal radiation emitted by the blast bleached the surface of roads and walls in Hiroshima; where people stood in the way, permanent 'shadows' were left behind. Most of these silhouettes have faded or been lost during the rebuilding of the city. But some are preserved in Hiroshima Peace Memorial Museum, including the steps of Sumitomo Bank. These slabs of stone are indelibly marked with the shadow of a person who was sitting there when the bomb fell.

🖝 *The museum is part of Hiroshima's moving Peace Memorial Park complex.*

ⒶLICE ⓈPRINGS, ⒶUSTRALIA, −23.8021 / 134.4368

HENLEY ON TODD REGATTA

A uniquely Australian boat race that takes place on a dry river bed (yes, dry), the Henley on Todd Regatta was first held in 1962 to poke fun at the formality of traditional British regattas (ie those held in water). 'Boats' made from metal frames covered in advertising are carried, pushed or pulled by 'rowers,' culminating in the Battle of the Boats – trucks modified to resemble boats, armed with confetti bombs and water hoses (warning: despite this being a dry race, spectators may still get wet). The spectacle is whimsical, nonsensical and a whole lot of fun, and anyone can take part – just turn up early to enter.

🖝 *Held annually on the third Saturday in August, on the Todd River outside Alice Springs. For more info, see henleyontodd.com.au.*

Les Archives du Coeur

At Christian Boltanski's installation Les Archives de Cœur, a 'heartbeat archive' in a plain building beside a scrubby cove on the island of Teshima, I entered the dark 'heart room'. Suddenly I was surrounded by the loud thump of a human heart, a single light pulsing in rhythm glancing across black-mirrored walls. Recordings of heartbeats taken from thousands of people (and at least one Swedish dog) are played one after another, creating an oddly intimate experience – how often do you hear another person's heart, unless resting an ear on their chest? Stepping out of the dark, I went to the 'recording room' and added my own beat to the library.
By Laura Crawford

🐏 Teshima is in the Seto Inland Sea with ferry links to various nearby destinations.

© De Agostini / Getty Images

RAI STONES

What is money? Chances are you pay for things with fancy paper, but the people of Yap, in Micronesia, rarely use bills for big purchases. Instead, they use giant limestone wheels. Sound crazy? Get this: there's not a single source of limestone on the island. So where did Yap get all of its so-called rai stones? Local lore has it that 500 years ago some fishermen washed up in Palau, 400km away, and traded goods for quarried limestone. The stones were then carved, brought back to Yap by canoe, and refashioned into donut-shaped discs that served as the island's main currency. Rai stones can measure up to 3m high and weigh five tonnes. Rarely moved, ownership is simply recorded in the oral history.

🐏 United Airlines offers a few flights each week to Yap via Guam or Palau.

'The daytime heat is so oppressive that I opt to play at night with a glow-in-the-dark golf ball. The course is utterly lunar-like in appearance'

SA. AUSTRALIA. -29.0069 / 134.7294

Coober Pedy's Grassless Golf Course

Mining towns tend to be pretty soulless places inhabited by gruff grunts and slick-suited businessmen with dollar signs for eyeballs. I, like most tourists, don't visit these places. But then I heard about a mining town located in the rear end of the Australian outback that was anything but typical. I was going through a phase where I wanted to be the kind of traveller who visits not just pretty places, but the ugly ones, too. So I booked a ticket.

Flying into Coober Pedy, I couldn't spot a town anywhere in sight. In fact, it looked like a team of extremely large, hungry earthworms had invaded the land below, leaving behind towering pits of rubble and little else. Turns out those holes are mines and what you find in them are opals. Lots of opals. In fact, an estimated 80% of the world's supply comes from Coober Pedy,

whose subterranean layers are bejewelled with incandescent stones.

Vibrant, too, is the life residents have carved out of this burnt-red earth. Yanni Athanasiadis, owner of the Umoona Opal Mine, is among the vast majority of residents who live in manmade caves. 'When I first came to Coober Pedy from Greece 41 years ago, I said, "Oh no. What have I done?" he recalled, as we toured his underground home. After sleeping beneath the earth for decades, however, he tells me he couldn't imagine ever living above ground again.

Dugouts like this one maintain a pleasant year-round temperature of about 24°C, making them a great escape from outback extremes. Coober Pedy also boasts glorious subterranean churches and cavernous underground hotels.

Yet its most curious attraction may be the one aboveground.

There's only one golf club in the world with reciprocal rights at 'the home of golf,' St Andrews, and it's right here in Coober Pedy. The daytime heat is so oppressive that I opt to play at night with a glow-in-the-dark golf ball. The only grass this ball will touch is the carpet of artificial turf I'm holding in my hand for teeing. The rest of the 18-hole course is utterly lunar-like in appearance. It's also so difficult that the last of my three glowing balls goes missing down one of Coober Pedy's signature wormholes, destined to become yet another shimmering orb lost to its kaleidoscopic underworld. *By Mark Johanson*

Five flights per week link Coober Pedy with Adelaide. Head to the Old Timers Mine to hire clubs and book the course.

①NARA, JAPAN, 34.6855 / 135.8421
NARA DEER PARK

For thirteen centuries, the most prominent residents of Nara have been the wild Sika deer who roam the city freely. Legends says that in the 8th century, a mythical deity rode into town on a white deer, proclaiming himself protector of Heijō-kyō (as Nara was then called). Until the end of the Second World War, the deer were considered sacred, and they are now considered national treasures.

More than 1200 deer wander freely through stores, restaurants, and homes in Nara. Be prepared for them to head-butt you to prompt you to feed them – they aggressively eat anything, including belts, purses and cameras. Many have learned to bow when fed, and they are so used to humans, they will think nothing of coming right up to you to ask for a snack. Think Bambi with attitude.

🐾 *Nara is 375km south of Tokyo; the Nozomi bullet train makes the journey in 3½ hours.*

②SA, AUSTRALIA, -34.6453 / 138.8465
WHISPERING WALL

Most people come to South Australia's Barossa Valley to taste its wines, but a few visitors venture here from nearby Adelaide for a different reason altogether. They come to whisper. The curved concrete dam of Barossa Reservoir is known for its parabola effect, wherein even a soft whisper can be heard on the far side of the dam some 140m away. Legend has it that the astounding acoustic properties of this nine-storey-high beast were first discovered by a construction supervisor who, after hearing his workers complaining about him, fired them from the opposite side of the dam.

🐾 *Located on the northern edge of Barossa Reservoir, about 50km northeast of Adelaide, the wall is free to visit from 8am to 5pm daily.*

ⒻFUJI ⓇREGION, ⒿJAPAN, 35.4626 / 138.6544

AOKIGAHARA FOREST

Some enter the dense forest of Aokigahara with no intention of ever coming out. Aokigahara has become the world's second-biggest suicide location, beaten only to this macabre title by the Golden Gate Bridge.

Located on the northwest slopes of Mount Fuji, this disorienting forest bestows an instant feeling of isolation. Its volcanic soil is pockmarked with caves, roots knot the ground, and densely packed trees act as sound insulation (and often block GPS signals). This impenetrability gave the forest its name, meaning 'sea of trees', and it can conceal victims of suicide for months, even years, before they are found via trails of their discarded belongings.

Up to 100 bodies were being recovered from the forest annually until the early 2000s, when authorities decided to stop sharing the numbers. Today, signs near the forest read 'life is a precious gift from your parents'. Occasionally, anti-suicide patrols pass through, hoping to help distressed individuals before they enter the forest. The cultural stigma attached to suicide isn't as strong in Japan as in many western countries, due to a historic tradition of honourable suicide among the Samurai. References to romantic suicide are sewn in to popular music and film.

🐦 *Drive to the forest from Fujikawaguchiko or, if you're coming from Tokyo by rail, change at Ōtsuki.*

ⒿJIGOKUDANI, ⒿJAPAN, 36.7330 / 138.4611

JIGOKUDANI HOT SPRINGS

We have 98% of our DNA in common with monkeys, so why shouldn't they share the very human joy of soaking in a hot bath? Jigokudani was named 'Hell Valley' because of its steaming springs and saw-edged cliffs. But there is nothing infernal about the sight of Japanese macaques (or 'snow monkeys') lolling in the naturally hot pools, particularly during the four months of the year when the valley is coated in snow. Japanese macaques are the most northerly primates in the world. Bathing isn't their only human-like habit: scientists have seen them washing food before eating it, and even making snowballs.

🐦 *The park is open year-round but bathing macaques are only guaranteed in winter. Buses run between Nagano rail station and the car park, a 30-minute walk from the springs. See en. jigokudani-yaenkoen.co.jp.*

TASHIROJIMA, JAPAN. 38.2955 / 141.4179

CAT ISLAND

As your boat glides towards the harbour, a furry welcoming crew stands on the dock. Dozens of cats, the dominant residents here, greet the arriving boats, mewling for food scraps and checking that no forbidden dogs make it ashore.

Cats outnumber humans by six to one on Tashirojima, and the ratio seems likely to increase in their favour, given the island's ageing population. Feline numbers swelled thanks to enduring beliefs that they bring good luck, and that fortune can be further cultivated by caring for them. Keeping them as pets is considered unseemly, so the kitty population roams freely on the island: perching on roofs, stalking through alleys, and making a lovable nuisance of themselves around the island.

Tashirojima's two historic industries, silk and fishing, have ensured centuries of red-carpet treatment for cats. During the Edo period, cats were encouraged to chase mice away from silk worms, thereby safeguarding the source of the island's wealth. Later on, it was the fishing industry that cared for Tashirojima's cats. Fishermen became accustomed to the sight of cats begging for scraps of the day's catch. Soon, feline mood swings were being interpreted in an attempt to predict weather at sea. Superstitious locals even consider cats to be lucky charms that protected the island from worse destruction during the 2011 tsunami.

 Catch a ferry to the island from Ishinomaki in northern Honshu; it is best explored as a day trip.

MELBOURNE, AUSTRALIA.
−37.8722 / 144.9759

SOLAR SYSTEM TRAIL

Navigate our solar system from the sun to the outer planets without ever leaving earth on Melbourne's geektastic Solar System Trail. This self-guided path between St Kilda and Port Melbourne offers a model of our solar system to a scale of one to one billion. That means you can cut the astronomical 5.9-billion km journey from the sun to Pluto down to a more earthly 5.9km stroll. Not only that – because of the crescent shape of Port Phillip Bay, you can actually view the sun from all nine model locations along the way. A team of artists and scientists came together to build this marvel in 2008 and it's been blowing minds ever since.

☛ Start at the sun sculpture at the south end of St Kilda Beach. The entire walk should last about 90 minutes.

MELBOURNE, AUSTRALIA. −37.8171 / 144.9453

COW UP A TREE SCULPTURE

If asked to interpret the twin Australian themes of flooding and camouflage cows would you think of an 8m sculpture of a cow in a tree? Well, that's what blossomed from the imagination of artist John Kelly – a tiny-headed, grotesquely bloated cow stuck upside down in a gum tree. Wait a minute: camouflage cows? What the heck? Well, during WWII, artist William Dobell crafted life-sized papier mâché cows and moved them around air fields and military bases in an attempt to fool Japanese pilots. Though if Dobell's camouflage cows looked anything like Kelly's bizarre block-bodied cow in the tree, then it'll come as no surprise that the Japanese airmen weren't fooled for a second.

☛ Cow up a Tree is on Harbour Esplanade in Melbourne's Docklands. Hop on tram 35, the free city circle tram.

CANBERRA, AUSTRALIA. -37.6333 / 145.0833

FUTURO HOUSE

Visitors to the University of Canberra could be forgiven for thinking a UFO has landed on campus. Supported by four steel legs, the space-age, pod-like structure may look like something from the Jetsons – complete with a hatch-like entry and drop-down staircase – but it's actually one of the world's only remaining examples of a Futuro House, designed by visionary Finnish architect Matti Suuronen in 1968. Originally intended as ski chalets or holiday houses, the prefabricated Futuros could be transported in several pieces and assembled in just a few days – or even airlifted in one piece by helicopter! The revolutionary design attracted global attention,

but its fanfare was short-lived; the 1973 oil crisis pushed up the price of plastic (a key component of the buildings), customers cancelled their orders, and only about 100 were ever constructed. Few were used as dwellings; some were turned into cafes or real-estate agencies in the USA, some were used as Swedish watchtowers, and this one was shifted around Canberra before eventually being used, fittingly, at an observatory. In 2011 the damaged and disused Futuro was donated to the university, where it was painstakingly restored and reassembled. Now the space is a student workspace, and a must-see for anyone who's ever wondered what the future might look like.

 Futuro House is next to Building 5, University of Canberra; take bus 3 from City Bus Station.

© Rob Cleary / OEH

NSW, AUSTRALIA, -30.2733 / 150.1643
GIANT PINK SLUGS OF MOUNT KAPUTAR

Arrive at Mt Kaputar National Park on a rainy night and you're in for a slimy surprise in the form of a creature that's better fit for the pages of R.L. Stine's Goosebumps books than the mountains of northern New South Wales. It's a creature that's as wet as your tongue, as long as a cucumber and as fluorescent pink as a nylon tutu. Picture, if you dare, a giant pink slug. This creepy crawler can grow up to 20cm long and is only found in the damp alpine forests atop Mt Kaputar, a remote peak that's the tallest of Australia's Nandewar Range. These hot pink slugs (*Triboniophorus aff. graeffei*) spend most of their time feeding underground, but rise to the surface after it rains to munch on lichen and tree moss. Remarkably, they're but one of many endemic invertebrates who've lived here in relative isolation for millions of years. Their brethren include the equally flamboyant red triangle slug and at least three species of carnivorous, cannibal land snails that roam Mt Kaputar in search of prey. These creatures are all marooned together 1500m above sea level atop the remnants of an extinct volcano, which was active about 18 million years ago. Scientists say this unique high-altitude habitat on Mt Kaputar offers a remarkable glimpse into Australia's geological past.

Mt Kaputar National Park is a 30km drive east of Narrabri, with campgrounds and bushwalking areas.

RUNIT ISLAND, MARSHALL ISLANDS, 11.5527 / 162.3474
RUNIT DOME

On a tranquil coral atoll surrounded by turquoise water lies something that looks like a half-buried UFO – but the reality is much more sinister than that. In 1958, US nuclear testing (dubbed 'the Cactus test') left a huge crater on Runit Island. Other nuclear tests in the surrounding area had led to high levels of contamination and something had to be done to clean it up. So, in the late 1970s, the radioactive debris was mixed with contaminated topsoil, dumped in the crater, and sealed beneath a 46cm-thick concrete dome. It's a bizarre and lasting legacy of nuclear war that's rendered the island uninhabitable ever since.

Runit Island can be seen by boat from neighbouring islands – since it's home to radioactive waste, visiting is not recommended.

◉ NSW, AUSTRALIA, -33.8333 / 151.0766

SS AYRFIELD

Plenty of cities sink decommissioned cargo ships off their shores to create artificial reefs, but what happens when you let a 1140-tonne hunk of steel languish on the surface unused for nearly 50 years? In the case of the SS *Ayrfield*, located just west of Sydney, you get a majestic 'floating forest' where bushy mangroves fight for space atop a rusted hull. The *Ayrfield* was built in 1911 and became a vital tool in helping the Australian Government deliver supplies to US troops stationed in the Pacific during World War II (when it was know as SS *Corrimal*). The ship spent the rest of its life as a collier running supplies between Sydney and Newcastle, until it

was retired from service in 1972. It was then sent to a ship-breaking yard in Homebush Bay, near the present-day Olympic Park, where it remains alongside three other decommissioned ships that were never torn apart. None of the other wrecks clinging to life atop this ship graveyard boast as spectacular foliage as the oft-photographed *Ayrfield*. Its resident mangroves have grown in size over the years and now billow over both sides of the hull, slowly ripping the ship apart at its seams. The *Ayrfield* may have survived a war and evaded dismemberment, but it's only a matter of time before it succumbs to the encroaching hand of nature.

🚂 *Take the train from Sydney's Central Station to Rhodes. Cross Bennelong Bridge for the best views.*

KAMCHATKA PENINSULA, RUSSIA, 54.4360 / 160.1363

VALLEY OF GEYSERS

Stretching towards Japan, the Kamchatka Peninsula in Russia's far east is a place where the Earth's fuming fury is never far from the surface. Kamchatka's 6km-long Valley of Geysers is fed by the 250°C heat of the stratovolcano Kikhpinych. More than 100 hot springs and geysers huff steam into the frigid air. This basin in Kronotsky Nature Reserve is so far-flung that its geological marvels were only fully explored in the 1970s. One of the most chilling discoveries was the Valley of Death, a narrow 2km-long creek where volcanic gases accumulate in such a high concentration that they kill animals and birds who stray too close.

Reach the Valley of Geysers by helicopter on a tour with Travel Kamchatka (www.travelkamchatka. com). Flights from Moscow reach the closest airport, Petropavlovsk-Kamchatsky.

TOP 10

AUSTRALIA'S BIG ROADSIDE ATTRACTIONS

Qld. Australia. −26.6726 / 152.9913

① Big Pineapple

Australia has a plethora of ridiculously over-sized roadside attractions designed to attract passing traffic and distract kids from asking 'are we there yet?' on long road trips. Sure, they're kitsch, but that's part of the fun. The Big Pineapple has been visited by the British Royal Family – if it's good enough for royalty, it's good enough for you.

☛ *The Big Pineapple is a 20min drive from Maroochydore in Queensland. The free observation deck is open from 9am to 4pm daily.*

NSW Australia. −31.127869 / 150.922708

② Big Golden Guitar

Instrumental in cementing Tamworth's reputation as Australia's country music capital, the Big Golden Guitar fronts a tourist centre with a wax museum, a display of Sir Donald Bradman memorabilia and, of course, a music shop.

☛ *The Big Golden Guitar is visible from the New England Hwy in Tamworth, NSW. See www.biggoldenguitar.com.au.*

TOP 10

SA. AUSTRALIA. -34.8211 / 138.8922

③ The Big Rocking Horse

Ever wished your toys were bigger? The world's biggest rocking horse opened in 1981 to attract visitors to the onsite toy factory, which is still working today. Climb onto its head for great views.

☛ The Big Rocking Horse is outside Gumeracha, 40km from Adelaide. www.thetoyfactory.com.au.

NSW. AUSTRALIA. -30.2746 / 153.1342

④ Big Banana

As sunny as the smiles it elicits from passersby, the Big Banana adds visual ap-peel to its eponymous fun park, which has waterslides, a banana plantation and, oddly, a cheesemaking workshop. Go bananas!

☛ The Big Banana is on the Pacific Hwy, just outside Coffs Harbour, NSW. www.bigbanana.com.

SA. AUSTRALIA. -36.0243 / 139.0625

⑤ Big Lobster

There are some cracks showing in this colossal crustacean, but that doesn't stop the locals loving him. 'Larry,' as he's affectionately dubbed, has been enticing folk to a seafood restaurant since 1979. If only the kitchen had a super-sized saucepan...

☛ The Big Lobster is on the Princes Hwy in Kingston, South Australia.

VIC. AUSTRALIA. -38.0713 / 145.6556

⑥ Big Pheasant

Sesame Street's got nothing on the big bird at the entrance to Gumbuya Park. The amusement park was once a pheasant farm, and is home to an 8m-high concrete pheasant that once had its bottom blown up by an arsonist. Talk about ruffling feathers!

☛ Gumbuya Park is on the Princes Hwy near Tynong. See www.gumbuya.com.au.

QLD. AUSTRALIA. -17.9342 / 145.9280

⑦ Golden Gumboot

Three Far North Queensland towns regularly compete to see who has the highest annual rainfall. The prize is a rubber boot; to commemorate the competition, a 7.9m Golden Gumboot was built in Tully.

☛ The town of Tully is on the Bruce Hwy between Townsville and Cairns, in Queensland.

NSW. AUSTRALIA. -34.7727 / 149.6905

⑧ The Big Merino

Ramming home the sentiment that Australia rode to prosperity on the sheep's back is this 97-ton 'Rambo'. Built in 1985, it houses an exhibition on wool, with a viewing platform and shop – not baaad at all.

☛ The Big Merino is just off the Hume Hwy in Goulburn, NSW. See www.bigmerino.com.au.

VIC. AUSTRALIA. -36.4641 / 146.2212

⑨ Big Ned Kelly

If you do the crime, you pay the time. If you're Australia's most infamous outlaw, however, you get immortalised by a 6m fibreglass figure in the town where your gang had its last siege. Go figure.

☛ The Big Ned Kelly is in Glenrowan, just off the Hume Hwy near Wangaratta, Victoria.

VIC. AUSTRALIA. -36.9185 / 142.5145

⑩ Giant Koala

This towering, slightly scary-looking critter was recently renamed Sam in memory of a koala that suffered burns in a bushfire and later died of chlamydia. Only in Australia...

☛ The Giant Koala is on the Western Hwy, on the edge of the Grampians National Park in Victoria.

GRANDE TERRE, NEW CALEDONIA,
-20.9377 / 164.6584

THE HEART OF VOH

In normal circumstances, the words 'romantic' and 'mangrove swamp' rarely occur in the same sentence, but in the north of New Caledonia's main island of Grande Terre, the local mangroves seem to have learnt about romance from 165 years of French rule. In an extraordinary show of passion, they have grown to form a natural heart shape that has local microlight pilots in a spin. Best observed from above, La Cœur de Voh has spawned a new business, with enthusiastic romantics taking to the skies to see it – adding a whole new meaning to 'love is in the air'. Most local Kanak people just wonder what all the fuss is about.

🕿 Drive or bus the 270km from Noumea to Koné, then fly by microlight.

HIDEAWAY ISLAND, VANUATU, -17.6991 / 168.2633

UNDERWATER POST OFFICE

Here's a little something to add to any list you may have of things you never dreamed of doing, but totally need to accomplish now that you know they're possible. Things like, say, sending mail underwater. In a marine sanctuary just off the shores of Vanuatu's Hideaway Island there lies an underwater post office where visitors can dive 3m down and drop off mail. This official branch of the Vanuatu Post accepts waterproof postcards that are embossed with an inkless stamp by scuba-diving postal workers. While their brethren on land fight off neighbourhood attack dogs, the intrepid postal workers of Hideaway Island need only to fend away a few curious reef sharks.

🕿 Opening hours are posted on the beach at Hideaway Island resort. A floating flag denotes the post office location.

Ⓝ NEAR QUEENSTOWN, Ⓝ NEW ZEALAND,
-44.8641 / 169.0214

CARDRONA BRA FENCE

Ladies, if when you're driving through
the jaw-dropping mountains of central
Otago you feel the urge to pull over, take
off your bra and hang it on a fence, you
won't be the first. Hundreds of women
have done exactly that. Starting with just
four bras fluttering on the wire, soon there
were hundreds – of every colour and
size, patterned and plain, from sturdy
sports bras to lacy lingerie. Originally not
everyone was supportive of the quirky
attraction; the local council removed the
undergarments (they said the display
was a traffic hazard). However, banning
the bras was a flop and additions soon
appeared from visitors around the globe.

⌁ Find the Bra Fence on Cardrona Valley
Rd, around 50km from Queenstown.

Ⓓ DUNEDIN, Ⓝ NEW ZEALAND, -45.8492 / 170.5343

WORLD'S STEEPEST STREET

Fans of optical illusions take note: there's a 350m-long
residential street in New Zealand's southern city of Dunedin
where, if you snap a photo at an angle, all the houses
appear to be sinking into the ground. That's because the
Guinness World Records calls Baldwin St the world's
steepest drivable street, with a gradient of about 35%.
Historians say its steepness was unintentional and merely
the result of a city grid built with little regard for local
topography. Baldwin St is famous across New Zealand
for its annual Cadbury Jaffa Race, an event that sees some
50,000 coloured chocolates tumble down the hill in the
name of charity.

⌁ Open to traffic year-round, Baldwin St is about 3.5km
northeast of Dunedin's city centre.

PENTECOST ISLAND, VANUATU. −15.7605 / 168.1897

LAND DIVERS OF PENTECOST ISLAND

If you thought bungee jumping was madness, wait till you meet the people who invented it. They start building the wooden towers in April. Young men work feverishly in the jungle, sawing and tying, measuring platform heights and sturdiness. When they're ready, village teenagers will fling themselves off headfirst with only a liana vine tied around each ankle to break the fall. All this in the hope of a successful yam harvest!

This is the ancient *naghol* (land diving) on Vanuatu's Pentecost Island, perhaps the most bizarre ritual in the South Pacific, a test of courage and rite of passage. It's heart-stopping to watch, like a terrible accident unfolding, but soon enough come cheers and singing as the young diver pulls up with a snap, his head barely grazing the ground.

🐾 *Naghol takes place weekly from April to June. There are twice weekly flights from Port Vila to Lononore on Pentecost Island; day trips can be organised from Port Vila.*

© David Kirkland / Getty Images

TANNA, VANUATU. −19.5155 / 169.3578

PRINCE PHILIP MOVEMENT

Emi blong Misis Kwin (Him belong Mrs Queen) – the Bislama language of Vanuatu clearly puts Prince Philip in second place to his wife, Queen Elizabeth II. Yet for the inhabitants of Yaohnanen village on the island of Tanna, he is the main man, their divine and beloved deity.

According to Yaohnanen legend, a spirit living in the nearby volcano travelled far over the seas to a distant land. There he won the heart of a powerful queen and, in time, would return to them. Seeing Prince Philip resplendent in his uniform alongside the Queen during a 1974 royal visit to Vanuatu, the villagers had their messiah. And so began a curious relationship: the people of Tanna sent the prince a traditional war club (a nal-nal), Prince Philip reciprocated with signed photos. But the prince has never been to the village of Yaohnanen.

In a 2006 interview with the *Daily Mail*, Chief Jack Naiva said that their greatest wish was for Prince Philip to visit. 'We want him to spend the last years of his life here, because we believe that when he returns as our god, his powers will make our wrinkles disappear and we will have many wives to attend to our every need. He won't have to hunt for pigs or anything. He can just sit in the sun and have a nice time.'

But what about the Queen? 'Oh, she can come, too,' says Chief Jack.

🐾 *Air Vanuatu has daily flights to Tanna from the capital, Port Vila.*

Hokitika Wildfoods Festival

I'm trying not to gag as I put the cockroach into my mouth. It's artfully presented in a dainty cup of pink jelly, but there's no hiding that it's a massive bug. At least it's not still alive, unlike the grasshoppers at the next stall. The roach kept down – just – what next? Earthworm sushi, pickled huhu grubs, giant chocolate-coated beetles, mountain oysters (sheeps' testicles) – the Hokitika Wildfoods Festival is not for the faint-hearted or the weak-stomached. I can't overcome my revulsion enough to swallow a huhu grub. As it is, for the rest of the day I'm picking cockroach feelers from between my teeth. By Tracy Whitmey

☛ Held annually on the second Saturday in March in Hokitika. See www.wildfoods.co.nz.

© Brian Fairbrother / Getty Images

STEAMPUNK HQ

A steam train with a dragon figurehead explodes from underground, coming to rest on a pile of rubble outside Steampunk HQ. Part art collaboration, part exuberant celebration of steampunk – a genre which imagines neo-Victorian, post-apocalyptic or fantasy worlds where retro-futuristic inventions are driven by steam-powered technology – this is a riotous reassembly of cogs, gears, pipes and machinery into phantasmagorical contraptions that grind, clank and whir their way into your imagination. If HG Wells or Jules Verne were in Oamaru, this is where you'd find them, playing the Metagalactic Pipe Organ or tinkering with a light sculpture of glowing skulls: it's quirky and fun, funky and steampunky.

☛ In Oamaru, 250km southwest of Christchurch. Open daily from 10am to 5pm. See www.steampunkoamaru.co.nz.

GIBBS FARM, NEW ZEALAND. -36.5206 / 174.4486

ELECTRUM

It's a sculpture, it's a science show, it's a crazy mad-scientist lightning fountain: Electrum, by Eric Orr and Greg Leyh, is a work of mind-blowing imagination. Looking a bit like a four-storey-high lollipop, it features the world's largest Tesla coil, harnessing over 3 million volts and flinging them out in retina-blasting bolts of lightning. And, peering hard into the heart of this electrical fury, you may see someone crouched atop it all inside the metal sphere, seemingly summoning the maelstrom like a maniacal conductor.

For the geeks, here is the techy stuff. The Tesla coil, invented by Nikola Tesla around 1891, is used to produce high-voltage, low-current, high-frequency, alternating-current electricity. The spherical cage atop Electrum forms a Faraday cage to protect the operator. For the non-geeks, this means the massive voltage sucks electrons from the surrounding air, letting rip 15-metre-long streams of electricity in crackling arcs – instant lightning.

Commissioned by millionaire businessman and art patron Alan Gibbs, and installed at Gibbs' farm on the Kaipara Harbour, Electrum is one of dozens of huge artworks displayed against a sweeping backdrop of rolling greenery, coastal waters and shimmering mudflats. After all, if you have bags of money, you can buy the coolest toys.

☛ *Gibbs Farm is open to the public for one day each month. Book free tickets at www.gibbsfarm.org.nz.*

© Robert Harding / Alamy

Ⓦ WAITOMO, Ⓝ NEW ZEALAND, −38.2609 / 175.1035

WAITOMO GLOWWORM CAVES

New Zealand isn't short on otherworldly oddities. After all, this is a country that's made a fortune marketing itself as the ideal backdrop for big-budget fantasy films. But of all its curious attractions, the Waitomo Glowworm Caves may just be the most surreal. Visitors descend from the enchanted forests above into an underground cave discovered 120 years ago by local Maori chief Tane Tinorau. They then hop aboard a boat and float down the underground Waitomo River into a glow-in-the-dark wonderland known as Glowworm Grotto, where thousands of tiny critters are hard at work emitting a turquoise glow. It's here that the roof of the cave morphs into a psychedelic planetarium with untold galaxies of living lights. Despite their name, Waitomo's resident population of *Arachnocampa luminosa* aren't actually worms; they're fungus gnats. Endemic to New Zealand, they thrive in its damp caves and become luminescent in both the larval and imago stages (the latter is the last stage an insect attains during metamorphosis). Though found throughout the country, nowhere is there a colony quite as large or flamboyant as in caves of Waitomo. Even if you hate damp and dark spaces, or are the kind of person who absolutely detests bugs, it's hard not to be enchanted by the spectacular subterranean kingdom of these bioluminescent maggots.

 Open daily, 9am to 5pm. Many hop-on hop-off buses from Auckland include the caves in their passes.

Hot Water Beach

A rumour reached my ears about a mythical spot on New Zealand's North Island where a steamy geothermal spring fizzles to the surface from golden sands. The rumourmonger spoke of a small window either side of low tide when the beach becomes a DIY spa. I arrived in the Coromandel Peninsula and strolled along Mercury Bay until I found a group of beachgoers bent over like gophers digging up heated holes. I joined the burrowing brigade and fashioned myself a sandy tub, but when I jumped in I instantly burnt my bum pink in the mineral-rich waters. It seems the rumourmonger forgot one important tip: use the ocean to control the temperature.

By Mark Johanson

Bus it from Auckland to Whitianga, then catch the seasonal bus to Hot Water Beach.

© Andrew Bain / Getty Images

THE BRIDGE TO NOWHERE

Deep amid the native forest of the Whanganui National Park stands a concrete bridge. Yet there is no road at either end, nor any signs of industry or human presence. It truly is a bridge to nowhere. It was built in 1936 to provide access to the remote Mangapurua Valley, where returned WWI soldiers were hacking farms out of the bush. But what began with hope and ambition ended in crushing disappointment: after years of battling poor soil in the valley, the economic catastrophe of the 1920s saw the final few families abandon the settlement. Soon the bush took back control, obliterating all signs of human habitation apart from the bridge that leads to the valley of abandoned dreams.

Take a jet boat from Pipiriki to Mangapurua Landing on the Whanganui River. It's then a 40-min walk to the bridge.

TAUMATAWHAK

KOAUAUOTAMAT

PIKIMAUNGAHO

WHENUAKITANA

ATANGIHANGA

EATURIPUKAKA

RONUKUPOKAI

TAHU

HAWKE'S BAY, NEW ZEALAND. -40.3704 / 176.5704

Were it not for its monstrous moniker few people would bother to visit this unassuming hill, but at 85 letters the Guinness World Records awards it the longest single-word place name in the world. Roughly translated it means 'the summit where Tamatea, the man with the big knees, the slider, climber of mountains, the land-swallower who travelled about, played his nose flute to his loved one'. What a name! According to the legend, Maori explorer Tamatea, fought a battle near the hill during which his beloved brother was killed. Grieving, Tamatea lingered near the battle site, playing a lament to his lost brother on a koauau, or Maori flute. Locals just call it Taumata Hill.

 Taumata Hill is near Porangahau in Hawke's Bay. A sign displaying the name is situated 5km along Wimbledon Rd.

'As a great cloud of sulphurous steam drifts across us my eyes start to sting. The island belches and burps, hisses and spits, grumbles and roars'

ⓃNEW ZEALAND, -37.5226 / 177.1797

White Island

On the boat on the way to White Island we are issued with hard hats and gas masks.

'This is an active volcano and eruptions can occur at any time with little or no warning,' we're told. 'Stick to the paths. In some places the crust is very thin and you don't want to fall into scalding mud and boiling water.'

The biggest surprise is that we step from the boat directly into the volcanic crater, the sharp rock walls rising above us to the crater's rim: we're actually inside the volcano. We're surrounded by a desolate, otherworldly landscape of bald grey rock, with blooming vivid patches of yellow sulphur crystals but not a speck of vegetation. The crater lake – its water more corrosive than battery acid – is milky jade, the hot surface glimpsed through billows of steam. I follow the guide step-for-step as we edge past piles of ash and cinder, stepping gingerly over acid-steeped streams and peering into pools of furiously boiling viscous grey mud. Sherbet-yellow fumaroles, like melted candles dripping down the neck of a wine bottle, spurt steaming gas. As a great cloud of sulphurous steam drifts across us, my eyes start to sting, and at the back of my tongue I taste the bitter tang of a struck match. The island belches and burps, hisses and spits, grumbles and roars. There's a sense of barely-contained menace; it's disquieting to be close enough to see, hear and smell the Earth's potential for destruction.

Moving away from the lake, we come to face to face with grim evidence of what happens when that pent-up energy blasts out. Destroyed buildings, rusted machinery, corroded cogs and wheels are all that's left of a once busy sulphur mine. In 1914 a terrific explosion occurred, killing all ten miners. It's thought that the force of the eruption blasted the miners and their quarters over the 50-metre high crater into the sea. Only the camp cat, Peter the Great, survived.

Later, we hear grim tales of life as a sulphur miner on White Island, including that the miners had to clean their teeth three times a day to stop them going black. Back on the boat I surreptitiously check my teeth – all good – but my silver necklace is sooty black. *By Tracy Whitmey*

☞ *White Island (Whakaari) is 50km offshore from Whakatane, and can only be visited with a registered tour operator.*

INDEX

A

B

C

D

ACKNOWLEDGEMENTS

Published in August 2017 by
Lonely Planet Global Limited
CRN 554153
www.lonelyplanet.com
ISBN 978 1 7865 7865 5
© Lonely Planet 2017
© Photographs as indicated 2017
Printed in Malaysia

Managing Director, Publishing Piers Pickard
Associate Publisher Robin Barton
Commissioning Editor Jessica Cole
Art Direction & Design Daniel Di Paolo
Illustrator Lauren Crow @ YCN
Editors Samantha Forge, Nick Mee, Christina Webb
Image Researcher Jael Marschner
Print production Larissa Frost, Nigel Longuet
Special thanks to Anita Isalska

Written by Alex Howard, Alexis Averbuck, Amy Balfour, Amy Karafin, Anita Isalska, Anna Kaminski, Anthony Ham, Bailey Johnson, Brandon Presser, Brendan Sainsbury, Brian Kluepfel, Bridget Gleeson, Carolyn B. Heller, Celeste Brash, Craig McLaughlin, Dominic Bliss, Duncan Garwood, Emilie Filou, Etain O'Carroll, Gregor Clark, Helen Ranger, James Bainbridge, James Dorsey, JB Carillet, Joe Bindloss, Jonathan Thompson, Karla Zimmerman, Karyn Noble, Kate Armstrong, Kate Morgan, Kevin Raub, Laura Crawford, Lucy Corne, Luna Soo, Marc di Duca, Mark Johanson, Matt Phillips, Nana Luckham, Pat Yale, Paul Harding, Phillip Tang, Ray Bartlett, Rebecca Warren, Regis St Louis, Steve Fallon, Tamara Sheward, Tom Hall, Tom Masters, Tom O'Malley, Tracy Whitmey, Trent Holden, Virginia Jealous

STAY IN TOUCH lonelyplanet.com/contact

AUSTRALIA
The Malt Store, Level 3, 551 Swanston St,
Carlton, Victoria 3053 T: 03 8379 8000

USA
124 Linden St, Oakland, CA 94607
T: 510 250 6400

IRELAND
Unit E, Digital Court, The Digital Hub,
Rainsford St, Dublin 8

UNITED KINGDOM
240 Blackfriars Rd, London SE1 8NW
T: 020 3771 5100

Paper in this book is certified against the
Forest Stewardship Council™ standards.
FSC™ promotes environmentally responsible,
socially beneficial and economically viable
management of the world's forests.